THE
IRISH
KOP

YOU'LL NEVER WALK ALONE

LIVERPOOL
FOOTBALL CLUB

EST·1892 ®

STORIES 'ROUND THE
FIELDS OF ANFIELD ROAD

The Irish Kop was written and researched by JOHN HYNES.
Cover design: RICK COOKE, LEE ASHUN, GLEN HIND.
Design/sub-editing: MICHAEL HAYDOCK.

With thanks to Liverpool FC Press Office and Marketing Department
and everyone who contributed or helped in any way.

Produced by
Trinity Mirror Sport Media:
Business Development Director: Mark Dickinson.
Executive Editor: Ken Rogers. Editor: Steve Hanrahan.
Production Editor: Paul Dove. Art Editor: Rick Cooke.
Sub Editors: Roy Gilfoyle, Adam Oldfield, Michael Haydock.
Sales and Marketing Manager: Elizabeth Morgan.
Designers: Barry Parker, Colin Sumpter, Lee Ashun,
Glen Hind, Alison Gilliland, Jamie Dunmore, James Kenyon.
Writers: Chris McLoughlin, David Randles,
Gavin Kirk, John Hynes, Simon Hughes.

Photographs: Trinity Mirror, PA Photos, John Cocks, Lee Ashun.
Historical content: Rob Gowers, Ger Scully.
Printed by Broad Link Enterprise Ltd.

Love of LFC knows no boundaries

LIVERPOOL is the capital of Ireland.

It has always been a famous saying in the city, never questioned by the Scousers who have grown up with a massive Irish presence in the shadow of the Liver Bird. Indeed, it has been a source of real pride for Liverpudlians.

Down the centuries, the historic Mersey port has been either a home from home for hundreds of thousands of Irish families from the North and South, or the launching pad for a new life in far away places in those days when ships left the Pier Head daily for the new world or one of the major ports of Australasia.

Of course, there has been another significant passage through Liverpool of individuals from across the Irish Sea. Their dream destination has not been another country, but rather a spiritual visit to a football shrine that is home to one of the most famous football clubs in the world.

Liverpool FC has warmly embraced its links with the island of Ireland through many famous players, but it is the fans themselves who have inspired and cemented a relationship that goes back to the club's formation at the end of the 19th Century.

This is what this book is all about. It's right to ask: "Why write a book about Irish Liverpool fans? Aren't Liverpudlians the same wherever they're from?"

There is a semblance of truth in this. We are all the same, part of one big family as Shankly put it all those years ago.

We feel the same passion for the club and talk about the same things. Is Gerrard on the same immortal plane as Dalglish? Why has Rafa picked that team? Who's the best partner for Torres and so on. The same debates will be heard every Saturday afternoon (or whenever Sky decide we play), debated by Reds' fans the world over. We all felt the pain of Athens and the ecstasy of Istanbul.

But like it or not there is a difference. Irish Reds don't have the club on their doorstep and have to make a huge commitment to follow Liverpool. They have to pay more (and take more time off work) to get to home games, getting to Anfield by whatever means possible. Many will think nothing about a 24-hour round trip to a midweek Champions League game involving six or more hours on the coach and a return ferry trip leaving Holyhead at 3am. If that's not commitment then what is?

It's not just in terms of travel that some Irish Reds go the extra mile. Scousers have Everton for neighbours while in Ireland, there are plenty of United fans to be found. Flying the red flag in modern times hasn't always been easy with the silverware count heading in the wrong direction, but the passion has never dipped.

This book is a salute to all those fans who are united in their love of all things Liverpool. Devotion to the Liver Bird knows no boundaries and every month ferries and flights from Belfast and Dublin will be packed with supporters making the pilgrimage to Anfield and other stadiums where the Redmen are playing across England and, indeed Europe.

The Irish Kop is also a tribute to the men who have proudly pulled on the red and green shirts.

The legendary Elisha Scott, the goalkeeping giant from the North, was one of only three immortals who secured automatic selection to the club's official Hall of Fame alongside Kenny Dalglish and Billy Liddell. Then there are more modern day Republic legends like Steve Heighway, Ronnie Whelan, John Aldridge and unsung heroes like Champions League winner Steve Finnan.

Indeed, I know that this book has been an incredible journey for the author, John Hynes. He has sat and listened to greats like John Aldridge and Ronnie Whelan talk about their love of Liverpool and spoken to many more legends and former players about their time at the club as well as interviewing celebrity fans whose devotion clearly runs deep.

When the club made an appeal through the official Liverpool website and magazine for fans' stories, you flooded us with letters and photos. We have printed as many as we could but it was impossible to include them all – that would make another book in itself.

Like any family, the Liverpool family is made up of many different parts and this book is an official club salute to those men and women who have contributed so much to the Anfield cause.

Wherever we're from, there's no distinction when the scarves go up and Gerry Marsden's powerful anthem is belted out on one of those famous European nights.

The words of the song sum up what it means to follow Liverpool . . . walk on, with hope in your hearts and you'll never walk alone.

KEN ROGERS

**Executive Editor Sport Media, and former
Sports Editor and LFC correspondent, Liverpool Echo**

THE IRISH KOP

Author's introduction: John Hynes...........................p6

THE PLAYERS

A chat with Aldo and Ronnie.....................................p12
'Ronnie was a Manc and he scored for Man Utd at the Stretford End against us once back in 1990!'

Steve Finnan...p26
'You didn't hear the Finnan song too often, but it did make me feel appreciated'

Steve Heighway p32
'There were times when Shankly would withdraw me from Irish squads without telling me'

Ray Houghton..p40
'It wasn't my decision to leave. That was down to Graeme Souness'

Jason McAteer..p46
'I found myself sitting in a room with my idol asking if I'd join his club'

Phil Babb and Mark Kennedy....................................p53
'Babb and Kennedy were part of one of the most unmemorable periods of Liverpool history'

Irish Liverpool Fantasy XI....................................... p54
Who would you pick in the ultimate team?

Jim Beglin...p58
'Chelsea had been my team, but as soon as I moved to Liverpool that went out of the window'

Steve Staunton..p66
'Roy Evans tried to get me back almost every summer'

Michael Robinson...p72
'It turned out I was the highest-paid player in British football at the time'

Shane O'Connor..p76
'I'd been used to facing Blarney, Mallow and teams like that. My first start for Liverpool came against AC Milan'

Mark Lawrenson...p78
'After Heysel I ended up in hospital with some of the dead and the dying'

Robbie Keane..p84
'In my household and amongst my extended family everyone, including my brother, uncles and cousins, are all Liverpool supporters. The club is huge in Ireland'

Elisha Scott...p90
'Elisha Scott gave 21 years and 52 days of his life to Liverpool Football Club, and deserves legendary status'

Memorabilia.................................p92
Programmes, tickets and souvenirs from an amazing collection of the Reds in Ireland

THE CELEBRITY FANS

Chris de Burgh...p100
'We took my private jet to Istanbul'

Colm 'Gooch' Cooper..p106
'I'd probably swap one of my All-Irelands for a Champions League medal'

Colin Murray...p110
'Four of us were all in Dundee on the day of the 2006 FA Cup final. We paid £800 each to get a plane down'

Dave Kelly...p115
'I've probably got all the home programmes since the mid-'80s'

Stephen Lucey...p116
'There was a mix-up and we ended up in the middle of the Milan end'

Dara O Cinneide..p120
'I've a long way to go before I reach Hansen's level'

Tommy Tiernan..p124
'When I was growing up in Zambia the most famous team were a side called the Kabwe Warriors'

Bernard O'Byrne..p130
'Shankly's passion was the hook for me'

Conor Mortimer..p134
'I could score any goal but I still wouldn't get a buzz like I do when Liverpool hit the back of the net'

CONTENTS

Felipe Contepomi....................................p138
'Football was always my first love. Whenever I get into a discussion on the game it can last for hours'

Eamon Horan.......................................p142
'McAteer decided to nudge me in the back and I went flying straight into Roy Keane, almost head-butting him'

THE WRITERS

From Zanzibar to Istanbul.......................p146
'You've spent three years living in Liverpool, and on their greatest night you were on a beach in Africa!'

David Randles......................................p150
'Of all our Irish Reds, there was one who stood head and shoulders above the rest'

Gerry Ormonde....................................p152
'The cattle would be boarded first, so they got all the best seats, and the people would squeeze on later'

Peter Sweeney....................................p154
'The taxi driver's head was completely bald, but he had a handlebar moustache that he grew all the way back to his ears'

James Hayden.....................................p157
'I can confidently say I have every home and away Liverpool shirt for the past 30 years'

Brian Reade..p158
'The cover of Warwick University's booklet leaps out at me. There is Stevie Heighway. My future was decided'

William Hughes...................................p160
'The landscape of Merseyside's footballing future could have been very different'

Keith Costigan....................................p162
'The Liverpool comeback only enforced my new belief that any situation can be overcome'

Liverpool v United in Dublin...................p164
'We spot two red jerseys walking side by side; one of the good Red persuasion, the other has 'Berbatov' adorned across the back'

Paul Hassall.......................................p170
'Aldo may have been a born 'n' bred Scouser, but he was fiercely proud of his Irish heritage'

Jackie Cahill.......................................p172
''Greats' such as Ziege, Kewell and Sissoko have adorned my various home and away tops'

Simon Hughes....................................p174
'I vaguely recall Staunton's face at the final whistle, moments after Michael Thomas scored. I cried'

Dion Fanning......................................p176
'Hillsborough took Kenny somewhere else and that sadness never left him'

Paul Tomkins.....................................p182
'We only hit the big time in the mid-'80s when the west of Ireland finally got BBC and Match of the Day'

Chris McLoughlin.................................p184
'Out-of-towners should not be branded as inferior to local Kopites because they aren't from Liverpool'

THE FANS

The Irish Kopites.................................p186
Your stories and pictures of following the Reds

Useful information...............................p204
Supporters clubs addresses and contact numbers

'This book is **a tribute** to the fans who go to **incredible lengths** and the players who **lived the dream** by pulling on the Red shirt . . . I'm glad to be **part of it**'

By author of The Irish Kop and proud Liverpool fan JOHN HYNES

IT'S strange, surprising, highly unusual and makes little sense. When you sit down and think about it, quite why so many people from Ireland – north and south – support English football teams is a mystifying subject.

The country already possesses its own proud sporting history, with Gaelic games and rugby union having particularly strong, unique identities in the Emerald Isle.

The Gaelic Athletic Association (GAA) has been a part of everyday life there since 1884, and continues to flourish with the magnificent Croke Park as its 21st-century centre.

Meanwhile, the advent of professionalism in rugby has sent the game soaring to new levels, with the national team

and the provinces enjoying unheralded and previously unimagined success.

All the sides that compete in those particular sports are instantly recognisable, and Irish soccer – as it's commonly referred to – also has plenty of tradition, albeit without ever enjoying huge popularity at club level.

So why turn your attentions to those that compete in England's top division?

Spending plenty of your hard-earned cash to undertake maybe a couple of trips to Anfield, Old Trafford or the Emirates every season certainly doesn't make good business sense. And only on increasingly rare occasions do Premier League teams include Irish stars.

Arsenal once had Pat Jennings, Liam Brady, Frank Stapleton and David O'Leary. At Anfield, it was all about the likes of Ronnie Whelan, Mark Lawrenson, Jim Beglin, Michael Robinson, Ray Houghton, John Aldridge or Steve Staunton. During the '80s, there were usually at least two Irish names on the Liverpool teamsheet, and often more.

In the '90s, Manchester United had Roy Keane and Denis Irwin, while Houghton, Staunton, Paul McGrath and Andy Townsend caught the eye when they all linked up at Villa Park. Recent seasons have featured Reading and Sunderland sides with plenty of Irishmen on their books.

But with the game now as global as it is, the days where a few lads we can call 'our own' run out together on the Premier League stage seem to be drawing to a halt.

Still, that doesn't prevent thousands of supporters catching low-budget flights to England every weekend to follow the fortunes of their chosen teams.

If anything, the numbers making these journeys are probably increasing, year on year. Explaining this phenomenon is difficult, and all I can do is draw from my own experiences. Where I grew up in Nenagh, County Tipperary, soccer was just as popular as any other sport, if not more so. Jack Charlton's team had just done well at Italia '90 and the game was on an upward curve.

As it is now, all of the players from that squad plied their trade outside Ireland, and maybe that is one of the reasons why so many people instantly turn their attentions to the Liverpools, Manchester Uniteds or Arsenals.

Even if the national teams do well, the domestic game very rarely, if ever, contains any of the players that make up the side. The vast majority of talented youngsters from Ireland, north and south, usually move across the water at an early age. As a result, the game at home isn't as attractive to supporters.

The bigger, brighter and better option is English football, and therefore it is only natural for lovers of the beautiful game to be attracted to it and want to become part of it.

When I attended school, and later university, soccer jerseys were a common sight. The list included obvious names such as Liverpool, United, Arsenal, Leeds, Spurs, Chelsea, Everton, Man City, Villa and Newcastle. Surprisingly, I've encountered QPR, West Ham, Nottingham Forest, Blackburn Rovers, Crystal Palace, Millwall and Swindon Town, too. It's a bizarre mix that illustrates just how far the fascination with the English game goes.

In our house it was all about only two clubs, both Red. My dad was a Manchester United fan and, as the oldest of four boys, it would probably have been normal for me to follow in his footsteps. Thankfully I escaped that affliction, although my next brother took up the mantle. I can't remember the exact reasons for leaning towards Liverpool, but my mind was firmly made up. Even watching United win the 1990 FA Cup couldn't change it. Strangely I can't recall us finishing top of the table during the same season as we claimed title number 18.

The two youngest siblings would later follow the same divided path, with one opting for the Anfield Red while the last of the clan unfortunately went in the opposite direction. As we all got older, this naturally led to some heated debates about which club was better, bigger, more successful, etc, etc. Again, it was an illustration of just how powerful the lure of Premier League football was to us.

I dreamt of going to Anfield some day, while two of my brothers probably had their own ambitions about a jolly to another venue at the other end of the East Lancs Road. Unfortunately, that was still a long way off, and the nearest we came to tasting 'real' soccer involved Crewe Alexandra coming to play a North Tipperary selection. We cycled miles as the rain bucketed down, just to get a glimpse of some professional players. In the end it was a stroll in the park as the pros easily notched up double figures. We eventually lost track of just how many they scored.

All the time I'd been wishing, as good as it was, that the opposition had actually been Liverpool, and I'm sure I wasn't the only spectator who thought so during that summer evening. When the Reds visited Ireland in the '90s they usually headed towards Dublin or Belfast; Tipperary was understandably never part of their itinerary. So watching them live had to wait for a number of years. That was mainly due to financial reasons.

All the time I imagined what it would be like to hear the Kop in full cry. By the age of 21 I'd decided I wanted to study journalism and was already casting my eye towards the UK. Options included London, Southampton, Stirling, Liverpool...

There was no choice to be made. I even mentioned the fact that Anfield wasn't too far from the campus on my application form. It was the best of both worlds, and suddenly the Kop was only a half-hour walk from my house.

'I dreamt of going to Anfield, while two of my brothers probably had their own ambitions about a jolly to the other end of the East Lancs Road. Unfortunately, the nearest we came to tasting 'real' soccer involved Crewe Alexandra coming to play a North Tipperary selection'

UEFA CUP 1ST ROUND 2ND LEG
LIVERPOOL V OLIMPIJA LJUBLJANA
Wed 15 Oct, 2003   8:00 pm
MAIN STAND
BLOCK   ROW   SEAT   PRICE
MD   9   205 -   15.00
Turnstiles   S Gr 1 - 4

Glove affair: Author John Hynes dons the goalkeeping jersey at half-time at Anfield (top left); John outside the ground with the Shankly statue (top right); Anthony Le Tallec scores against Olympija Ljubljana

The first time

ANTHONY LE TALLEC. Most Reds will remember him as a highly rated youngster who never lived up to his reputation.

When the Frenchman arrived at Anfield in 2003, along with his colleague and cousin Florent Sinama-Pongolle, he was rumoured to have been wanted by every top club in Europe. Of course, both are no longer Reds, with Le Tallec having endured loan spells at St Etienne, Sunderland, Sochaux and Le Mans. But he will always hold a special place in my heart.

Growing up, I'd imagined Rushie, Barnesie, God or – later – Michael or maybe Stevie would score the first Liverpool goal I'd see live. And that it would be a stunning strike in a huge game.

It was none of those illustrious names on the scoresheet that night when I made my maiden visit to L4 for a UEFA Cup tie.

Stevie was on the pitch; it was his first game after taking over as captain from Sami Hyypia.

Olimpija Ljubljana were the opposition as Le Tallec pounced on a goalkeeping error before placing the ball in the roof of the net.

It was hardly a classic effort, or occasion, but the first time always lives long in the memory.

Making that trip to Anfield was the culmination of almost two decades spent imagining such a day.

I didn't know it then, but it would unbelievably become a regular occurrence.

As a student on Merseyside most of the time was spent without enough cash to fund our very relaxed lifestyle.

That was made harder by the fact that I wanted to go to the match whenever possible, and even avoided paying my rent to do so. Still, it was mainly a diet of UEFA Cup football that year, as tickets were a lot cheaper and easier to obtain.

The day after one of those particular Thursday night encounters, a 1-1 draw against Marseille, I went to Everton's Bellefield training ground to attend a press conference, as part of work experience.

'Even if in the future no players from Ireland can gain a place in the first team, I believe that incredible backing will still exist. It's knowledgeable, loud, loyal and, when you consider the cost involved in terms of money and time, incredibly committed'

While there I got chatting to two journalists who informed me they were on their way up to Melwood for another press briefing. A very kind invitation to come along was immediately snapped up.

Driving through the gates of the place where Shanks, Paisley, Fagan and Dalglish had moulded their great teams sent a shiver down my spine.

But before I could enter the pressroom I had to explain to the vigilant press officer who I was and what I was doing there.

Thankfully I was allowed in, and when Gerard Houllier sat down to chat at the table with the print journalists, his head suddenly turned in my direction before he asked who I was.

Being caught completely unawares and already nervous enough, I muttered something about "student" and "work experience", which seemed to do the trick and he soon relaxed.

A few years later, I was back sitting at the same table, albeit with a new manager on the other side, after somehow landing a dream job writing for the club magazine.

Since moving to the famous city, I've been lucky enough to experience many magical Liverpool moments first hand. Olympiakos, Cheyrou's brace, Crouchie's first goals against Wigan, his FA Cup winner against United, seeing Robbie come back and score, beating Chelsea at Old Trafford and in the 2007 Champions League semi, Xabi's second goal from his own half, Crouchie's bicycle kicks, Barcelona, just watching Fernando Torres playing – they were all brilliant days and nights.

Even Athens, as much as the defeat hurt, was still something I'll always cherish.

Being here to witness Torres, Jamie Carragher, Sami Hyypia, Javier Mascherano and Stevie in action is a privilege on each and every occasion. And along the way there are always familiar accents mixed in amongst the crowd.

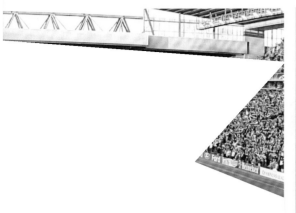

Explaining it?

WHETHER it's when you're standing outside the Albert or landing in some far-flung corner of Europe, every time there is a presence from across the Irish Sea.

The links between the Emerald Isle and Liverpool are well known and go back centuries.

As the first stop when you head out from Dublin bay straight across to the UK, it's only natural that millions should have chosen the banks of the Mersey as their new home.

The person who came up with the line that Liverpool is "in England, but not of it" was spot on when they suggested the city of King John was different to any other in the country. It might sound corny or patronising, but there is something unique about the place, especially on a match day, and Irish fans always feel at home when we come here.

Another obvious reason for the large fanbase that exists is that at one stage Liverpool seemed to go on pre and sometimes post-season tours to Ireland almost every summer, even bringing 'old big ears' with them in the '70s. Such exposure obviously increased the devotion that was already present.

Having plenty of Irish players down through the years also creates a natural link that people quickly latch onto.

But even if in the future no players from Ireland can gain a place in the first team, I believe that incredible backing will still exist. It's knowledgeable, loud, loyal and, when you consider the cost involved in terms of money and time, incredibly committed.

This book is a celebration of that: a tribute to the fans who go to incredible lengths to be Reds and the players who lived the dream by pulling on the Red shirt. The passion of this particular fanbase knows no bounds, and I'm just glad to be part of it all.

'Pulling on the **red shirt** was special and **the Kop** still blows us away'

They're Anfield and Ireland legends – and they're pretty good mates too. Irish Liverbird author John Hynes joined JOHN ALDRIDGE and RONNIE WHELAN at a Liverpool hotel for a cup of tea and a chat about their careers at club and international level . . .

Put it there: John Aldridge and Ronnie Whelan were reunited for our special interview

PHOTOS: LEE ASHUN

Both of you went on to become Liverpool legends but you arrived at Anfield via very different routes:

JA: Yeah that's true. I knew teams were watching me at Oxford United because I was doing well for a struggling side; I'd scored 20 league goals in one season.

Then one morning – before we played Manchester City – the phone rang in my hotel room. I was sharing with Bobby McDonald at the time and he answered the call and said the manager wanted to see me. I thought it was a bit odd. Bobby joked about someone coming in for me and we were laughing. Then, when I went to meet Maurice Evans he said they'd accepted an offer.

With this being on the day of the game it was all very strange. Arsenal were rumoured to be interested and I thought it might be them. Maurice said: "I think you'll like it." I said: "It's not Liverpool is it?" more in hope than expectation. And I couldn't believe it when he said yeah.

When I was young I went to all the games on a Saturday. I never missed a match until I started playing myself so this was my dream come true.

The problem was I had a poor performance after hearing that news. I think it was strange to be told about it before kick-off and it definitely affected me.

Then Robert Maxwell, who was very naïve about football, made me stay while we were still in the FA Cup, and again I thought that was bizarre.

Looking back now, Liverpool had probably told them that they didn't want me until the following season when Rushie was going to Juventus. But as it happened we got knocked out of the cup by fourth division Aldershot, who battered us 3-0. None of us played well, including me, and I got a load of stick from people who suggested I didn't perform because I knew I was leaving. That was rubbish.

Fortunately Oxford's loss was my gain, and I went to Liverpool the following week. On the Monday after the

Aldershot game I met with Kenny Dalglish, John Smith and Peter Robinson. Thankfully it all went through and I signed a contract. To be perfectly honest, money was irrelevant. I didn't care how much it was, I just wanted to get the deal done.

Liverpool probably knew that because they only offered me a little bit more than I was on at Oxford. But I didn't care. I was fulfilling a dream I'd had since I was six years old.

RW: My story was obviously different to Aldo's. It always looked like I'd go to Manchester United. I was over there during every school holiday from about the age of 14 onwards. I even played for them against Liverpool in a friendly game at The Cliff one Saturday morning.

JA: Yeah, he was a Manc and he scored for Man Utd at the Stretford End against us once back in 1990. He did it on purpose!

RW: (Laughs) I was only trying to help out Bruce Grobbelaar by playing the ball back to him, unfortunately it went over his head.

Anyway, United had offered me an apprenticeship when I was 15 but I didn't want to leave home at that stage and stayed at Home Farm instead.

Then a few years later Jim McLoughlin, who was manager of Dundalk, wanted me to go there but I said no because I wanted to go abroad, well not abroad really, England.

The story was that he got in touch with someone at Liverpool and then I think Tom Saunders came and watched me.

After that I was invited over for a two-week trial during the summer of 1979, and they asked me to sign at the end of that September. I didn't need any time to think about it.

It all worked out pretty well for me so I made the right choice.

Was homesickness a major problem for you Ronnie?

RW: Yeah it was. My dad had been at Chelsea on trial when he was a kid so he knew all about how difficult it could be for a youngster in a strange city.

Thankfully I always had him to turn to for advice. He never pressured me into playing but he always pointed me in the right direction.

For example, I remember getting ready to go out to a disco on a Friday night and he'd ask where I was off to.

His response was always: "If you think that will help you to play better in the morning then go."
(Aldo starts laughing)

'It's difficult to single out just one. On a personal note, mine was probably lifting the FA Cup as skipper in '89. That's something you imagine doing when you're a kid. Winning the European Cup in '84 was obviously special too'

RW: Of course I'd have to get changed again and go to bed instead. But he knew about all those pitfalls and that was a big help to me.

His experience at Chelsea came into my thinking. The first six months at Liverpool were horrible, but he told me to give it more time.

Initially I wasn't playing well and got moved down to the A team, but I stuck it out and it came good for me in the end.

Surely there were no such difficulties for you John?

JA: Not when I joined Liverpool because it was like a homecoming.

But when I went down to Newport County in South Wales I was completely lost at first and found it really hard. It was like another world.

I moved there in March and obviously the season was ending in May. Of course I wanted to go home for the entire summer and take it easy. That was my plan, then the manager told me I was too lean and he wanted me to stay down there to build myself up. I didn't fancy that, so I said I'd organise a weightlifting course in Liverpool if I could go home. Thankfully he agreed. But making that move was tough, although it did put me in good stead for the future. I was a toolmaker by trade so those first 12 months sorted me out because I never had an apprenticeship in football.

What was your best moment as a Liverpool player?

RW: It's difficult to single out just one. On a personal note, mine was probably lifting the FA Cup as skipper in '89.

That's something you imagine doing when you're a kid. Winning the European Cup in '84 was obviously special too.

JA: For me it's very difficult too. The team that we had was just awesome.

RW: With you being a Scouser and a Liverpool fan it must have meant everything was even more amazing.

JA: Yeah, definitely. All of it. Winning the Championship and the FA Cup was great, but just playing for Liverpool was the best.

In your time at Anfield, who was the best player you lined up alongside?

JA: *(Moves in and hugs Ronnie)* Got to be Barnesie. *(Both burst out laughing)* I presume Ronnie will say the same, although you played with Kenny too so maybe not.

RW: The likes of Kenny were magnificent but I always go for Souness. It might be because centre-forwards nearly always go for centre-forwards, and midfielders usually look at what other midfielders did.

I don't think Rushie and Kenny would have been as good without Souey in midfield. Okay, they were still good after Souey left for Italy, but he was the one who made everything tick. He started everything, controlled the pace of the game, led by example and orchestrated the whole thing.

Having played in the middle of the park, I know exactly what's involved. Graeme made it look pretty easy when it's definitely not, so because of all that, he's the best player for me.

Of all the goals you scored for the club, what's your favourite?

JA: For obvious reasons the most important goals I ever scored were in the replayed FA Cup semi-final of 1989, just after the Hillsborough disaster.

Some people don't agree, but I think that game against Nottingham Forest was the most vital one for us to win, more so than the actual final, so that meant a lot. In pure football terms, the semi-final goal the year before that – also against Forest – really stands out.

It was a great team move, and I managed to get on the end of it. That underlined what we were all about.

RW: For me it has to be '83, the Milk Cup final against Manchester United. Having been a Manc as a kid made it even sweeter.

JA: Yeah, that bender against United was just terrific.

RW: To win the game at Wembley, after also scoring two the year before against Spurs was great.

People said it was a cross but it definitely wasn't. I meant it all the way.

And I think when you deliberately attempt something and it comes off, that makes it just that little bit better. Winning the cup with that goal was brilliant.

'Any regrets? Yeah, that I took that damn penalty. Steve Nicol should have taken it! Regrets? Not winning the double in '88 and '89. My penalty and Arsenal's late goal were devastating moments because we were so close to achieving it'

Setting the record straight: Aldo's first kick of the 1989 final against Everton resulted in a goal – his last kick in the 1988 final saw him miss a penalty

Any regrets?

JA: Yeah, that I took that damn penalty. Steve Nicol should have taken it. *(Both laugh)* Regrets? Not winning the double in '88 and '89. My penalty and Arsenal's late goal were devastating moments because we were so close to achieving it.

That team we had was terrific and deserved to win the double back to back, which has never been done. But it wasn't to be.

RW: We can't really have too many regrets. I probably should have taken a 12-month contract they offered me near the end of my time at the club.

I wanted two years and they said one. I eventually agreed but by that stage the original offer had been withdrawn. I should have signed it because it was a good deal. But I wanted a second year just to take me up to retirement. But if I look back, I can't argue with anything else.

JA: Going on 'You're A Star' is another thing I'd like to change. *(Laughs)* I went into it a bit blind. I can't sing so it felt like a prison sentence.

RW: But look at the end result, which was all that money you raised for those kids.

JA: That is what it was for at the end of the day. I swear to

God I had to have a few drinks beforehand because I was so nervous.

It was a real nightmare and probably the hardest thing I've ever done in my life. Playing in front of 40,000 people was easy compared to it.

But when I went to see those kids in that hospital it was all worth it. That made me feel very humble.

I agreed to it and thought once they heard my attempts to sing that I'd be quickly out of it and they'd give me a pat on the back and say thanks, but no thanks. Instead I somehow ended up winning it.

RW: I was asked to go on it too. But I'd had a few drinks before I was talking to one of the organisers. After a few minutes I started singing down the phone. *(Sings)* 'Take your time, think a lot, why, think of everything you've got...'

So I told the kids I'm going on some kind of 'X Factor' – style show. Then when I woke up the next morning they asked me if I was really going to do it.

I didn't have a clue what they were on about because I couldn't remember the conversation from the previous evening. Having heard about it from Aldo there is no way I'd ever put myself through it.

Ronnie's Irish links are obvious, but how did it come about for you, Aldo?

JA: I'd always followed the fortunes of both England and Ireland when I was growing up.

Then when I went to Oxford I played with a guy named Dave Langan, who'd won a few caps for Ireland.

We used to chat about it and I remember him saying to me that I'd qualify to play through my gran. I thought he was just having a laugh.

But he must have had a word with Eoin Hand and there were some enquiries made. Then Eoin got the sack and Jack Charlton came in. Again someone must have made him aware of my link.

He came to watch me play against Aston Villa in the semi-final of the 1986 Milk Cup and I scored two goals.

After the game he asked me and I immediately said I'd

be honoured. Then it was a case of getting the paperwork sorted and off I went.

Before that I'd never really thought about international football: I just wanted to play for Liverpool.

Even now people still say to me that I should have waited and played for England.

That was never an option. As soon as I was asked by Ireland my mind was made up. Thankfully it's one of the greatest decisions I ever made.

Euro '88: The best moment of your international careers?

RW: Yeah, because I didn't really play too much in the two World Cups – half an hour in 1990 and something similar four years later – so '88 is always what I remember most fondly. Beating England was terrific and we played well against Russia too. Unfortunately we couldn't go that final step in the last group game against Holland.

JA: The performance against the USSR, who were a very strong side, was brilliant.

RW: Definitely one of the best Irish displays ever and we were very unfortunate not to win. That would probably have put us in the semi-finals. But the whole experience of playing in the Championships for the first time was unbelievable.

At one stage we didn't even think we were going to qualify, it looked like Bulgaria would top the group. Then Gary, what was the guy's name...

JA: Mackay.

RW: ...for Scotland scored the goal that put us through. I was in the pub that night with Jim Beglin not even thinking about it.

To get there that way was unexpected and we didn't let anybody down when we went to Germany.

JA: Really it was justice that we made it because we were the best team in that qualifying group and if the referee

Memories of 1988: Aldo in action against England and Ronnie against Holland

'Even now people still say to me that I should have waited and played for England. That was never an option. As soon as I was asked by Ireland my mind was made up. Thankfully it's one of the greatest decisions I ever made'

hadn't cheated us in Bulgaria we would have done it ourselves.

We were robbed over there, it was an absolute disgrace some of the decisions he made, so justice was done when we got there. Isn't that right Ron?

RW: Yeah, similar poor calls had cost Ireland before that too when a Frank Stapleton goal in Belgium was disallowed late on and that would have got them through.

So we'd been knocking on the door for a while and to be part of the team that finally got there was terrific.

What's your best memory from that summer?

RW: Just experiencing it all, the whole set-up was great.

Security around it was unbelievable. You're kept away from the supporters, or as much as you can be when it's the Ireland fans. They still managed to get in though.

JA: It was all brilliant. To be part of the first Ireland team to qualify for a major tournament was the stuff dreams are made of. And if that wasn't enough then we came up against England in the opening game. People ask me what was the most memorable day of my international career.

The quarterfinal of Italia '90 against Italy in Rome was tremendous. But I have to say defeating England was the best, it even topped beating Italy in Giants Stadium in New York. The result against England put us on the map. It announced to people that we'd arrived as a football team and we're going to stay here as long as possible.

RW: People fancied England to win the tournament but we beat them and they never won a game after that.

I can't imagine a better opponent for Ireland in a major tournament. But then again if it had just been a kick-about out on the street we would wanted to have won just as badly. Our team was classed as second-rate compared to England, and in a lot of ways we were.

They'd be up the front of the plane while we were down the back. When it came to hotels, they stayed in the best while we didn't. They'd have the best training facilities and we'd have the worst. So we didn't help ourselves in that

'It was all brilliant. To be part of the first Ireland team to qualify for a major tournament was the stuff dreams are made of. And if that wasn't enough then we came up against England in the opening game'

sense. But we knew that on a pitch we weren't second best.

JA: We had more hunger and desire when we faced them.

Of course, Ray Houghton netted the winner in Stuttgart from your assist, Aldo . . .

JA: Yeah, I out-jumped Tony Adams. That wasn't hard. *(Laughs)* Although I have to say it was a shock to see Ray just head the ball, never mind score from it.

Then, a few days later, that goal was bettered against the USSR . . .

JA: I don't know if it came off Ronnie's shin or toe but it was definitely a great goal.

RW: That was a group of lads who were playing with confidence and weren't bothered if we were going to make an idiot of ourselves by falling down or nearly breaking our necks. The boys would have laughed if I had done that, thankfully I didn't and it just flew in.

JA: If Ronnie had put that effort in the stand it wouldn't have been all serious like it is today. We would have just all smiled about it and run back to the halfway line.

But he stuck it in the top corner so he had the last laugh on all of us.

RW: The '88 squad was a great group, we knew how to play

football and enjoy ourselves.

JA: Definitely, another example of that was when we played against Luxembourg away and I still hadn't scored an international goal so I was nearly pulling my hair out.

Then someone knocked the ball down in the box, I got onto it and banged it in, and off I went behind the goal going mad with all the fans. Of course I hadn't realised the flag was already up for offside.

Next minute I hear Ronnie shouting: 'Aldo get back.'

I'd probably been standing there for about 30 seconds while the game continued and all the lads on the pitch were taking the piss out of me. *(Both laugh)* It was never offside by the way!

You had an even more famous moment in the USA, didn't you Aldo?

RW: *(Laughing)* Aldo's most famous for that stupid disagreement rather than the goal you scored in the same game against Mexico that actually put us through to the knock-out stages.

JA: *(Laughs)* That, and the FA Cup final penalty miss are what I'll be remembered for.

RW: You've scored nearly a million goals but it's those two incidents people always recall.

JA: *(Still laughing)* The official didn't have a clue and I was

Milk Cup Kid: Whelan in action during the 1983 Milk Cup. **Left:** With Irish PM Bertie Ahern and the European Cup in Dublin; pundit Aldo opens a new club shop

The Irish Kop: Ireland fans at Anfield for the play-off against Holland. Top: Aldo famously makes his point to the official during USA '94

just underlining that fact. Unfortunately for me the cameraman spotted it straight away and highlighted it. The fourth official – or was he the fifth official? – wouldn't let me on. We had two people come off and only one sub on, so we're 2-0 down and suddenly reduced to 10 men for no valid reason. Anyone in my position wants to help their teammates and I just lost it.

In the end I was stood there for four minutes while the lads were running around like lunatics trying to keep up with the Mexicans. All my frustrations came out, and when I did eventually get on I was really pumped up. Thankfully I got an opportunity and took it.

At the time I thought it was just a consolation. But it actually gave us the opportunity to go into the last game against Norway knowing a draw would put us through, so it was a big goal in the end.

RW: *(Laughs)* I was sitting in the dugout while all this was going on. I think that was the best place to be because there was air conditioning on the bench. We had lovely cold air blasting around the back of us so none of us wanted to get up. We saw it all happening and we were going mad too, but also laughing at Aldo at the same time.

It was obvious we only had 10 men out there, so we couldn't understand why they wouldn't let him go on.

JA: I got fined $2,500. Jack got involved and ended up being fined $12,500. *(Both laugh)* He wasn't happy about it and didn't pay it.

While there were many good days in an Irish shirt, did the fact that the 1995 play-off defeat against Holland came at Anfield make it even harder to take?

RW: I couldn't attend it because I was down south working as Southend manager at the time.

JA: With the game being at Anfield and loads of Irish fans guaranteed to be there, I thought it was all set up for us to do the job. But Holland were far too strong. We couldn't live with them. I don't think I got a sniff of a chance that night. I was absolutely gutted because I think we knew that was the end of an era.

We got a great ovation from about 20,000 supporters afterwards. But it was very frustrating because we couldn't give the Dutch a real game like we had done in the past.

The Irish squad then had a large number of players born outside the country. Was that ever a problem?

JA: It was never an issue within the squad. If anything, it probably knitted us together a bit more and made us clannish. The lads like Ronnie probably protected us and we protected ourselves by doing it out on the field.

RW: We were obviously aware that they came from different backgrounds, the likes of Ray, Aldo, Andy Townsend and Tony Cascarino.

JA: Well Cas isn't Irish anyway: he's admitted that now.

RW: Yeah, he's Italian. But we noticed guys like them and David Kelly, even going back to Gary Waddock and lots of others, how much they really wanted to be part of it. Irish ancestry is very important to lots of people even if they don't come from the country, and it was the same for those guys, Cas aside obviously!

They're brought up on the history and know what the people expect. Once the fans saw them on the pitch and what they wanted to give for the cause, no one cared if they were from England, Scotland, Wales or Italy.

I think it was mainly the English media who joked about it. But England had done it for years with the cricket team.

JA: And we used to have a laugh with Barnesie too about him being Jamaican and playing for England. I remember the papers over here describing us as mercenaries. How could that be true when we were only on 250 punts per game?

So whenever we faced England, we wanted to show those reporters and prove a point. It gave us ammunition and a teamtalk. I think it worked too because England never defeated us during Big Jack's time in charge.

Would you ever take the job as Ireland boss?
RW: I went for it once when I was manager of Southend and Mick McCarthy got it. The chairman of the club said: "If you go we want compensation", and I think that put the FAI off. Although they probably didn't really want me.

JA: I thought I had a good chance in the past and it wasn't to be. Now I just want whoever has it to do well.

Can you ever see an Irish team enjoying similar success again?

RW: Mark Lawrenson said a while back that we might not see Ireland qualify for a major competition in our lifetime. That was taken in jest by some people, but if you think about it, he might be right. The more defeats we suffer put us further down the rankings, and as a result we get drawn in harder groups. It's a vicious cycle.

JA: I think Lawro said it tongue-in-cheek, the way he

'We had lovely cold air blasting around the back of us so none of us wanted to get up. We saw it all happening and we were going mad too, but also laughing at Aldo at the same time'

usually does, but he could be spot on. At the moment we need somebody to galvanise the side and instil belief. There are some really good players there and they need to gel into a decent unit.

RW: We're all hoping it works out and comes good again. Unfortunately, we've always had six or seven decent individuals but the squad strength probably isn't up to scratch. If you can get the main guys out on the field and give them some balance as a team, then you've got a chance. That's what Jack did with us.

JA: You've got to look at what Greece achieved in 2004. They showed Europe that if you get the right manager with the right players and the correct tactics then you can do it. If I were the manager, I'd be putting that across to my players every day. They weren't household names and probably weren't a fantastic team, but they won it.

RW: You saw them at Euro 2008 and that was probably their true level. But they were set up to play a certain way that could work. It was the same story with us.

Did it take a while to adjust to Jack Charlton's style of football?

RW: Yeah. It was completely alien to us and it certainly wasn't the Liverpool way. But if it gets success then you're happy to play like that; happyish, anyway. A lot of the time you'd see a pass you wanted to play but instead you'd have to put the ball in the corner and let Aldo chase it.

JA: *(Laughs)* But I bet you had a smirk on your face while you were doing it and shouting at me to get after it.

RW: Yeah, but continuously pressing the opposition was hard work.

JA: It was probably the hardest I've ever had to do.

RW: But I think it all came together in that Russia game at Euro '88. We put them under pressure, continuously won the ball back and we decided – for some unexplained reason – to pass it around. When we did we tore them to pieces. Maybe Jack at that time should have mixed it up a little more.

It's a famous cliche and you've already touched upon it but the spirit of that side seemed special . . .

JA: Yeah, we always had a laugh every day in training. It was second to none.

RW: You're never happy if you're not playing regularly as I wasn't after 1990, but I always turned up and wanted to be with the lads. The things Jack did really helped that bond develop. I remember being on the bus one time when he started picking the side. I can't recall which player it was, but Jack just said: "I want to look at him at right back so Aldo you're dropped."

JA: Oh yeah. I remember that. Jack just didn't care. He'd just laugh and all you could do was laugh along.

RW: A lot was made of the things we got away with but Jack was clever in how he dealt with us. Although we often overstepped the mark, we never went too far.

We would go and have a laugh and a drink. But at the same time there were a lot of good pros in the squad so we knew when to draw the line.

JA: We knew the time to get serious.

Do you think the game has changed for the worse since then?

JA: It's a different world now, a real goldfish bowl for footballers. You can't move without somebody spotting you. People have mobile phones and cameras with them all the time.

RW: We could go to a race meeting and get absolutely

Living the dream: Nothing beats the buzz of playing

Liverpool Legends: Still proudly wearing the red shirt for reunions with former team-mates

bladdered in Dundalk even though we weren't supposed to be there and it was the week of an international game.

We all had a few beers, won a few quid and came back on the bus to Dublin having a singsong telling Jack we wanted more beer. We stopped, and Kevin Sheedy had won some money so he bought a load of drink. Then we stopped at another pub and another and another. Today you couldn't get away with that. If we were at the races now everyone would be taking pictures of us having a pint. Back then Jack obviously knew what was going on but he also knew we needed a break.

JA: Yeah he just turned a blind eye to it and gave us a chance to relax.

Looking back now, do you think you played the game at the right time?

JA: People always mention the money in football now but back then we had the normal life to go with it.

RW: We earned half decent money, better wages than most people and unlike today we could enjoy it too. But for £100,000 a week I'd change! *(Laughs)*

How often do you get back to Anfield and do you wish you could do it all over again?

RW: With doing the commentary work, Aldo obviously goes back more often than me, but I try to get to the Champions League games whenever I get the chance and it's great.

We had some terrific European Cup nights at Anfield during my time. But I think the last few years have been extra special.

JA: Yeah, it's amazing. As a kid I was at the St Etienne game and the atmosphere was brilliant. But all the noise was mainly coming from the Kop. For the 2005 Chelsea game it was coming from all over the ground. That was incredible.

RW: For us it's probably better when the team play badly because fans say 'you should get your boots on again lads! 'If only we could. Nothing will ever replace playing but we had our time. Having said that I still get a tingle whenever I see the Kop. The atmosphere blows me away.

JA: Yeah, on every occasion. Thankfully we got to experience it all during our careers and nothing will ever come close to that.

'With **the history** of Liverpool it was special. You've got to **be proud'**

Finn was Mr Consistent for Liverpool, making the right-back spot his own and even winning a Player of the Season award. He looked back on his career before he left Anfield for Espanyol

AT the end of the 2007/08 season, Steve Finnan's Liverpool career appeared to be drawing to a close. An injury-plagued campaign had seen him in and out of the side, and rumour had it he would be moving on to pastures new.

When the transfer window eventually shut on 1 September, the Irish international had indeed departed. As usual with Finnan, it was in a quiet, unfussy manner, so typical of his displays on the field, with him moving to Espanyol as part of the deal that took Albert Riera in the opposite direction.

The move brought to a close a five-year stint as a Red, which had begun in similar fashion to how it concluded, with rumours circulating before the deal was eventually concluded.

"I think at the time there was something about it in the papers every couple of weeks," he laughs. "When it actually came about there were a lot of changes taking place at Fulham.

"Jean Tigana had just left and I think the club wanted to cash in on me. It was a great opportunity. So I think the transfer probably suited both parties. Even right before it happened there was still lots of gossip; it would have been nice if it had been done earlier. Unfortunately, as we all know, it rarely works like that in football.

"But I knew it was going ahead and I couldn't wait. My family were all delighted that I was moving to such a big club where I could win major honours.

"I was always an admirer of Liverpool and their approach to the game," he continues. "I wasn't a supporter but I was definitely able to appreciate just how good that team was.

"No football fan would say they didn't enjoy watching Kenny Dalglish, Ian Rush, Peter Beardsley and John Barnes when they were at their best."

Finnan's first season on Merseyside was disrupted by injury; he only made 22 league appearances and the fans rarely witnessed him at his best. Such difficulties would have got most individuals down.

"When I arrived here I was still recovering from an injury and trying to find my fitness," he confirms. "During the year I picked up one or two other knocks.

"And the team probably wasn't performing as well as we knew we could. But I still loved being at the club."

When 2003/04 came to a halt, the Reds finished fourth, and secured

the last Champions League place, but it wasn't enough to keep Gerard Houllier in the managerial seat.

The Frenchman departed to be replaced by Rafa Benitez. We all know what happened less than 12 months later. Even now, Finnan still seems amazed when he remembers that rollercoaster campaign.

"It was the first time I'd played in the Champions League and it doesn't get any better than going on to win the trophy, especially the way we did it against AC Milan. I went to Liverpool to win honours, and that's one of the top medals in the game. For everyone at the club it was an amazing achievement. Winning the FA Cup the following year was another fantastic memory. That's what the game is all about."

In between picking up those two pieces of silverware, the Irish defender was also part of a Red rearguard that set a new record in 2005 when they kept clean sheets for 11 consecutive games in all competitions.

"With the magnificent history of Liverpool, it was special to do that. You've got to be proud of it because it requires a real team effort. And if you're the goalkeeper, or part of the defence, then it obviously means even more. Trophies are the priority for every player, but if you can set records like that, it gives you a great chance of achieving success."

Of course, before moving from London to Liverpool, Finnan had caught the eye at the 2002 World Cup as part of Mick McCarthy's squad. The fact that he was pulling on a green shirt would have shocked those who understandably expected the Cockney-sounding Finnan to be an English man.

"My dad's from Limerick city, all his family still live there and I was born there," he explains. "We lived there for about a year before moving to London. I still have lots of family back in Ireland: uncles, aunts and cousins. But I haven't been over to visit for quite a while. I used to have quite a few ticket requests from Ireland as a lot of my relatives are

Melwood: Finnan trains with Fernando Torres in November 2007

In control: Shielding the ball from AC Milan's Andrea Pirlo in Istanbul, 2005

Liverpool fans.

"The World Cup was never really something I'd thought too much about," he says in reference to his participation.

"When you're playing in non-league, you never think about something like that. It's probably the last thing on your mind. And even when you become an international, you can never be sure you're going to reach a major tournament. Obviously you want to, but you can't be certain it's ever going to happen."

Finnan more than played his part in helping McCarthy's men make it to South Korea and Japan. It was his cross that led to Jason McAteer scoring the only goal in a game that ended Holland's chances of making it to the Far East on an unforgettable afternoon at Lansdowne Road.

"I only came into the team near the end of the qualifying campaign, but just coming through the group ahead of the Dutch was an achievement in itself," he says with justifiable pride. "Then we overcame Iran in the two-legged play-off. I didn't start the first game of the tournament but featured in all of them. We did well and were perhaps a little unlucky to lose out on penalties against the Spanish."

It's often forgotten that Finnan stepped up that day to convert a spot-kick during the shoot-out, and it was a penalty he couldn't afford to miss.

"If it hadn't gone in, we were out, but I didn't worry about it too much. You can't afford to." Of course the defender displayed his usual calmness to find the net; alas it wasn't enough to prevent elimination. "If we had gone through to the next round, it would have meant a quarter-final against South Korea, so who knows how far we could have gone. The whole experience was absolutely fantastic, from start to finish. It's definitely one of the highlights of my career."

It's a memory that can't even be tarnished by the infamous manager-versus-captain episode that made headlines across the globe.

"No, not at all," Finnan honestly admits. "Everyone knows what happened with Roy Keane, but that was between him and the boss. When I look back now, it didn't dilute any of the experience. We all wanted Roy to be there, he was the best player in the team, but – strange as it may sound – it took the spotlight off the rest of us in a way. Roy went home and we still had a job to do. We had to continue and I'll always fondly look back on it."

When we delve a bit further into Finnan's childhood it's easy to see why the World Cup means so much to him. Mexico '86 is remembered for various reasons. For some

'It was the first time I'd played in the Champions League and it doesn't get any better than going on to win the trophy, especially the way we did it against AC Milan'

Rising to the challenge: Finnan jumps with John Terry in the second leg of the 2005 Champions League semi-final

it's the 'Hand of God' that still makes their blood boil, while others only recall Diego Maradona's magical second goal on the same afternoon.

For Finnan, it's his first real football memory. "I would have been 10 years old and watching it was special," he fondly recalls. "It was a great tournament. As everyone knows, Maradona was the star of the show, he was amazing. I think watching that really got me into the game. I was obviously playing it before then, but it was during that summer when my interest really started to grow."

Fast-forward four years and the world's biggest sporting event had moved on to Italy. And once again a young Finnan was glued to the box.

"It was massive. Overall, the quality probably wasn't as good as Mexico but I enjoyed it. Ireland reaching the quarter-finals is obviously something that stood out for me. My dad made sure we never missed any of the games. David O'Leary's winning penalty against Romania, Toto Schillaci's goal, I can still remember it all. When you're a kid it doesn't get any better than watching football almost every day for a month."

Of course Finnan is now part of Irish World Cup history, and the only complaint anyone could possibly ever aim at him would be his lack of goals. With that in mind, it's a shock to discover that he once managed to get on the scoresheet three times in just five games for club and country in November 2000. When we remind him of this, his first reaction is laughter.

"I think we had a few injuries at Fulham around then," he explains. "I was used up front and as a winger, so I managed

'Finnan is a player who will always play at a consistent level. He will be seven, eight, nine or even 10 out of 10 every week' – Rafa

to find the back of the net a few times. Unfortunately it's not something I've been able to repeat."

Finnan's quiet manner meant he was always, without fail, described as an unsung hero during his time as a Red, although that scenario eventually changed. Nobody can put an exact date on when it was first aired but, after much debate and many suggestions, a song for Finnan finally materialised prior to Christmas 2005.

A request for the man himself to perform the tune is instantly knocked back with a smile. "I vaguely know the words," he confesses, "although I'm not going to sing it now. You didn't hear the song too often, but it did make me feel appreciated."

That appreciation was well earned by solid displays against some of top widemen in the modern game. Even Rafa Benitez, who rarely offers individual praise to anyone, took time out to talk up Finnan on more than one occasion.

"A player who will always play at a consistent level. He will be seven, eight, nine or even 10 out of 10 every week," was how the boss summed up one of his most reliable charges. Despite that approval being well deserved, 'Finn', as he is affectionately known, is his usual modest self when it comes to such acclaim.

"It was nice to hear the boss say stuff like that," he says. "Sometimes you can't allow yourself to listen to comments, but if the manager thinks that, then it's great."

At his peak, few attackers have ever got the better of our former number three. But how would he have fared against some of the best wingers to ever wear the Liverbird on their chest? Steve McMananaman, John Barnes and Steve Heighway are three names from that group that immediately spring to mind. So would Finnan be up to the challenge?

"All at the same time?" he jokes. "Facing any of those guys would have been a real test. Any defender would certainly have their work cut out. McManaman and Barnes are a bit nearer to my age and I clearly remember watching them. They were superb talents with great attacking ability who could win a game on their own. You'd never get a moment of peace if you were against either of them. Heighway was a bit ahead of my time. But I'm well aware of the high regard he's held in by the supporters at Anfield, so he must have been absolutely fantastic."

Of course the two will never come head-to-head, but if they ever had, we're sure Finn would have dealt with him in a quiet and efficient manner, just as he always did.

Mr Reliable: Stopping Arsenal's Theo Walcott in his tracks in 2008

'I think everyone involved would pick **that night.** To win it in Rome like that was the **best moment'**

From playing a part in the glory of Rome '77 to nurturing Academy talents like Steven Gerrard, Shankly signing STEVIE HEIGHWAY has always helped us to be the best

S TEVIE Heighway on the wing, we had dreams and songs to sing.' Those words are heard at Anfield on almost a weekly basis. Every Red is well aware of just how good the winger was, but it's only when you look at the other LFC greats featured in the tune that you realise what kind of an impact Heighway had.

'Shankly', 'Kenny' and 'Paisley' are Liverpool legends so famous they don't even require their full title. The fact that Heighway sits alongside those names shows how highly he's regarded by the Kop faithful. A Liverpool player probably couldn't receive a bigger tribute. When this accolade is mentioned to the ever-modest Heighway, he simply chuckles as he replies: "I did okay."

Nearly 500 games and a host of major honours in 11

The start
of a new
era: Irish
Red Steve
Heighway
in action
in the
1977 final

seasons suggest the Dublin-born wideman did a lot more than that. In his time as a Red he collected League, FA Cup, UEFA Cup and European Cup medals as part of an all-conquering team. However, it could have been so different.

"I was 22 and still at Warwick University. I'd been playing with Skelmersdale United when Liverpool had spotted me and offered me a contract," he says. "In truth it was a massive surprise. I'd been a decent player; I was with Man City as an amateur when I was 17 or 18. But my plan was always to go to university and then get a job, so it was a bit of a shock when Liverpool knocked on the door. That was May 1970, and I was due to complete my degree in June, so it all came a bit out of the blue. I think Liverpool were in transition. The wonderful team of the '60s was being dismantled and a new side was being constructed. I certainly wasn't one of the big signings at the end of the 1969/70 campaign."

Bill Shankly obviously thought otherwise, and made the journey down the motorway to ensure he got his new winger. Answering the door to the great man might have left some people speechless. Heighway took it in his stride.

"Obviously I knew about him and how well-regarded he was. But I wasn't nervous when I met him. I suppose the fact that I wasn't a 16-year-old kid made a difference. I was 22, about to graduate and get married."

Of course all those factors entered the equation when he weighed up his options. "I was getting ready for a different career. Now my attitude was 'I've got a professional contract with a top club, and the money's okay'. It was a decent way of starting my first year of marriage and first year out of university. I'd been training to be a teacher and knew I'd always have the option of going back to that. So we decided to give it a shot and see what happened."

It proved to be a great choice, as weeks later he was in the first team, making his debut as a substitute against West Brom. Going from relative obscurity to a place in the Anfield set-up alongside the likes of Ian St John, Emlyn Hughes, Tommy Smith, Ian Callaghan and Ron Yeats would have intimidated most newcomers. "No, not really," Heighway says. "I guess football was just something that never really made me nervous. Other things did, especially a lot of other sports, but never football. I suppose you just take to something or you don't and it was never a problem for me. I just fitted in without any nerves."

Bobby Graham's broken leg that October gave Steve his real opportunity and he snatched it with both hands. The following month he won the affection of the crowd by playing a starring role in a stunning Merseyside derby victory at Anfield. Shankly's men were 2-0 down against the reigning champions with just over 20 minutes left when Heighway squeezed home a shot at Andy Rankin's near post. Then his cross enabled John Toshack to nod in an equaliser before Chris Lawler grabbed a sensational winner six minutes from time.

By the end of the 1970/71 season – less than a year after he'd become a Red – he was scoring in the FA Cup final at Wembley; unfortunately it wasn't enough to prevent an extra-time defeat against double winners Arsenal. That was a rare loss, as over the years that followed, Heighway's blend of pace and trickery tormented numerous opponents both at home and abroad, and helped bring huge success.

A whole host of medals came his way as Shankly, and later Paisley, conquered England and Europe. So many glorious occasions and big wins obviously create a host of special memories, and there's one that stands head and shoulders above all the rest.

"I think everyone who was involved in our first European Cup victory in 1977 would pick that night if you asked them to single out one particular success. To win it in Rome like that was the best moment. It came after winning the league and just four days after losing the FA Cup final. We'd never won it before and I think that was the crowning moment of my time at the club."

If singling out the top triumph is tough, how do you pick

Hats off: In high spirits after Rome '77 and (right) scoring in the 1974 FA Cup final

'I knew about him (Shankly) and how well-regarded he was. But I wasn't nervous when I met him. I suppose the fact I wasn't a 16-year-old kid made a difference. I was 22, about to graduate and get married'

a best player from that era? "It's obviously a really high standard," Heighway says. "As everyone knows there were loads of fantastic talents at the club, but for me Kenny Dalglish was simply the best. He was a terrific team player and a terrific individual, which is a rare combination. For those reasons, I'd put him just slightly ahead of Kevin Keegan because he was fabulous too."

Naturally being part of such a successful side put Heighway in the spotlight and probably would have resulted in an England call-up had his international future not already been sorted out. "My memory's a little suspect, but I think I'd been asked to play for Ireland even before I became established at Liverpool," he reveals. "I guess someone in the Republic set-up must have heard I had an Irish connection and made an enquiry."

That link came about because Heighway was born in Dublin in 1947. "I spent a decade there, but it never fully felt like home because I think we were always going to move back to England where all the rest of my family originally came from," he explains. "I think that was always on the

cards. They'd come across to Ireland when my dad got a job as a consulting engineer at Busaras in Dublin. I was born around then and that's why I was eligible for the green shirt."

Unfortunately he didn't always get the chance to wear it, as Shankly sometimes intervened. "There were times when the boss would withdraw me from squads without telling me," says the man who won 34 caps. "I'd only find out after the game had taken place. It was easy for him to do that because I was the only Irish player at the club, so if he didn't tell me about it, nobody else would. Back then Ireland didn't receive much coverage, it was all about the England and Scotland fixtures."

Owing to the rigorous demands of domestic football nowadays, players often have to pull out of international duty, so it looks like the legendary Scot was once again ahead of his time when he ensured one of his key assets didn't overdo it. "It made sense. I wasn't a big powerful player so I needed to look after myself. Near the end of every season I had to be careful that I didn't play too much, so that's what Bill was guaranteeing. Because I came into football so late I think I did need some of those games off. If I'd been part of the England squad with all those extra fixtures I'm not sure I would have survived at the highest level for so long."

When Heighway did actually hear about international action and made the trip across the Irish Sea it was a slightly unusual experience. "For most of the players it was a chance to return home and see their family and friends. In my case it was different because I didn't know anyone there. As a result, my trips were sometimes a little lonely. I'd go over and it felt like nobody at Liverpool realised I'd gone and I had nobody to see in Dublin, outside of the squad obviously. But I loved playing for Ireland all the time."

While success at club level might have come easy, on the international stage it proved elusive. "We were very close to qualifying for some major competitions on more than one occasion. I think we were very unfortunate not to do it," Heighway reflects. "It was a good team with some cracking players like Liam Brady, Frank Stapleton and David O'Leary. I think, if we had been a bit more high profile, we would have received a lot more attention for some of the refereeing decisions that went against us in key matches."

The qualification campaign for the 1982 World Cup in Spain is still a particularly sore point. Eoin Hand's men only lost two of their eight outings, finishing above Holland, a point behind Belgium and narrowly missing out on second place to France through goal difference. That French side, including Michel Platini, Jean Tigana and Didier Six, went on to reach the semi-finals before losing to Germany on penalties. "There was more than one controversial call that didn't go in our favour. If they had, it would have made a huge difference and we probably would have qualified. Afterwards we felt like we'd been cheated, and that it should have been us in Spain rather than the French."

Reaching the World Cup would have been a major achievement for Heighway, although he's not sure he would have actually played at the tournament. "I'd left Liverpool at the end of the 1980/81 season to go to America so there are no guarantees I'd have been in the Ireland squad the following summer," he says. "One of the problems with starting so late in the game was that it felt as if I finished

fairly quickly. As a result that tournament came at the back end of my career but I would definitely have gone if selected." It wasn't to be, and by the time Spain '82 began, Heighway had been part of the North American Soccer League for almost 12 months. "I took my whole family over there; we effectively emigrated," he says. "We stayed for eight years and had a wonderful time."

The only downside was that soccer's brief period of popularity in the States was drawing to a close just as Heighway arrived at the Minnesota Kicks. "A lot of clubs, including mine, were going bankrupt quite quickly. After about a year, Minnesota went bust and then I moved on to the indoor league before eventually retiring.

"It was certainly very different. In terms of playing I found it quite difficult. When you're surrounded by fantastic teammates – like I was at Liverpool – you can never be sure about how good you are. The standard obviously wasn't as high and, as a result, I didn't feel I was as effective. The fact that I was coming near the end of my career was obviously a factor in that too."

Despite the playing side of life not going exactly to plan, Heighway clearly loved his time in the USA. "Most people who go there don't come back and I can see why," he continues. "Everything about it is fantastic; the lifestyle, the weather and the cost of living are all great. My kids grew up there and they loved it too. I've still got a house in America and go over a couple of times every year because I like it so much."

With his playing days behind him, Heighway obviously needed a new challenge, and that came in the form of coaching. Originally working in his new homeland, it was a choice that would eventually bring him back to Merseyside. "I started coaching in America, and around 1989 I returned to Liverpool to join the Academy," he says. "It was a role I occupied for 18 fantastic years, during which I worked with some terrific kids and great players."

Graduates from the youth system in that time include the likes of Steve McManaman, Robbie Fowler, Michael Owen, Dominic Matteo, Jamie Carragher, Steven Gerrard, David Thompson and Stephen Warnock. "I'd like to think we helped bring the club's underage system into the 21st

'There were times when the boss would withdraw me from squads without telling me. I'd only find out after the game had taken place. It was easy for him to do that because I was the only Irish player at the club, so if he didn't tell me, nobody else would'

Outside the Shankly Gates
I heard a Kopite callin'
Shankly they have taken you away
But you left a great 11 before you went to heaven
Now it's glory 'round the fields of Anfield Road

Chorus
All 'round the fields of Anfield Road,
Where once we watched the King Kenny play (and could he play),
Stevie Heighway on the wing, we had dreams and songs to sing,
Of the glory 'round the fields of Anfield Road

Outside the Paisley Gates I heard a Kopite callin'
Paisley they have taken you away
But you left a great 11 back in Rome in '77
And the Redmen they're still playing the same way

All 'round the fields of Anfield Road
Where once we watched the King Kenny play (and could he play)
Stevie Heighway on the wing, we had dreams and songs to sing
Of the glory 'round the fields of Anfield Road

century," Heighway says. "We improved the facilities, took on more staff and invested a lot of time and money. As a result the Kirkby facility is a fabulous place for a kid to learn the game." Along the way, the U18 side won the prestigious FA Youth Cup on three occasions, including retaining it in 2007 thanks to a penalty shoot-out victory over Manchester United at Old Trafford. "They were good achievements," he again states modestly.

Some people would be quick to point to those pieces of silverware as signs of a job well done, but Heighway has a different way of looking at the situation. "It's an interesting trophy because you don't actually set out to win it. The main objective is to nurture players. So you could do a fantastic job of developing players and never make an impact in it. Or you could win the Youth Cup and do a lousy job bringing players through. Once you get to the later rounds you focus on it a little bit more. Winning it in '06 and '07 meant we almost had a full two-year span of involvement.

"That particular bunch of kids was absolutely fantastic in terms of talent and behaviour. I'd have taken them anywhere in the world to face any opposition in their age group and been very confident of them holding their own. It was great fun and I'm sure they'd all say the same. It was also pleasing to see some of them play a part in the reserves' league win in 2008. For me it was a natural progression. But that's all only worth something if they go on to enjoy top careers."

After the Youth Cup hat-trick was completed, Heighway stood down from his role at the Academy, a decision that couldn't have been easy. "I wanted to take a step back," he informs us. "I'm in my 60s now. I'd had 18 years of it. You work with youngsters to make them as good as they can be.

"But I think in the game today it's harder and harder for young guys to come up through the ranks. That's just an unfortunate fact of the modern game, and you see it happening all over the world. There's more money involved now and more competition for players. In the end it became a little bit frustrating. I think I'd had my time. There are other things I want to do. I'm still involved with the club, I watch the first team and the youth team on a regular basis

'I've been asked if I wanted to manage senior teams and my answer has always been 'no'. I don't think I'd have slept very well at night'

so I'm quite happy."

Having been a top player and cut his teeth in coaching underage sides, surely a move to senior management would have been a natural step for Heighway at some stage? "I've had the opportunity," he reveals without naming any clubs. "But I've spent my time working with younger players and that's what I enjoy. The nice thing about it now is you can specialise in that if you wish to. In the past it was a stepping-stone to somewhere else. Not now. I've been asked if I wanted to manage senior teams on more than one occasion and my answer has always been 'no'. I don't think I'd have slept very well at night if I'd been a first-team manager. It's not for me."

It means that although Heighway's name may proudly stand alongside Shankly, Kenny and Paisley as a quartet immortalised in song, he won't be following them into the Anfield hotseat. That fact matters little, as his exploits 'on the wing', and at The Academy, mean he will always be a Liverpool legend.

Career choice: Heighway opted to work with younger players

BRIAN DE SALVO originally hails from London and now lives in Wexford, Ireland. He signed pro-forms at Charlton as a teenager and was a goalkeeper with Brighton reserves before moving into the world of advertising. In 1971 RTE commissioned him to produce an anti-smoking advert.

I AM suspicious of good causes. As Frankie Howerd, quivering with righteous indignation, once pronounced on the subject of charity concerts: "Is the band doing it for nothing? Are the usherettes?"

So when I was asked to direct a television commercial to launch Ireland's anti-smoking campaign, I feared the worst.

First: they would pay the film crew union rates plus overtime and subsistence.

Second: they would ask me to accept a much-reduced fee because of the nature of the campaign.

Third: I would lack the bottle to refuse. I was right on all counts.

There was, however, a reward beyond money. The commercial was to star Steve Heighway of Liverpool.

It was my chance to get inside Anfield. For a former Brighton third-team goalkeeper, it was like offering a retired village priest's housekeeper tea with the Pope. In the Vatican.

Anfield's holy father was, of course, Bill Shankly, and the snag was that I had to invite myself to tea.

Contacting Mr Shankly from Dublin turned out to be about as easy as persuading Sir Alf Ramsey to manage Argentina.

Every day I rang Anfield to be told he had just left for the training ground.

Every day I rang the training ground to be told he was in the bath. They didn't even bother to vary the excuse.

"Why don't you come over to Anfield and I'll introduce you to Shanks?" suggested Steve Heighway, revealing a slight speech impediment that made my eyes glaze. He had dialogue to camera.

It was good thinking, but Heighway failed to realise how much I was in awe of Bill Shankly.

I heard the great man before I saw him. I had been left behind the corner of the Main Stand while Steve went to find him.

"No, no!" Shankly was saying, "he canna film the match!" I felt a weakness behind both knees.

"Next time he phones I'll talk to him!" Shankly was getting louder. My mouth was getting drier.

"He's here now." Steve sounded apologetic.

"WHAT!!!"

Bill Shankly rounded the corner of the stand leaving Heighway, who was no slouch over the first 10 yards, trailing.

It took an enormous effort on my part not to run away. Possibly the fact that now both my knees had seemed to lock helped.

But suddenly I was galvanised into action because after a handshake the conversation took place on the run.

"How d'you do, Mr de Salvo. You canna film the match. No, no, no. You don't want that.

"What you want is training shots. I will destroy Stevie Heighway on the training ground for you."

I never discovered why he thought bringing their hero to the point of collapse would encourage young people not to smoke.

"But Mr Shankly I want a montage cutting between Steve playing and Steve training. The atmosphere of Anfield on a big matchday contrasted with the discipline of the training ground."

"No, no! You canna film the match!"

He repeated his concept for the commercial. I repeated mine.

We must have covered 50 yards by now.

I reminded myself I was no longer Brighton's third-team goalkeeper and heard myself say: "Mr Shankly, I wouldn't dream of telling you how to pick the Liverpool team. You mustn't tell me what I need to make my commercial."

He stopped suddenly and peered up at me intently. There was an endless short pause during which, for once in my life, I felt gangling at five feet nine.

"If Mr Robinson says it's all right, it's all right," he said and moved on. Even Steve Heighway was impressed.

Saturday 13th February 1971. Liverpool versus Southampton in the 5th Round of the F.A. Cup.

The man from the BBC makes his paternal rounds rather like a commanding officer visiting a partisan unit rumoured to be friendly.

He apologises for not having space for us on the gantry and congratulates me on putting a camera in the dugout.

"What a good idea!" he muses. I am too tactful to point out that the rival channel has been doing this for some time.

The commercial is completed. "If you wanna be fit, schmoking's out," opines Steve Heighway in big close up; the lisp will be carefully filtered out in the dubbing studio.

It goes on to win the obligatory award for guilt given by the advertising industry to public health commercials.

Liverpool go on to Wembley, where Steve Heighway scores but they lose to Arsenal.

My mum, who thinks anyone from north of Watford is a foreigner, can't understand why I, a Londoner, support Liverpool. But then she never met Mr Shankly.

LIVERPOOL

STEVE HEIGHWAY

Razor sharp: Houghton takes a shot in a 1991 game against Norwich at Anfield

'Liverpool fans **genuinely love** their club, that's the special thing about them'

RAY HOUGHTON played a key role in bringing success to Anfield yet he is remarkably critical about his strike-rate in front of goal and he talks honestly about the way he suddenly left the club

NETTING the only goal against England just six minutes into Eire's first-ever game at a major tournament is enough to guarantee you legendary status in the Emerald Isle, and probably a few free drinks too.

If that wasn't enough, firing home another winner, this time in the 1994 World Cup victory over a star-studded Italian team, ensures you a place in the history books and probably free meals to go with the complimentary beverages. Those two moments are something no supporter of Jack Charlton's successful side will ever forget. But Ray Houghton, the Scottish-born midfielder with the Donegal dad, never thought of himself as a great

goalscorer, despite the protests of millions of Irish people.

"I think Ron Atkinson once said if I had six shots at John Lennon he'd still be alive today," he surprisingly says. "That probably summed it up. Both for club and country I was terrible in front of goal. It doesn't sit well with me at times. I still think about it now, some of the chances that I missed and the goals I could, and probably should, have scored."

But what about those efforts mentioned earlier? "You had to get it right now and again," he chuckles. "It took me quite a while to get my first international goal. I can remember plenty of bad misses before that header against England actually went in. I can recall others after that too, such as

Rivals: On the trail of Ryan Giggs in 1992. Below: Houghton celebrates his goal against Italy in 1994 with Terry Phelan and the 1988 win against England with trainer Charlie O'Leary

when we drew 1-1 with England at Wembley in a qualifier for Euro '92. I missed an absolute sitter with around five minutes remaining and that was probably the difference between us qualifying and not going to Sweden the following summer."

Again we argue the case by quoting Houghton's strike ratio for Liverpool: almost a goal every five games. For a midfielder at the top level that's more than respectable. Again the little man refuses to budge. "Those stats aren't bad, but in that team you were always going to get goals because you were encouraged to get forward as much as possible," he reasons. "No matter who played in that position it was the same. Before I came along Steve Nicol was playing there and he got plenty, including a hat-trick against Newcastle. Because of the way the team worked

you would always get chances."

Houghton enjoyed nearly five years as a Red, making 202 appearances in that time, but it's fair to say he made his name on the international stage, particularly with THAT header in Stuttgart. "It was our first-ever time at a major tournament and we were pitted against England, one of the favourites for the trophy. For us to get a win was brilliant. The whole day and everything that went with it was fantastic and something I'll always treasure. It was undoubtedly our best game."

Houghton's pinpoint dipping, cushioned effort has probably been replayed a million times. And for the Eire number eight it was as much a relief as a joy to see the ball hit the net. "To get your first goal for your country is special, no matter who it comes against," he points out. "Doing it in

Ireland's first match in a big tournament against England? It doesn't get much better. It really was a dream come true. People have asked me whether I prefer that goal or the one against Italy. It's got to be '88 because it was my first. I'd waited a long time but it was certainly worth it."

Like many of his international colleagues at the time, Houghton's Eire qualifications were often questioned. He has no doubt about the validity of his 'Irishness'. "Others might have mentioned it but it was never a problem for me. My dad was from Donegal, so I never really thought of it as a big issue. Even now, when I hear the Irish national anthem being played the hairs on the back of my neck stand up. It's a really passionate song and always makes me think of my father."

When Houghton started out in the game, his dad had mentioned the possibility of one day pulling on a green shirt. "He'd suggested it, but at the time trying to just become a professional footballer was tough enough. That was the first challenge for me. I got all the 'you're too small' rubbish that players of my stature usually get. So I had to overcome those hurdles first. Thankfully my attitude was always to never give in, and I eventually made it."

Before then the midfielder had been let go by West Ham before moving on to Fulham. While at Craven Cottage he played against the Reds in a League Cup tie during which he allowed himself to dream about one day running out in Red. "I can still remember thinking it would be amazing to play for that team. I'd grown up watching a lot of Liverpool and I always admired the type of football they produced. It was always exciting, I loved one-touch football, and I loved pass-and-move stuff. They were one of the best teams around when I was a kid, and of course they also had Kenny who'd played for Celtic, so I always kept an eye on his progress. But a transfer never materialised and I moved on to Oxford United. By then I thought a switch to a really big club had probably passed me by."

Instead, Houghton's impressive form for The Us eventually earned him the move he'd longed for. "Playing with Oxford in the old first division gave me a real opportunity to show what I could do, and thankfully Liverpool came in for me in October 1987."

Just like his path through football, Houghton's signing in at Anfield didn't follow the usual procedure. "Most former Liverpool players talk about walking into Melwood or the ground to sign for the club, but I didn't do that. I played for Oxford against West Ham on a Saturday, then got in the car with my wife and drove up to Liverpool. There I met Kenny Dalglish, Peter Robinson and the chairman, John Smith, at a hotel.

"We went through the deal that night, I stayed over and the next day I went for my medical while my wife went home. Then I went straight up to Scotland with Kenny because there was a testimonial game for Jim Duffy. I don't think many players would do that today.

Ray Houghton boasted a decent scoring ratio during his Anfield career

'It was a joy to be on the park with so many legends. Everyone on that team knew exactly how to pass and move and play the game'

'It wasn't my decision (to leave). That was down to Graeme Souness. I'd just had what I thought was one of my best campaigns. Graeme had also told me how well I'd done for him so it was all out of the blue'

"They usually get a chance to sit back and take it all in. But I went straight in at the deep end," he laughs.

At the time the midfielder was described as 'the final piece' of the great team Dalglish was assembling. It's a phrase we've heard in relation to LFC on many occasions over recent summers. Houghton paid absolutely no attention to it. "We hear that analogy all the time but it doesn't exist, there's never a final piece," he explains. "You've got to keep adding to what you have. It can never be complete. I never thought of myself in that way so there was no pressure on me. I think Kenny thought I was a player who could slot into the system and be comfortable with the way Liverpool played. I'd been up to Anfield to watch the team a few weeks before that and the lads were absolutely flying. They didn't need me to solve any problems or be 'a final piece'."

He mightn't have been the last part, but Houghton certainly fitted in perfectly alongside the likes of John Aldridge, Peter Beardsley and John Barnes. Having debuted in October, he went on to feature a further 34 times, netting seven goals in all competitions as the Reds stormed to the title, suffering only two defeats along the way.

"It was a joy to play that kind of football and be on the park with so many legends," he says. "Everyone on that team knew exactly how to pass and move and play the game. All the lads knew instinctively what to do and where to run. I'd been at other clubs where you might have had one, two or maybe three players who wanted the ball all the time. At Liverpool, everyone looked for it. They were always in a position to receive it and you had to be a bad player not to pick the right option. That first season we won the league and just missed out on a double after the defeat against Wimbledon. The following year we won the cup and just missed out on the league. They were great times. Then there was the famous 5-0 win over Nottingham Forest, which has been described by many people as the best performance from an English club side ever. I also managed to score the winner in an FA Cup game against Everton, so there were many, many highs and very few lows."

In action during a famous night – the epic comeback against Auxerre in 1991

Wembley: Shooting on goal during the 1989 FA Cup final

As Houghton says, his time at the club was mainly a joy, although April 1989 and the death of 96 supporters at Hillsborough was obviously a very difficult period for everyone connected with LFC. "That was undoubtedly the toughest time," he says. "It was bigger than football. Liverpool fans genuinely love their club, that's the special thing about them, and to lose so many was tragic. Finishing runners-up in the league or losing a cup final could never compare to that."

Less than three years after that fateful day in Sheffield, Houghton was on his way out of the club he'd served so well as he surprisingly joined Aston Villa. If those on the Kop found it strange to see him leaving, it was also a shock to the player.

"It wasn't my decision," he continues. "That was down to Graeme Souness. I'd just had what I thought was one of my best campaigns.

"I'd been one of the six players nominated for the PFA Player of the Year and won many fans' player of the year awards too. Graeme had also told me how well I'd done for him so it was all a bit out of the blue. He offered me wages

that were a lot lower than what some other players were on so it was clear my time was up and he didn't really want to keep me."

Instead, Birmingham was his next stop where he teamed up with former Red and international colleague Steve Staunton. Houghton almost landed a third league title as part of Ron Atkinson's side, and enjoyed his football there before eventually hanging up his boots after spells at Crystal Palace, Reading and Stevenage Borough. Nowadays he works as a pundit. "I really like the media side of the game," he says. "Obviously I can't play any more but football is still my passion and I want to remain involved in some capacity."

The former Red loves the game so much that he still hasn't given up hope of one day becoming a manager. "I wouldn't say it definitely isn't for me. It's something that eats away at me.

"However, I feel modern management is a complete lottery. At times there doesn't seem to be any rhyme or reason as to who gets what job. That's what probably puts me off. But I'll never say never."

'Just being on that pitch was a **thrill**. You've got to savour **every** moment'

Birkenhead-born JASON McATEER talks about his rise through the ranks at Marine and Bolton before the call came from his boyhood heroes. Saying no to King Kenny wasn't easy, though . . .

"ONE minute I'm lining out for Marine at Burscough on a wet and windy evening. Then, all of a sudden, I'm playing with my heroes like John Aldridge, Steve Staunton and Ray Houghton against Franco Baresi, Paolo Maldini and Roberto Baggio at Giants Stadium in New York on my birthday, and we win 1-0! It doesn't really get any better than that. It was probably the best few weeks of my life. Everything about it was perfect. 'Jim'll Fix It' couldn't have sorted it so well."

That was the summer of 1994, but even now Jason McAteer can still recall his rapid rise from non-league to the World Cup just like it was yesterday. Of course, it didn't happen that quickly. It actually took the Birkenhead lad a few years to go from the Mariners to the magic of the USA, but it's still an impressive achievement. And even more so when you consider that the likeable midfielder had at one stage given up on his dream of ever becoming a footballer.

"I thought my chance had passed me by," he explains. As a kid I'd had trials at Manchester United, Chester and Tranmere. Everton were interested in me too but it just never really happened. When I turned 20 it hit me that I'd have to start looking at another career. I thought my chance of playing professionally was all but gone."

It all changed when a Liverpool legend happened to spot McAteer in action and took a gamble on the youngster. "Phil Neal was Bolton boss at the time. I had no contract at Marine so he offered me £110 per week and a 12-month deal. Unfortunately, I think the ink was barely dry on it when Phil got the sack and Bruce Rioch came in."

A new manager usually means a new beginning for most players, and that was certainly the case.

"From a personal point of view it was probably the best thing that could have happened. Suddenly we were all starting again on an even keel. Bruce gave all the kids a chance. I thought: 'I'm not going to let this opportunity pass me by', and grabbed it with both hands. I knew if I didn't take it, that was it. Coming from a boxing family, I was always a fit lad. My dad pushed us hard and I think that stood me in good stead."

The extra effort paid off when injuries to others left Rioch with little option but to pitch McAteer in at the deep end during an FA Cup tie with Rochdale. "Thankfully I scored and managed to stay in the team."

Over the seasons that followed, Wanderers established themselves as the country's biggest cup giant-killers. "Bruce built a really good side," McAteer recalls. "There were individuals like Alan Stubbs, Alan Thompson and John McGinley who got a lot of praise. But there were a lot of guys who never really got the credit they deserved. Guys like Andy Walker, Mark Seagraves, Keith Brannigan and Phil Brown. We were a team full of very different ingredients and they all clicked. On top of that, Bruce was a good manager and Colin Todd was a fantastic coach. So it all worked well.

"I remember occasions when we were 3-0 down and came back to win 4-3. Or 2-0 down at half-time and won 3-2. The spirit was fantastic and we gained promotion twice and had some terrific results against big sides like Everton, Aston Villa, Arsenal and Liverpool. It was a good place to learn about the game and provided me with a great determination to do well."

As one of the star performers in a side that seemed to consistently defy the odds, it was no surprise when the chance to play international football came his way. Obviously, hailing from Birkenhead he could have worn the three lions but, with an Irish grandfather, there was also the option to pull on a green shirt.

"Until it actually happened, it wasn't something I'd ever really thought about," he confesses. "There had been a few rumours about it, then Jimmy Armfield who was working with the FA at the time asked me to play for England. A week later, Jack Charlton turned up to watch our FA Cup match with Everton. Afterwards he called me to one side in the players' lounge and mentioned the World Cup in America. He didn't guarantee anything, but said I had a chance. So I asked him to let me have some time to think about it. With my family's Irish roots, I'd always kept an eye on the team's progress. Plus, for me, I also had Ronnie Whelan, Ray Houghton, John Aldridge and Steve Staunton, who were all great players for Liverpool and legends I really looked up to."

Despite those factors, it obviously required serious thought, and McAteer had some experienced heads to call upon for advice. "Bruce (Rioch) was born in England but played for Scotland so he understood my dilemma."

Then, still undecided, McAteer made the short trip to Anfield to watch the Reds in midweek action, although it was events after the game that would actually influence his future.

"I met Ronnie (Whelan) and he told me playing for Ireland would be the best thing I'd ever do in my career. When Ronnie – one of your all-time heroes – tells you that, you can't do anything else. My mind was made up and I remember ringing Jack and saying I'd love to come over to Dublin. I remember me, Gary Kelly and Phil Babb made our debuts against Russia at a very windy Lansdowne Road. That was the start of something great. Shortly afterwards, we went away and beat the Germans in a friendly and that game booked a place on the plane for us, 'the three amigos' as we were christened later. It really was special. Ronnie doesn't get many calls right, but he was spot on with that one!"

Making the giant leap from the footballing outskirts to the biggest sporting event in the world is something out of the realms of fantasy, or maybe a Carlsberg advert. So does McAteer see it happening again?

"Would it occur nowadays? It's unlikely," he believes. "Football's changed a lot since then. People don't really take chances on players as much. They want them to have a pedigree. What they don't know they don't like. They want to know you've had a good schooling in the game and been brought up in the right ranks at an academy. And I think that's a shame because there are some great players out there who've slipped through the net or developed at a slower rate.

"It's very rare now for someone who hasn't made it by the time they're 20 to go on to play top-flight football, never mind reach the World Cup."

It was almost the perfect story. Only one thing was missing from McAteer's dream, and that was the opportunity to wear the famous Red jersey with a Liverbird on the chest. "I'd been a fan since I was 12 years old," he

says. "My uncle was a season ticket holder, and some of his mates couldn't make it, so he took me and my cousin instead. It was against Manchester City at Anfield, the place was buzzing and Kenny Dalglish was absolutely amazing. He instantly became my hero, and after that I was always Kenny whenever I played in the park."

Unfortunately, those 90 minutes were a rare treat for the youngster, rather than a regular occurrence. "Where I came from money was tight. Instead of spending quite a bit of cash on a match ticket, we were busy buying essentials like clothes and shoes. Even that was hard work at times but that's the way it was. It was only when it was a freebie that I actually got to go to the game."

'It's very rare now for someone who hasn't made it by the time they're 20 to go on to play top-flight football, never mind reach the World Cup'

League big guns. Then in the summer of '95 he was on his way to training when the phone rang. Roy Evans had been one of his supposed admirers, but it was his hero who had actually made the first move. "Bolton put a £4.5m price tag on my head and it turned out that Blackburn had offered a combined fee of £9m for me and Alan Stubbs. That was accepted and the next step was talks with Kenny. So I found myself sitting in a room with my idol asking if I'd join his club."

Most professionals would have signed the contract without hesitation, although McAteer had other ideas. "My heart was always set on playing for Liverpool and I asked my agent to find out if they were really interested. During the meeting with Kenny they came back to us saying they'd also now agreed the fee and wanted to talk. I told Kenny about this and he basically called off our discussions there and then because he knew what would happen. It was strange because on one side I had my hero - the manager who'd just won the Premier League with Blackburn – and everything sorted for me and Stubbsy to go there. And on the other, Liverpool were knocking on the door – and it was actually Kenny's fault that I supported the club! I obviously agreed to go to Anfield and then rang him back. I told him thanks very much but this is your fault. I only want to do what you did. And Kenny took it on the chin and wished me all the best, which was great to hear."

Turning down the King was the only minus of McAteer putting pen to paper on a deal that finally made him a Red. "I was a kid from Birkenhead who spent most of my childhood running around pretending to be Kenny," he says now, still with disbelief in his voice. "I'd thought I'd never be a footballer, then had four great years at Bolton and was on the crest of a wave already. I'd sat on the bench when we'd won in the FA Cup game at Anfield, and lined up in the Coca-Cola Cup final against the lads, and thought that was as good as it could ever get. Then it somehow gets even better when I'm running down the tunnel with 'You'll Never Walk Alone' blasting out. You can't put into words how good that is. I used to say to one of my mates: 'If I could buy you this as a present, I would, because nothing beats it.' It was special, fantastic, amazing."

McAteer spent nearly four years at the club and when you ask him to pick his best memory it's impossible to select just one. "Everyone I bump into has some story from that period. I loved it all. I remember Ronnie (Whelan) once telling me to enjoy every moment of my career because it will go quickly. At the time I thought he was talking rubbish and it wouldn't end for another 10 years. But again, he was right. People always mention the Newcastle 4-3 game as a highlight and it was great but there are many others, some not so obvious.

"My first goal came against Rochdale in the FA Cup and that was a great feeling. Unfortunately it was the last in a 7-0 win and nobody else seemed to care. I wanted to go mad celebrating while the rest of the lads were already on the way back to the halfway line! That nearly always happened to me. I managed to get on the scoresheet in our 3-0 FA Cup semi-final win over Aston Villa at Old Trafford but it went

Happy memories: Signing in and (top) the team celebrates the famous 4-3 win against Newcastle

That situation occurred sporadically, although there was always a ticket available for the stadium on the opposite side of Stanley Park. "A lot of my older mates were Everton fans who used to go to Goodison every Saturday and they nearly always had a spare, so I'd end up tagging along with them." In such circumstances the temptation to turn blue might have entered the heads of most teenagers, but with McAteer that was never a possibility.

"After I'd been to watch Liverpool and then seen Everton there was no comparison," is his emphatic stance.

"Everything, from the atmosphere to the players on show was better at Liverpool, particularly Kenny. He lit up my life and as a result there was no chance of me ever becoming a bluenose."

Having seen his profile rise considerably with Bolton and Ireland, a move to a larger club seemed inevitable, and paper talk linked McAteer with almost all of the Premier

On his return from injury, McAteer bags a brace against West Ham (left) and celebrates as Ian Rush scores his 100th FA Cup goal against Rochdale in 1996 – McAteer got his first goal in the 7-0 win

completely unnoticed because Robbie Fowler had already netted two crackers.

"Breaking my leg and then coming back to score a brace against West Ham was a great moment too. I probably would have got a hat-trick if Karlheinz Riedle had squared the ball to me in the second half. I've always cursed him since then, the greedy German! It obviously wasn't an important game but it was special for me, a great memory.

"To be perfectly honest, just being on that pitch was a thrill. You've got to savour every moment because you think it's going to last forever but it doesn't. The way the game is now, you might be in the team on a Saturday and get sold on Sunday, so you have to make the most of it."

And would he change any of the events?

"The fact that we didn't win anything," is the instant response. "We were as close as any Liverpool side to winning the title during that period. Manchester United bought the right players at the right time. We didn't. If we had, we could definitely have won the league. I think a couple of top-class centre-halves and a top-notch centre-forward, allied to the squad already there, could really have made an impact. Also, I should have remained at the club a bit longer. Unfortunately, Roy Evans and Ronnie Moran were gone and some of the players were going their separate ways. Gerard Houllier came in and he had new ideas which I wasn't part of. But I still should have stayed."

Instead, a move to Blackburn materialised, four years after he'd turned down the initial opportunity to become a Rover. By that stage Kenny had long since left, and life at Ewood Park was far from perfect, although on the

international scene the good times appeared to be beckoning once again.

Jack Charlton had brought his incredible reign to an end after a painful play-off defeat against Holland (at Anfield of all places) meant the side wouldn't be taking part in Euro '96. Then Mick McCarthy took over. "He was like my uncle," McAteer reveals. "Mick's one of my closest friends in football even though we don't speak on a regular basis. I could ring him up now, and it would be as if we'd spoken just an hour ago. He's been an important figure in my life and I loved working with him. He's a great fellow. At first he found it difficult when he took over from Jack, because they were very big shoes to fill. It took him a while to realise he had to put his own stamp on it. But he eventually did work it out."

It started badly: qualification for France '98 proved elusive, and then an injury-time equaliser for Macedonia and eventual away-goal play-off defeat against Turkey prevented them making it to the next European Championships. "We'd been unbelievably close to reaching Euro 2000, and because of that there was a real belief amongst the squad," McAteer says. "Roy Keane was at his peak around then, definitely one of the best midfielders in the world. We'd also got a good crop of other experienced guys like Shay Given and Niall Quinn, while the young lads such as Robbie Keane and Damien Duff were also on the scene. So I was confident we could make it to the next World Cup." The qualifying draw for the 2002 competition pitched them in alongside Holland and Portugal.

"It looked difficult, very difficult," he laughs. "And having those two away from home early on also appeared to make it even tougher. But we knew if we could come back from Amsterdam and Lisbon with even a draw in each, we'd have it in our own hands."

It was a tough ask, but McCarthy's men did exactly that. "If you're being honest, we should have won in Holland," he continues. (Robbie) Keane opened the scoring before McAteer netted a great goal with his left foot to put the boys in green 2-0 up before the Dutch fought back to secure a 2-2 draw. In Lisbon a few weeks later, the scoreline was 1-1, and after progressing unbeaten through the next half a dozen fixtures, it all boiled down to a home clash with Holland. "By half-time they could have been three or four-nil up that day," he says without over-exaggeration. "Thankfully they couldn't put the ball in the net."

With just over 30 minutes remaining, Gary Kelly received his second yellow card and victory for Louis van Gaal's men appeared to be only a matter of time. That was until (Roy) Keane set off on a typically determined run and the ball was eventually worked to Steve Finnan. His cross from the right wing evaded everyone and allowed McAteer to arrive in the box, slam the ball past Edwin van der Sar and send Landsdowne Road wild.

"It was our spirit and camaraderie that got us through that game," he says. "I know everyone always mentions that about the Irish camp, but it was true. You become really close to the lads and you looked out for each other. "We had to really hang on and dig deep, but everyone played a part. Even Roy, who was man of the match, said as much afterwards."

Barring some huge upsets, that result virtually ended Dutch hopes of reaching Japan and Korea. However, with Portugal topping the group it meant the Irish couldn't book their plane tickets just yet. Before that, the small matter of a two-legged play-off against Iran had to be overcome.

"After the effort we'd put in, there was no way we were going to lose," he says with the determination that was obviously present at the time. A 2-0 first-leg victory in Dublin put them on the way, and a 1-0 reversal in Tehran was enough to get the celebrations started, or almost. "It was something I'll never forget. The final whistle that night brought tears to my eyes.

"It was a strange trip. We were kept in the dressing room for two hours after the game. Then we were delayed for ages at the airport, and of course we couldn't have a drink. So our emotions were all over the place. We'd qualified for the World Cup but we were sitting around the departure lounge as if we'd just been beaten. But as soon as we got into international airspace the champagne opened. That was special. Apart from the '94 World Cup, qualifying for 2002 was my best moment in a green shirt."

Unfortunately, the following May that feeling evaporated, as we all know what happened before the squad got to even kick a ball in the actual competition. "It's probably one of the biggest disappointments of my career," is how McAteer sums it all up. "My thinking on it was you don't just get to go to a World Cup. You've got to earn it, and it's a lot of very hard work spanning nearly two years. We travelled from Andorra to Iran to do it. We got there and it wasn't a case of

Famous goal: Scoring against Holland at Lansdowne Road

Still living the dream: Turning out with the Liverpool Legends team keeps McAteer involved with the club

job done, far from it. But it was an achievement to qualify. Then Roy went and did what he did, and that put a massive dampener on it all. What happened shouldn't have, and then the media descended on our hotel and that made it really difficult."

With the skipper on his way back to the Emerald Isle, the squad, supporters and the country were left in chaos, and it didn't get any better for McAteer.

"I'd worked hard to get there, overcoming a lot of problems with Graeme Souness at Blackburn to do so. Then I got a nasty injury after an awful challenge in a warm-up game. My medial ligaments were gone and I got an injection and took some painkillers to try and play. I told Mick I was okay and he trusted me but, realistically, I was probably only 70 per cent fit for the opener against Cameroon.

"My knee gave away and I had to come off at half-time. I didn't play at all in the next game, got on against Saudi Arabia and wasn't involved against Spain. And then it was all over. It was an awful way for things to go."

In the months that followed, the pressure on McCarthy built and he eventually quit the post.

Brian Kerr took up the reins but the 31-year-old McAteer, who was now at Sunderland and once again working with 'Uncle Mick', knew his time on the international scene had

come to a halt. "I retired and rang Brian. It took him four days to get back to me, which doesn't need any comment. So it was a sad conclusion to my time with Ireland, but Ronnie was spot on when he said it would be a good decision. It was, and I loved it."

With his Irish career at an end, McAteer started to think about his next step, and in 2004 left the Stadium of Light to join Tranmere where he started coaching under the guidance of Brian Little. "I loved that, especially working with the young lads. They give you so much respect. Then unfortunately Brian got the sack.

"There was a chance of Aldo and me taking over, but he decided against it, which I totally understood. And I wasn't ready to do it with anyone else.

"So I decided to try and stay on when Ronnie Moore came in. It didn't work out and, in the end, I had to walk away. I hung my boots up and thought enough is enough."

A move into the media materialised and, although it was enjoyable, an even more tempting offer eventually came along. "I started lining out for Liverpool legends and it's absolutely brilliant," he says, sounding like an excited kid again. "I'm back playing with the likes of Ronnie, Aldo, Rob Jones and Steve McManaman. It's a combination of my heroes and my mates from my Liverpool days. For me it doesn't really get any better than that."

'I started lining out for Liverpool legends and it's absolutely brilliant. It's a combination of my heroes and my mates from my Liverpool days. For me it doesn't really get any better than that'

Mixed fortunes: Phil Babb and Mark Kennedy

Phil Babb & Mark Kennedy

WHEN you look back over the greatest Irishmen to don the Red shirt, the images that spring to mind are Steve Heighway sprinting down the wing, Ray Houghton jinking through the middle, Ronnie Whelan at his all-action combative best or John Aldridge scoring. Few people would think of either Phil Babb or Mark Kennedy.

Unfortunately for Babb, typing his name into a search engine results not in a montage of his best pieces of defending, but the lasting image of his Liverpool career – an eye-watering collision with a post at the Anfield Road end. No one who watches that clip can doubt Babb's commitment to the cause, but the fact that he could not prevent Pierluigi Casiraghi's shot finding the net that day encapsulates Babb's Liverpool career in a nutshell.

Arriving from Coventry on the back of a glorious 1994 World Cup, the future seemed bright. His stock had risen considerably in the Giants Stadium of New York, where he was part of a backline that kept Roberto Baggio and co quiet in one of Ireland's greatest-ever victories. Centre-half had seemingly been the Achilles heel of Liverpool's failed title challenges up to that point, so in the summer of '94 both Babb and John Scales arrived.

The £3.6m price shows how highly the then 23-year-old was rated, setting a British record for a defender. But the London-born Irishman's Liverpool career could scarcely have gotten off to a worse start. Making his entrance at Old Trafford, he watched the first 70 minutes from the bench as his new colleagues were battling out a 0-0 draw. Within minutes of replacing Jan Molby to secure a point, Liverpool were 2-0 down, with one of the goals rather ironically coming courtesy of an error by fellow new boy Scales.

Shortly after Babb's arrival at Anfield, boss Roy Evans' attacking instinct led to the use of wingbacks in a 5-3-2 or 3-5-2 system. This meant that Babb, Scales and Neil Ruddock were to form a centre-back triumvirate in the hope that their variety of styles would ease Liverpool's defensive vulnerability.

Signs of improvements could be seen. In Babb's first three seasons at the club, Liverpool conceded fewer goals than the actual league winners. But having established himself as part of the side, the next step was to marshal a team that could genuinely challenge for the title, and this never materialised. The disappointing 1998/99 season was to be Babb's last in the first team.

Meanwhile, the name Kennedy will always have a special place in the history of Liverpool Football Club.

It evokes memories of European Cup wins in Paris and Rome. Alan Kennedy scored the goal that sunk the mighty Real Madrid during our first ever competitve meeting with the Spaniards, and three years later he netted the winning penalty against the Romans in their own back yard.

Namesake Ray was a vital cog in the Red machine between 1974 and 1981, and he scored a crucial goal in the '81 European Cup semi-final, second leg away to Bayern Munich. His six league titles and three European Cups will stand the test of time.

So it was with a whiff of excitement and optimism that a third Kennedy joined the ranks in 1995. 18-year-old Mark became the most expensive teenage footballer in our history when he was signed from Millwall for an initial fee of £1.5 million.

His debut as a substitute just two weeks later offered real encouragement, despite the result. A 1-0 home defeat by Leeds was a disappointing beginning, however Kennedy came closest to beating John Lukic in goal, having his shot tipped onto the crossbar.

Despite the initial optimism that his 18-minute cameo appearance provided, Kennedy's Anfield career never really got going. He found it difficult to break into the first team, and in his three years at the club he made only 16 league appearances.

As a result, footballing memories of Kennedy in a Red shirt are sparse. His career highlight was probably the opening goal in the Division One play-off final, which helped Wolves seal their return to the top flight in 2003.

By Gerry McGuinness

Irish Reds Fantasy XI

We've all spent an hour or two in the pub debating the greatest Liverpool XI of all time – but what about the best Irish Reds team? We reckon that with Whelan and Aldo in the side, Stevie Heighway on the wing and a decent defence this team would give anyone a game – and we've even got someone who will happily take the goalkeeper's gloves in an emergency

NATURALLY a lot of the side pick themselves, with individuals such as Elisha Scott, Steve Finnan, Mark Lawrenson, Ronnie Whelan, Ray Houghton and John Aldridge good enough to grace most teams.

At the back we've decided to employ Steve Staunton as centre-half, a position he occupied during the later stages of his career, and he forms a solid unit alongside Lawro, Finnan and Jim Beglin. 'Stan' could also don the goalkeeper gloves in an emergency, therefore negating the need for a sub keeper.

Midfield is probably the strongest area of the 11, with Jason McAteer and Steve Heighway on opposite flanks and the latter given licence to roam into other areas, dragging defenders out of position.

Whelan would easily pull the strings while at the same time protecting his back four, which would give Houghton numerous chances to get forward.

In attack, it's a case of two busy and nippy frontmen who would constantly harass defenders, as well as having the ability to put the ball in the net. With McAteer and Heighway providing service, goals surely wouldn't be a problem. On the bench, there's plenty of cover, with Michael Robinson giving us the option of changing our angle of attack. And there's also the option of pushing Heighway into a more advanced role if a tactical reshuffle was required.

John Hynes

1. ELISHA SCOTT
DOB: 24/08/1894
BIRTHPLACE: Belfast
JOINED LIVERPOOL: 1912
LFC APPEARANCES/GOALS: 468/0

A lack of height – he was less than six feet tall – proved no barrier to the agile Ulsterman. His older brother Billy lined out for Everton, and when Elisha eventually established himself at Anfield, he went on to win league medals in 1922 and '23. A real fans' favourite, Scott addressed the crowd before his final game in 1934, bringing a tear to the eye of many a Scouser before he returned to his native Belfast.

2. STEVE FINNAN
DOB: 24/04/76
BIRTHPLACE: Limerick
JOINED LIVERPOOL: 2003
LFC APPEARANCES/GOALS: 217/1

A MOVE to Merseyside had long been rumoured for Finnan and it eventually came to fruition in the summer of 2003.

The full-back went on to become a key component in the team that claimed the Champions League and FA Cup in 2005 and 2006 respectively.

As well as being solid defensively, his attacking play was a great weapon in our recent success.

3. MARK LAWRENSON
DOB: 02/06/57
BIRTHPLACE: Preston
JOINED LIVERPOOL: 1981
LFC APPEARANCES/GOALS: 356/18
QUALIFIED FOR IRELAND
THROUGH: Grandfather.

QUICK and good in the tackle, he formed a formidable central defensive partnership with Alan Hansen.

Lawrenson could easily have become a Red in 1977, but ended up at Brighton instead.

When he eventually arrived at Anfield he went on to claim five league championships, one European Cup and three League Cups, before injury brought his top-flight career to a premature halt at the age of 30.

4. STEVE STAUNTON
DOB: 19/01/69
BIRTHPLACE: Drogheda
JOINED LIVERPOOL: 1986 and 1998
LFC APPEARANCES/GOALS: 148/7

ORIGINALLY a talented left-back, Stan finished his international career at centre-half.

Graeme Souness sold Staunton only to see him become one of the most consistent defenders in the country at Aston Villa.

More recently, you won't need telling that he will be remembered for a brief spell in the Republic of Ireland managerial chair.

Elisha

Finn

Stan

Lawro

Beglin

Whelan (Capt)

Razor

Jason McAteer

Stevie on the wing

Robbie (not Keano)

Aldo

5. JIM BEGLIN
DOB: 29/07/63
BIRTHPLACE: Waterford
JOINED LIVERPOOL: 1983
LFC APPEARANCES/GOALS: 98/3

"HE has the ideal build for a full-back," was how Bob Paisley summed up his last-ever Liverpool signing.

Beglin arrived at Anfield in May 1983, played a vital part in the double success three years later, and appeared set for a bright future. Unfortunately, a broken leg suffered against Everton in January 1987 ended his Liverpool career and he is now a TV analyst.

6. RAY HOUGHTON
DOB: 09/01/62
BIRTHPLACE: Glasgow
JOINED LIVERPOOL: 1987
LFC APPEARANCES/GOALS: 202/38
QUALIFIED FOR IRELAND THROUGH: Father

SCOTTISH-BORN Houghton had already been on the books of West Ham and Fulham before he rose to prominence alongside John Aldridge at Oxford United.

A tremendous worker and an intelligent footballer, he could operate on either flank and had the great habit of appearing at the right time in the penalty area.

Two of his most spectacular strikes came on the international stage when he netted winners against England and Italy.

7. RONNIE WHELAN
DOB: 25/09/61
BIRTHPLACE: Dublin
JOINED LIVERPOOL: 1979
LFC APPEARANCES/GOALS: 493/73

"A good goalscorer, good passer and good runner. A determined and hard midfield player who was very underrated." That was how Kenny Dalglish summed up his teammate. The midfielder marked his Liverpool debut with a goal against Stoke in 1981, and over the next decade established himself as a vital part of the Liverpool line-up until injury disrupted his later years.

Whelan succeeded Ray Kennedy on the left side of midfield before eventually moving into the centre when John Barnes arrived.

He also had a useful knack of popping up with vital goals, including League Cup final strikes against Spurs and Manchester United. Whelan's the skipper of our side.

8. STEVE HEIGHWAY
DOB: 25/11/47
BIRTHPLACE: Dublin
JOINED LIVERPOOL: 1970
LFC APPEARANCES/GOALS: 475/76

HEIGHWAY had everything a winger requires: speed, dribbling ability, an eye for a pass and, although never prolific, he certainly knew where the net was.

The fact that his name is featured in a real Kop anthem illustrates just how good he was, and in the modern transfer market he would surely command a massive fee.

9. ROBBIE KEANE
DOB: 08/07/80
BIRTHPLACE: Dublin
JOINED LIVERPOOL: 2008
LFC APPEARANCES/GOALS: 28/7

ROBBIE Keane's arrival at Anfield was one of the most unexpected signings of recent times.

A clever, instinctive forward, he'd impressed for Wolves, Coventry, Leeds and Spurs, while he also enjoyed a brief spell at Inter Milan.

In pulling on the number seven shirt, he fulfilled a boyhood dream and made every Irish Red happy.

He took some time to find his feet but broke his duck against PSV Eindhoven in the Champions League

Unfortunately Keane failed to ever nail down a regular place in Rafa Benitez's starting line-up and moved back to Tottenham after just 28 appearances which brought him seven goals.

10. JOHN ALDRIDGE
DOB: 18/09/58
BIRTHPLACE: Liverpool
JOINED LIVERPOOL: 1987
LFC APPEARANCES/GOALS: 104/63
QUALIFIED FOR IRELAND THROUGH: Grandmother

'ALDO' only enjoyed a brief spell at L4 but, as his record shows, he's one of the best goal-getters we've ever had.

Having stood on the Kop as a kid, he thought the chance to pull on a Red shirt had passed him by.

But after prolific spells at Newport and Oxford he finally moved to Anfield at the age of 28.

The fact that he casually slipped into Ian Rush's boots as our leading striker illustrated exactly how good he was. Scoring in 10 consecutive league games in 1988 is a feat that nobody has surpassed.

11. JASON MCATEER
DOB: 18/06/71
BIRTHPLACE: Birkenhead
JOINED LIVERPOOL: 1995
LFC APPEARANCES/GOALS: 139/6
QUALIFIED FOR IRELAND THROUGH: Grandfather

'TRIGGER' was a boyhood Red who caught the eye as part of Bolton's cup giant-killers in the early '90s. Originally a central midfielder, he found a place in Roy Evans' side as an attacking wing-back; a move that initially appeared to suit him. But after 91 appearances he moved on to Blackburn.

On the bench

12. PHIL BABB
DOB: 30/11/70
BIRTHPLACE: London
JOINED LIVERPOOL: 1994
LFC APPEARANCES/GOALS: 170/1
QUALIFIED FOR IRELAND THROUGH: Mother.

UNFORTUNATELY for the central defender, he will always be remembered for THAT collision with the Annie Road posts. After some tremendous performances alongside Paul McGrath at the 1994 World Cup, Roy Evans moved quickly to seal his signature from Coventry City, in the hope of solidifying the Liverpool defence.

His first year was probably his best, as it contained 47 appearances and a Coca Cola Cup medal. He left on a free transfer to join Sporting Lisbon.

13. MARK KENNEDY
DOB: 15/05/76
BIRTHPLACE: Dublin
JOINED LIVERPOOL: 1995
LFC GAMES/GOALS: 21/0

EXPECTATIONS were high when the 18-year-old winger arrived from Millwall. On his debut against Leeds at Anfield, he was inches away from a stunning goal when his powerful shot rebounded off the woodwork. However, that was as good as it got, and over the next three years he only appeared a further 20 times.

14. WILLIAM 'BILLY' LACEY
DOB: 24/09/1889
BIRTHPLACE: Wexford,
JOINED LIVERPOOL: 1912
LFC APPEARANCES/GOALS: 259/29

THE versatile winger became a Red as part of the deal that took Harold Uren to Goodison Park, and it was Liverpool who profited more from the exchange.

After the First World War he went on to win league titles in 1922 and '23.

It was his ability to create chances for others that made him so important, although on the way to the 1914 FA Cup final he managed to find the net a remarkable five times.

15. MICHAEL ROBINSON
DOB: 12/07/58
BIRTHPLACE: Leicester
JOINED LIVERPOOL: 1983
LFC APPEARANCES/GOALS: 52/13
QUALIFIED FOR IRELAND THROUGH: Mother.

SEVILLE, Newcastle and Manchester United were rumoured to be chasing the powerful Brighton centre-forward before Joe Fagan swooped.

He mainly served as a back-up striker, with the highlight of his time at Anfield being a hat-trick against West Ham, after which Kenny Dalglish wrote "I don't believe it" on the matchball!

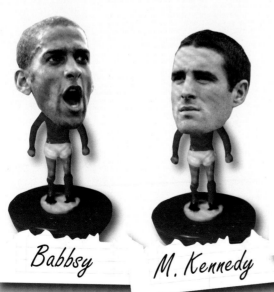

Babbsy   *M. Kennedy*

Billy Lacey   *Robbo*

'Whenever I **get the chance,** I go down the tunnel and **touch the sign.** It's a special place'

JIM BEGLIN's Liverpool career was tragically curtailed after a crunching challenge with Gary Stevens in 1987, but before that he enjoyed great success as the team overhauled Everton to snatch the league and FA Cup double. Now a pundit on TV and radio, he still loves being involved in football and savouring the unique Anfield atmosphere

BACK in November 1982, the Reds made the short trip across the Irish Sea for a friendly against Shamrock Rovers in Dublin.

On the night the game finished 1-1, with Liam Buckley's late header cancelling out Ian Rush's opener. Afterwards probably every member of the home side dreamt about one day lining up with the likes of Bruce Grobbelaar, Mark Lawrenson, Ronnie Whelan, Kenny Dalglish and Ian Rush.

Such wishes are obvious and usually futile, although it did come true for one member of the Irish team. "I remember being in awe of all those players that night," Jim Beglin says now. "So to find myself alongside them a few seasons later really was the stuff dreams are made of. Of course you imagine it as a kid, but to actually get amongst it all is a very special feeling."

Beglin became a Red in May 1983, although if things had been different, he could have ended up wearing similar colours at another English side. "I'd gone to Shamrock Rovers from Waterford Bohemians," he explains. "With the rivalry between those two clubs it probably wasn't the best move in the eyes of many locals, but in terms of progress it was brilliant for me. Basically I'd done my leaving cert and two weeks later I was in pre-season with Rovers. It was full-time then, and an attractive proposition in that I'd only be 100 miles up the road from home, learning my trade under the tutelage of Johnny Giles. It also meant I wouldn't have to switch to England at such a young age. I could mature a bit more before making the move across the Irish Sea at a later stage."

As Beglin says that was an ideal scenario for the youngster, unfortunately it didn't last long. "Things began to break up, the full-time system was falling apart. So the club was trying to find jobs for the players who could go part-time instead. I was doing a commercial course with Aer Lingus when I was informed that Arsenal had come in for me."

The Gunners had obviously been keeping tabs on the defender and felt he was good enough to make the grade. "Rovers were actually playing in Waterford that night so I said goodbye to the family, thinking I'd be going back to Dublin after the game and on to London the next day. Then Louis Kilcoyne told me that (Arsenal manager) Terry Neill had changed his mind and the deal was off. Within a week I was on my way to Liverpool. Of course I was absolutely delighted."

The Highbury club's change of heart was never explained to Beglin although he did bring the subject up recently. "Funnily enough I met Terry Neill at a golf event and I asked him about it. I think he thought I was still angry," Beglin laughs. "I wasn't, and he said he didn't handle the deal so he couldn't give me any explanation. I was just a kid and he wouldn't have had a clue who I was. But I thanked him because it all worked out for the best."

Initially Beglin was on trial at Anfield during which he played two reserve games. "As far as I can remember they were both convincing wins and, after 10 days, the club said they wanted to sign me permanently. I'd been all geared up and ready to join Arsenal, then heard it was off and I was going to Liverpool. In the space of just over a week I went from being delighted to disappointed to delighted again."

Beglin was the great Bob Paisley's last signing, and making the move from the Irish league to Liverpool was obviously a huge jump. "Definitely, but I think a lot of what Gilesy, who was a hard taskmaster, preached to me as a youngster was a great grounding. Liverpool's standards were sky high. Gilesy had a similar philosophy, and what I learned from him really helped me. I was fortunate that I'd

Beglin celebrates the 1986
FA Cup win over Everton
with his teammates

gone to Rovers and worked under him. That enabled me to hit the ground running when I moved over."

Like most kids in Ireland, Beglin grew up on a diet of English soccer and naturally he had his favourite team. "Believe it or not I was a Chelsea fan," he laughs. "It was mentioned recently and a lot of Liverpool supporters have accused me of being biased. But I suppose when you're commentating on a Champions League semi-final between those two teams anything you say is open to accusations of favouritism. My response was: 'I played in the Liverpool side that won the league at Stamford Bridge. I obviously wasn't supporting the home team that day!' When I was growing up all my family were soccer mad. My father – God rest him – was a Red. My older brother was Manchester United and my younger brother was Everton, so we all hated each other on matchday. Chelsea had been my team, but as soon as I moved to Liverpool that went out of the window."

Of course the young Beglin wasn't the only Irishman at Anfield in 1983. "Ronnie Whelan and Mark Lawrenson were already there, and I think Michael Robinson arrived shortly after that. Obviously Lawro and Robbo were born in England but had the Irish connection and were very much part of the scene. Lawro in particular was a legend in my eyes. What a defender. I really looked up to him. I'd been called for training with Irish teams for a bit of experience and encountered Ronnie there so it was good to see a familiar face. It also meant I didn't have to make international trips on my own which was another benefit."

Although Beglin had a natural connection to that trio he

> **'There was a lot of flak flying and you got picked up on any mistake, all in jest. But, put it this way, you could have a bad run. And you'd be made to feel pretty small. You could make a fool of yourself and you'd really know about it'**

had to bide his time before actually playing with them on a regular basis. "They were all first-team players, whereas I still had to complete my apprenticeship," he continues. "So I didn't have an awful lot to do with them at first. But they were friendly and went out of their way to make me feel welcome. It was only once the club actually felt I was progressing, and they started taking me with the first team, that I got to really know the lads."

Walking into any dressing room for the first time is a daunting prospect, even more so when the club in question is one of the most successful around and the place is dominated by living legends. "I was still a kid so I would have been very, very quiet at first," Beglin says. "Basically I spoke when I was spoken to. I wouldn't dare take the mickey out of a senior professional because I knew I'd end up regretting it. As a young lad you had to be on your guard

because everyone was trying to wind you up. It was very childish but also very funny.

"You didn't want to be the victim. But if you were the new kid on the block you were tested. They wanted to know if you could handle it and give some back. It was an essential part of things. I heard that Bob Paisley said one or two players, such as Avi Cohen, sometimes struggled with the sense of humour in the dressing room. There was a lot of flak flying and you got picked up on for any mistake, all in jest of course. But, put it this way, you could have a bad run. And you'd be made to feel pretty small. You could make a fool of yourself and you'd really know about it. On the other hand, you wouldn't necessarily be making a fool of yourself but you'd still end up getting a load of stick."

It's clear Beglin enjoyed the banter as he tells all this while laughing. He views it as a good thing that stopped any individual from getting carried away by success. "It was all part of the club's ethic. Keeping your feet on the ground was important. Ronnie Moran used to come out with some great psychological comments. He'd say: 'You guys might have beaten Manchester United yesterday but so what. Nobody cares about that. You've got to win the next game now.' That kept people in check. No one ever got to the point where they thought they were bigger than the club. The dressing room joking was an important part of that, and it was always a good laugh."

While Beglin was being tested in the dressing room banter stakes, there was also a huge challenge ahead on the pitch if he was to find a place in the first team, with one particular star already firmly cemented into the left-back slot. "Alan Kennedy was an absolute legend, so I knew I'd have to bide my time. Back then you did anyway. It meant a year or 18 months playing in the Reserve Central League side. I was doing that until I started going on the road with the first team, just for the experience. Actually that used to frustrate me because I'd miss a reserve game if I went on those trips and I always wanted to play. I remember some of the lads telling me to calm down, be patient and learn as much as I could."

Surprisingly, Beglin had originally started out as a wide man before becoming a defender when he got older. "Initially I'd been a left-winger as a kid and then occupied the old inside-left position," he recalls. "I was able to read the game better coming from deeper so I progressed into a more defensive-minded player who was able to nick the ball. Before I joined Rovers I was operating as a centre-half, although I wasn't the kind who'd go and win it. I'd rather play a bit, so if I had a bruiser beside me it was ideal. And when I got to Rovers I had a guy called Ronnie Murphy who was a great partner for me. Then there was a problem at left-back, and that became my position. I got a run in the side and never really looked back."

It was a similar scenario that gave Beglin his big chance at Anfield in November 1984. Injuries meant Joe Fagan had to shuffle his pack for Southampton's visit, with the Waterford man slotting into midfield. Making your senior debut for Liverpool is obviously a huge moment, unfortunately for Beglin it was almost ruined by nerves.

"Joe always picked his team the day before – unlike Kenny who named his side an hour and a quarter before kick-off –

Euro battler: Beglin and Dalglish challenge Juventus' Michel Platini in 1985 (far left) and Beglin has his own tussle with Zbigniew Boniek in the ill-fated clash

and that was the worst thing he could have done. All my family came over from Ireland and I was a nervous wreck. The excitement, and apprehension were awful. I hardly slept a wink that night."

Naturally, the following afternoon it all took its toll on the young Beglin. "I was a fit lad but I remember really flagging towards the end," he laughs. "I know the pace at that level was higher, but I think all the adrenalin and nerves I'd had prior to making my debut really caught up with me. In particular, the last 15 minutes were a massive struggle."

That day was something Beglin had been anticipating for a while as, understandable nervous tension aside, he felt he was ready to step up. "The hierarchy at Anfield might have thought different, but I was really chomping at the bit by that stage. I'd won two Central Leagues and we were playing well. I felt I couldn't really do any more to further my cause, and thankfully I got my chance. To play in front of the Kop in full cry was an unbelievable experience. It was everything I could have dreamt of."

Unfortunately, reality kicked in four days later when the Republic of Ireland travelled to Copenhagen for a mid-week World Cup qualifier with Denmark. A knee injury picked up

Riding a challenge from Celtic Legends' Joe Miller during a charity match at Celtic Park in 2006

that night meant Beglin was forced to sit on the sidelines again, and another opportunity didn't come his way until the following April, when Kennedy suffered a knock.

"I got in again and managed to play about 14 games then. It was great to get a run in the side and feel what it's all about, both physically and mentally. It's okay to make your debut and not feature again. But having a sustained spell in the team teaches you a lot. Playing with Dalglish, Hansen, Grobbelaar, Whelan and Rush was a real eye-opener."

During that 1984/85 run-in, Beglin even managed to score in the semi-final of the European Cup against Panathinaikos before featuring on that ill-fated night in Heysel. When the following campaign came around, Fagan had departed and Dalglish was handed the role of player-manager. The Scot obviously rated Beglin and started him in the first three league outings. By the end of the season, he'd featured a further 50 times and played his part in a glorious finale.

"From start to finish, it couldn't have gone any better for me. It was a tremendous learning curve and I really cherish that year all the more because of what eventually happened."

As we all know, Dalglish's side finished with the League and FA Cup double, although at one stage it looked an impossible target. "For Kenny to do that during his first season in charge was an unbelievable achievement. I don't think I've ever told him, but it really was magnificent. I remember Everton beat us 2-0 that February and it's probably fair to say we weren't looking great. Then Kenny came back into the team, his presence brought a real sharpness to the side and suddenly we were on a great run. We probably weren't playing the most attractive football, but it was businesslike and got the job done."

Getting it done involved an unbeaten run that began in early March and stretched to the end of the season. Along the way a 0-0 draw against Sheffield Wednesday might have been viewed as a bad outcome but one old head had a feeling it might be crucial. "I remember after the final whistle that day Ronnie Moran saying it could be the point that wins the title," Beglin recalls. "We won it by a few in the end but results like that certainly helped us gain momentum."

With the Reds on a fantastic roll, it all boiled down to a trip to Stamford Bridge where victory was essential. As now seems to be the norm, our record in that part of London wasn't the best, and many felt Dalglish's men would falter at the last. "It would have been nicer to do it at Anfield, but wherever we would have been playing it was going to be tough," Beglin continues. "I remember the great belief we had in the team. We were very solid at the back, and with the players we had we knew we could always score. So if we could keep things tight we were likely to nick one. Another reason for optimism was the fact that we'd won down there in the cup that January so we knew we could do it again."

In truth, the performance wasn't the best but the result was all that mattered as Dalglish famously netted the only goal. And it came courtesy of a Beglin assist, although on many other occasions he wouldn't have been in the position to turn provider. "I never went up for corners," he reveals.

Beglin scores the fourth goal against
Panathinaikos during Liverpool's European Cup
semi-final first-leg match at Anfield in April 1985

"Thankfully I did on that day and had a shot booted off the line. But instead of going back to the other end I decided to stay where I was."

The ball was only half-cleared by the Londoners to the edge of the box where Whelan eventually headed it towards Beglin who again takes up the story. "I knew Kenny was to my right so I just had to help it on. He took it on his chest and stuck it away. I'll never forget that ball hitting the net. It's nice to know that I played a little part in it. I'm sure it was one of Kenny's greatest moments, and he had dozens to choose from."

A week later the newly crowned League champions travelled to the Twin Towers for the first ever all-Merseyside FA Cup final. When Gary Lineker put our neighbours ahead prior to the interval, the situation didn't look good. Thankfully, a second-half comeback was enough to clinch more silverware. "That day probably mirrored our season," Beglin believes. "We stuttered at first before eventually getting it together. At Wembley we probably didn't play for about an hour and then it all clicked into gear. It was another example of our spirit. We had the confidence that

we could pull results out of any situation, and we did it when it mattered most. To clinch the double was special. My only wish is that my dad could have been there. He would have been the proudest man on earth. I had about 60 family and friends over from Ireland anyway. So we were well represented, but I would have loved for him in particular, as a Liverpool fan, to have witnessed it."

As we all know, that league and cup success was as good as it got for Beglin. The following year he continued to be a first-team regular, and having just turned 23 during the summer looked to have a glorious Liverpool career ahead. Then in January 1987 tragedy struck during a League Cup tie with Everton when Gary Stevens' tackle left him with a broken leg. His season and, although he didn't know it at the time, his Liverpool career were in ruins.

"I remember the doctors told me it was bad. I think there were certain people who felt when they saw me lying there on the pitch that I'd never recover. I suppose, in many respects, they were right."

Paisley said it was one of the worst broken legs he'd ever seen during his many years in the game. Beglin's reaction:

'To clinch the double was special. My only wish is that my dad could have been there. He would have been the proudest man on earth'

'Just before I broke my leg I'd played a lot of games and was feeling good. All my little inconsistencies, that you have when you first start out, were beginning to disappear'

"I'll come back stronger, that was my attitude. It had to be. I've always been fairly positive. Sometimes things can go against you but my attitude will always be good."

His broken bone was pieced together by the surgeon who, according to the Irishman, did an incredible job. Unfortunately that wasn't the end of the problems. "During the rehab my other leg was worked extremely hard. In a reserve game against Manchester United at Anfield I was playing in midfield to improve my fitness. I can still remember turning and my right knee cartilage tearing. Afterwards about 80 per cent of it was removed. Because of that, it was a case of bone on bone and when they're grinding together like that it's only a matter of time before you have to stop playing."

Beglin bravely battled on, but knew he was fighting against impossible odds. "I could see things unfolding on a pitch but couldn't react quickly enough anymore. That was a horrible feeling. I never got my real sharpness back again."

The writing was clearly on the wall, and by the end of the 1988/89 season everyone knew what was coming. "Kenny called me in and told me the worst. The club did me a favour by letting me go on a free transfer. That enabled me to get a better deal elsewhere."

To be in your prime and then have it all cruelly snatched away is a sobering thought. And Beglin's mindset around that time is completely understandable. "Simply devastated," he says with sadness in his voice. "It really was shattering. Just before I broke my leg I'd played a lot of games and was feeling good. All my little inconsistencies, that you have when you first start out, were beginning to disappear. I was starting to be seen as the main left-back – not guaranteed a place by any means, of course – but I felt it was coming together. Instead of continuing in that vein, I was brokenhearted. I didn't want to face up to the reality of

Reunion: With former Reds Phil Neal, David Johnson and Phil Thompson at a dinner in Liverpool

the situation. I thought I'd dealt with it well at the time. But, looking back now, I think it affected me much more than I realised. You blot a lot out because you're trying to cling onto a career. My confidence took a right battering, not just as a professional footballer but as a person, too. Basically the nature of the profession means you do want to carry on, but really I was fooling myself."

With his time up at Anfield, Beglin moved on to second division Leeds United, hoping that his injury horrors were firmly behind him. "I never wanted to leave Liverpool but I did join a very progressive club and I was praying that things would take off for me again."

Sadly, that was far from the case. "It was just one injury after another. Eventually I went back to the surgeon and he simply told me I had to stop. I did a lot of damage to my knee by trying to play on for 18 months too long. I couldn't do anything before games and when I did actually manage to get on the field I ended up walking around like John Wayne afterwards. In the end I wasn't enjoying it and it was actually a huge relief to hang up my boots. On top of what I'd already been through at Liverpool, it was another huge disappointment for me. To go from being part of one of the best teams in Europe – I know we were banned – to end up retiring a few years later was awful."

Few would blame him if he was bitter about the whole agonising end to his playing days. Most people would be. With Beglin that isn't the case. "It happened. There's no point in dwelling on it because all you'll do is beat yourself up. I eventually sorted it out in my head and I've moved on. I look back as being very fortunate to have experienced something that other pros with very lengthy careers don't ever get to sample."

That is certainly true. Beglin was just 21 when he played in a European Cup final and 22 when he won the double. He also won a second division title while at Elland Road. "I can take huge positives from it all," he says. "I got to pack in a lot at a young age. Playing for Bohemians was great, Rovers was a fantastic grounding and Liverpool was the best ever. Even at Leeds, where it sometimes felt like one frustrating injury nightmare, I still featured in over 20 games. It might have ended badly but I still look on it all as one huge plus."

With his playing days abruptly brought to a halt, Beglin had to find other options, and being a coach was something that naturally appealed. He started doing his badges, although it wasn't long before injury problems again intervened. "After doing double sessions every day my knee started to swell up. It meant putting ice on it when I got home in the evening and I didn't fancy doing that every day for the rest of my life."

With that avenue shut another one eventually opened, as during his time on the sidelines at Leeds he'd already done some media work with RTE Radio. "I remember Howard

Night to remember: Beglin now has the privilege of commentating on European nights at Anfield – the clash against Arsenal in April 2008 being one of his own personal highlights.

Top: With Five Live's Alan Green in 2004

Wilkinson asking me about it in his office. At that stage I hadn't really thought of it as an alternative career but he suggested I should."

Beglin's experiences at Liverpool and his calm manner made him a well-informed and natural pundit. The phone started ringing more frequently and before long he was a regular voice of football in the UK. "Thankfully I'm still getting away with it," he laughs again. "My mother used to say everything happens for a reason and maybe that's been the case. When I retired it was a bit easier to get into the media side because not as many guys were doing it. At the same time, I hadn't huge stature. Yes, I'd played for one of the top clubs. But not for 10 or 15 years, so I had to really work hard when I was starting out."

It obviously paid off, and the role has taken the former full-back to numerous World Cups and European Championships, and naturally it also means working on Liverpool games. "I always get a real buzz from Champions League nights at Anfield. Whenever I get the chance, I go down the tunnel and touch the sign. It's a special place. If

people ask me what's my favourite ground there's only one answer I can give. Not because I'm trying to butter up Liverpool fans. It's because it is awesome and I was lucky enough to play there. I managed to get my name on the scoresheet in a European Cup semi-final at the Kop End, and I'll treasure that for as long as I live. It's one of my best memories because it happened in such an awesome, awesome place. So to go back there on a regular basis as part of ITV's team is a real bonus for me."

Our recent runs in Europe mean Beglin has witnessed some amazing action up close, although it's almost impossible to choose the best 90 minutes. "On a couple of occasions I've turned to my colleague and said: 'I'm speechless.' As anyone who knows me will tell you, that's very rare. Istanbul was obviously one of those. But it's the nights in front of the Kop that really stand out. Olympiakos and Arsenal were absolutely stunning.Some people might suggest I was unlucky with the way my career ended but I count myself lucky to do what I do now. I'm still involved in football and I absolutely love it."

'Anfield is obviously famous for its **European nights** – I would love to have **sampled that** once'

HE broke into the team under Kenny and Roy Evans brought him back to Anfield but Houllier and Souness sold him. STEVE STAUNTON had an up and down time at the club but he never lost his affection for Liverpool. He looks back at his time wearing the red shirt – and on one memorable occasion, the goalkeeping gloves too

I N the long history of LFC, not many players can claim to have filled every position on the field. It's a rare distinction, but Steve Staunton did exactly that during his two spells at Anfield. Usually a defender, he also operated in midfield, occasionally attack and even donned the goalkeeper jersey during the heat of a Merseyside derby.

'Stan', as he is affectionately known, arrived at Liverpool in 1986 as a 17-year-old, before going on to establish himself as a vital part of Kenny Dalglish's squad, although he could have ended up plying his trade in a blue shirt at the other end of the East Lancs road. "I'd been playing for Dundalk and gone on trial at Man City, he recalls. "But I wasn't good enough and they didn't take me on, so I came back to Ireland."

While the Manchester blues mightn't have rated Staunton, Liverpool obviously felt he had something. "They offered me a trial and once I heard of their interest my mind was made up. I knew I wanted to go there. Back then Liverpool were obviously the best team in the country and, in my eyes, the best club in the world. Like many Irish people, I grew up as a Celtic fan but I always had a soft spot for Liverpool, so to be

going there was awesome. Thankfully they offered me a contract which I was only too happy to sign."

The teenager might have felt all his Christmases had come at once, but before he could sample first-team action, he had to overcome a common problem. "I was from Drogheda, a small town, and all of a sudden I was away from home in a big city and you had to grow up quickly, both on and off the field. It was a steep learning curve.

Could have
been a
Blue: Steve
Staunton
went on
trial for
Manchester
City – but
didn't make
the grade

'There were a few of us. I was in the reserves with Ken DeMange and Brian Mooney, we were all away from Ireland and experiencing the same thing. We'd go playing snooker together and looked out for each other so that certainly made life easier'

"But my dad told me I couldn't be running back home every few weeks. Of course he was right. I knew what I wanted, and I was prepared to sacrifice a lot for it. But it was tough and, even to this day, I still get homesick."

Of course at that time in the mid-'80s Staunton wasn't the only Irishman at Anfield. "There were a few of us. I was in the reserves with Ken DeMange and Brian Mooney, we were all away from Ireland and experiencing the same thing. We'd go playing snooker together and looked out for each other so that certainly made life easier."

There were also more established Irish stars on the scene, although it would be a while before Staunton rubbed shoulders with the likes of Ronnie Whelan, Mark Lawrenson or Jim Beglin. "Of course I knew who they were, but I didn't see much of the lads at first."

As was the Liverpool way back then, the young Staunton bided his time with the reserves, learning about the game. He also had a loan spell at Bradford City to further his development. Finally, just over two years after he'd moved across the Irish Sea, Kenny Dalglish gave him his debut when he came on for Jan Molby during the first half of a 1-1 draw with Tottenham at Anfield.

Staunton obviously impressed the Scot, and by the end of the campaign was a regular fixture in the side, picking up an FA Cup medal after the 3-2 triumph over Everton. "It was awesome," he says. "That season ended with a win at Wembley but, to be honest, every game for Liverpool felt like a cup final. The whole experience was brilliant. We won the cup and the league during my first period at the club, and you always dream about doing that when you're a kid. For me the only downside to it all was the fact that we never played in Europe when we were at our peak. Anfield is obviously famous for its European nights; I would love to have sampled that just once."

Staunton might not have faced the cream of the continent, but he did create his own piece of history in a League Cup tie. It came as part of a bizarre scenario that involved the Reds playing the away leg of their second-round fixture with Wigan Athletic at home.

Staunton replaced Ian Rush during the interval with the game still scoreless. By the 88th minute he'd unbelievably bagged a hat-trick at the Kop end in a 3-0 win. "To do it at any time would be special, at that end of the ground made it even more so," he states. "I've still got the matchball at home now. I'm sure not many players have come on and got three goals so it's a great memory for me."

More than a decade later, after Staunton had returned to the club following his time at Aston Villa, his versatility again earned him a place in the headlines during a clash with Everton. "Sander Westerveld and Franny Jeffers both got sent off for what was nothing more than handbags," Staunton laughs.

"We'd used all our subs, so obviously someone needed to take over the goalkeeper's jersey. I'd played a bit of Gaelic football during my youth, so Phil Thompson said I should go in goals. It was near the end of the game and I didn't have much to do really apart from stopping an Abel Xavier shot."

If you can recall the save, you'll know Staunton is being

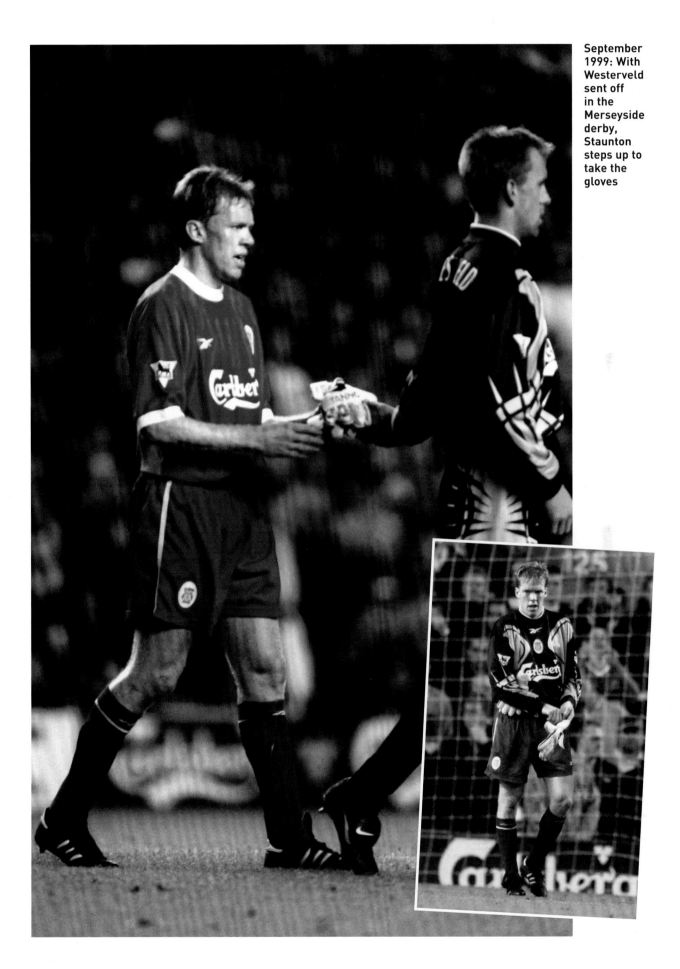

September 1999: With Westerveld sent off in the Merseyside derby, Staunton steps up to take the gloves

Staunton homes in on Lee Sharpe of Manchester United at Old Trafford, 1991

far too modest, as he had to stretch full-length to prevent the future Red getting on the scoresheet. That derby came during Staunton's first campaign back on Merseyside. Many Reds felt he should never have left in 1991, and the left-footer agrees. "It wasn't a case of me leaving," he quickly protests. "I was still only 22 and loved being at the club. But Graeme Souness came in and it was made perfectly clear to me that I might be better off looking for a new team. Unfortunately it was obvious that my playing days at Liverpool were finished."

The manager's ushering of Staunton towards the exit was based on a new ruling that classified Irish, Scottish and Welsh players as foreigners for European competitions, thus limiting selection options. "There were already three English guys at the club who could play in the left-back role so Graeme decided he didn't want me anymore. It was tough and I was gutted. But I didn't really have a choice. All

I could do was move on."

Staunton's new home was Villa Park where, alongside Ray Houghton, he was part of Ron Atkinson's side that pushed Manchester United all the way for the 1992/93 Premier League title. Despite his success there, Liverpool was never far from his thoughts.

"When Roy Evans took over, he tried to get me back almost every summer but it didn't happen for a while. Villa were playing some good football under Ron and doing okay – we almost won the league and also won two League Cups – while Liverpool were a team in transition with a new boss trying to build a side, so I wasn't sure about it."

Eventually, in the summer of 1998, Staunton gave in and agreed to return to Anfield. "It was special to walk into the club again. Of course I was more than happy to return." Unfortunately, as before, fate dealt him another cruel hand.

"Within a few months Roy had departed and Gerard

'Within a few months Roy Evans had departed and Gerard Houllier was in sole charge. Straight away I felt it wasn't good news for me'

'Ultimately I thought we received an awful lot of unfair criticism. I was helping out my country in a time of need but didn't get much reward for that'

Houllier was in sole charge. Straight away I felt it wasn't good news for me."

That proved to be the case, as Staunton featured in only 16 games of the following campaign before joining Crystal Palace on loan. In the treble season he appeared just twice, with his last ever Liverpool appearance coming during a 2-2 draw at Olympiakos in November 2001. The following month he left Liverpool for good, again joining Villa, this time on a free transfer.

At the age of 31, many felt his best days were behind him, but Staunton proved that wasn't the case by helping Mick McCarthy's Republic of Ireland side reach the 2002 World Cup. When the competition proper began in Korea and Japan, he became the only Irish player to have played at three World Cups. Along the way he featured in every game of Italia '90, USA '94 and the '02 competition.

"That's something I'll always cherish," he replies when the stat is mentioned. "1990 was brilliant, whereas I think the heat really killed us in America four years later. We did manage to beat Italy in the Giants Stadium in the opening game, of course, but really the temperatures took too much out of us."

That victory over the Italians was a special day for Irish football, although it's the last of his three World Cup adventures that Staunton looks back on with most fondness. "For me 2002 was the best," he says. "We knew we had a chance in that group if we could come out of the Germany game without suffering a defeat. Obviously we did that, but the way it happened with Robbie Keane's last-minute equaliser was special. It doesn't really get any better."

Again Staunton's modesty comes to the fore, as he doesn't mention that dramatic night in Ibaraki saw him win his 100th cap for his country and he also wore the skipper's armband in the absence of Roy Keane. The former Manchester United man's early return home was one of the stories of the year although, even now, Staunton refuses to comment on what actually occurred on the island of Saipan.

"Enough has been said on that subject and I'm not going to add to it now," is all the Drogheda man will concede. Dealing with player problems such as that are part of being a manager. Staunton himself would go on to experience it when he hung up his boots after further spells at Coventry City and Walsall. Brian Kerr had succeeded McCarthy, but after failing to qualify for the 2006 World Cup, the FAI decided to end his contract. Many names were tipped for the

Still hurting: Stan was given a tough time as Ireland boss

role, including Alex Ferguson, so it was a surprise when Staunton was unveiled as the new boss in January 2006 with Bobby Robson also part of the set-up in a consultant's role.

It was obviously a huge risk to chuck such an inexperienced coach into the testing environment of international management, and in the end Staunton's reign only lasted until October 2008. In that time his team finished behind Germany and the Czech Republic in Group D, and failed to reach the European Championships.

"Obviously the whole experience didn't work out as I'd planned," Staunton, who sounds like he is still hurting from it, says. "I was asked to do a four-year job and always viewed it as that. When I initially took the post the idea was for us to bring through young players with the aim of making it to the 2010 World Cup in Africa. That was the target. Unfortunately, other people had different ideas. I think we suffered one or two bad results in qualifying, especially away to Cyprus, but ultimately I thought we received an awful lot of unfair criticism. I was helping out my country in a time of need but didn't get much reward for that. We finished third, with two very good sides ahead of us."

Despite the treatment he received, Staunton would have remained in the role if he had been given the option. And he also refuses to rule out being Eire boss at some point again in the future. "I was very disappointed to leave the job and especially the way it happened," he continues. "Long term, I'd love to be a number one again. If I get more experience and the FAI asked me again, I wouldn't rule it out. That's yet to be decided."

Some might scoff at the idea, but Staunton has previous form for returning to old stomping grounds. Doing so with Ireland might be his toughest task, although, if he can fill every role on the pitch for Liverpool, then surely nothing is beyond the always-determined Louth man.

'Pulling on **that** shirt was the greatest trophy'

It was a dream come true for childhood Liverpool fan MICHAEL ROBINSON when he signed for the mighty Reds, and in his short career the trophies came thick and fast

SOME players can go their entire career without ever winning the European Cup or a league title. In the space of 16 months, Michael Robinson claimed both of those medals and also added a League Cup crown for good measure.

The centre-forward only enjoyed a brief, albeit glorious sojourn at Anfield, but even without such success it would still have been a dream come true for the boyhood Red. Robinson originally sprung to prominence at Preston North End before moving on to Manchester City and then Brighton, from where Joe Fagan swooped to land his services ahead of the likes of Manchester United, Newcastle and Seville. Having spent many afternoons on the Kop during his youth, the day he put pen to LFC-headed paper is something he will always cherish.

"I actually signed my contract at Schiphol Airport in Amsterdam," he recalls as he takes up the story. "Club secretary Peter Robinson and chairman John Smith asked me how much I wanted as I didn't have an agent to negotiate on my behalf. 'I'll pay you £100 per week,' was my response. In my mind there was no way I could sit there and argue with Liverpool Football Club over money. This was my dream for as long as I could remember so when it came to it I was basically incapable of negotiating a deal."

Such a scenario would obviously never occur nowadays so how was the pleasant problem solved? "Then Peter went away and rang my former club Brighton," Robinson continues. "He discovered how much I'd been on and it turned out I was the highest-paid player in British football at the time. Peter told Mr Smith this, at which point I intervened and informed them they didn't need to match my previous wage. As far as I was concerned they could have

paid me whatever they wanted to. They didn't listen and Mr Smith elegantly said they'd pay me what I was already on and also increase it. After that he turned around to Mr Robinson and said: 'Some of the other boys might want to renegotiate their contracts when they hear this!' But for me that was all completely inconsequential, it was just an enormous honour to become a Liverpool player. The first time I met my teammates I didn't know whether to shake their hands and introduce myself or ask them for an autograph."

It was usually the custom for any new signings to spend some time in the reserves before making their first-team bow. With Robinson, that approach wasn't used, and he was plunged straight into the side for the 1983 Charity Shield against Manchester United at Wembley. The following weekend the league campaign kicked off at Molineux, which meant Robinson had to wait until September for his first taste of Anfield as a home player.

"Of course I'd walked out there many times as part of the opposition team," he continues. "That meant coming out of the left-hand dressing room and, as the volume grew, it felt like we were being fed to the lions. The priority then had been to frustrate the Kop and maybe pinch a goal. As a visitor there was no pressure: you went there with everything to gain. You normally lost so nobody really expected any other result. Now it was different. When that famous wall of noise is for you and your team, the responsibility is enormous. Of course I touched the sign as we walked out. It was amazing. You were so aware of the history of the club. To play for Liverpool in the 1980s was unbelievable. So much was expected of you."

Despite fulfilling his childhood dream it was a burden that weighed on the new man's shoulders. "I remember being asked afterwards if the shirt felt heavy," he says. "And I joked: 'Yes, because I was used to wearing nine and now I was carrying two numbers, a one and a zero.' It was more frightening for me to run out at Anfield as a Liverpool player rather than a Brighton or Manchester City player. You were so aware of what it meant to fulfil the desires of the people.

They gave you everything and that meant you couldn't let them down. My first thought wasn't: 'Are we going to win or lose?' or 'Am I going to play well?' It was: 'I'm playing for those fans.' In a way it was almost a moral blackmail, albeit a good one. And with me being a Liverpool supporter, I think I never really got used to it."

That feeling is something that Robinson, through his role as a football pundit in Spain, has recently discussed with Fernando Torres. "It's amazing how much he identifies with it," Robinson reveals. "Fernando didn't have it at Atletico Madrid and it was the first time I ever had it in my career."

The pressure might have been huge but, by the following May, Robinson had pocketed three medals and helped create history. "I think it was the first-ever treble by an English top-flight team, and even now it's hard to describe the whole experience," he continues.

Along the way he got to play with some of the greatest players British football has ever seen. "The best of them all was Graeme Souness. In my opinion he was God," is Robinson's summary of the Scot's ability. "As a person and as a footballer he was amazing. When he left the club it was as if five players had departed at the same time."

He also has high praise for Ronnie Whelan, a colleague at both club and international level. "A genius, simple as that," is how he describes the Dubliner. "They were all great players, and not only that, they were nice people too. It was probably the most humble dressing room I've ever been in. If any group of players deserved to be arrogant or show off it was that Liverpool Football Club that won four European Cups in eight years. But those guys were the opposite."

Unfortunately for the burly frontman, that was as good as it got. Paul Walsh's arrival meant competition for forward places was at a premium and the thought of sitting on the sidelines didn't appeal to Robinson. "I thought he [Walsh] was a far better player than myself and that I'd just be a sub," he says. "So I asked Joe Fagan to ensure I'd never become cynical by listening to any offers for me. Joe tried to convince me to stay because he actually thought I was better than I did. He held me in higher esteem than I held myself."

Then Queens Park Rangers made an enquiry. "'Go and speak to them if you want to,' Joe said, 'but I'll prolong your contract here if you want to stay.' My reply was: 'I love playing for this club but if I become a reserve and end up cynical or jealous it will destroy it all for me. It will ruin this dream.' The problem was I felt I wasn't as good as other players that were going to come in, so the deal was eventually completed. Then on Boxing Day I went to collect my boots. I gave Joe a hug and immediately burst into tears. As I went to my car all the fans were coming to the game against Leicester. And then it really hit me that I was leaving and I cried like a boy who'd lost his first dog."

Despite his LFC love affair ending in tears, Robinson has no regrets, and would do it all again. "None at all," he confirms. "My life is happy because I got to defend the colours I'd loved since I was a kid and still do now." And the best moment of his brief time as a Red? "We won a lot and it doesn't get much better than the European Cup," he states. "But I got far more than the treble. Pulling on *that*

Sheer devotion: Michael Robinson is still a big fan of the club from his home in Spain

shirt was the greatest trophy. It was the ultimate honour. Every time our bus pulled up outside the ground it gave me a special feeling. Mine was absolute sheer devotion. Liverpool Football Club, in my short time there, fulfilled my dream and it made me a very happy man. It's for that reason that I'm still a happy man over 20 years later."

Robinson's desire to be a Liverpool player was something he'd held almost since birth. When it came to international football, that wasn't quite the case. "I never really thought about playing on that stage," he confesses. "Of course as a footballer you want to do it, but the idea hadn't really entered my mind. I'd never considered it."

But when he started making waves in the English top flight it was a subject he suddenly had to consider. "At one point I was leading scorer in the division while playing for a Brighton side who were fighting relegation. I didn't finish up in that position, but it obviously got me noticed."

Naturally his exploits led to newspaper speculation regarding his England chances. "All the press were suggesting Ron Greenwood would pick me; apparently I was a hot favourite to be centre-forward ahead of Paul Mariner and Peter Withe. Although I didn't think I was better than either of those guys. Then when the squad was announced I wasn't included. I was on standby for the B team."

It was Alan Mullery, Brighton manager at the time, who broke the news to Robinson. And Mullery also informed him that Eire boss Eoin Hand had been in contact on a number of occasions to enquire about his availability. "Alan didn't want me to play for Ireland because he felt I'd eventually make it into the England set-up. After he told me all this I decided to ring my parents."

As we all know, Robinson opted for the green shirt and went on to make over 20 appearances. But what was the deciding factor? "There were two massive influences that made my choice easy," he explains. "The first was my mother who had an Irish background and obviously would have loved me to do it. The second person was Alan Kelly who was my coach at Preston North End reserves. I basically owed my whole career to him. If it wasn't for his influence, I would never have become a footballer. He was the man who had most faith in me and always pushed me to improve.

"As a former Ireland international, I knew he'd be really proud of me. My only worry was that in my habits I could be seen to be very English. The way I spoke and the newspapers I read marked me out as different from the rest of the squad, and I didn't want that to affect the passion I felt about playing for Ireland. To be honest, even now I'm not someone who pays a lot attention to flags or badges as I find it all very claustrophobic. I tend to like most people regardless of what nation they're from. The bottom line was I really wanted to play for Ireland and that was all that mattered to me."

Even all these years later, Robinson is convinced he made the right choice. "I absolutely loved it," he laughs. "Each and every time I was part of the squad was a brilliant experience. Can you imagine travelling all over the world and – wherever you go – you've got Irish supporters giving you the benefit of the doubt? I knew that they'd always accept me as long as I gave everything for the cause. And I always did that. I found it harder to be good at football but I enjoyed it all."

'Liverpool fulfilled my dream and it made me a very happy man. It's for that reason that I'm still a happy man over 20 years later'

The next Irish Red?

It's every Irish Kopite's dream to win a place at the Anfield Academy. SHANE O'CONNOR is living that dream. Here's his story of what it's like trying to make it at Liverpool

 FOR one reason or another, plenty of youngsters become disillusioned with the beautiful game. Sometimes it's outside distractions, while on other occasions it can be the sport itself that causes so much frustration.

The latter was the situation Irish youngster Shane O'Connor found himself facing in the summer of 2006. Undoubtedly a talented player, he had been picked as part of the Cork squad for the prestigious Kennedy Cup competition but didn't make the starting 11. Also adept at both hurling and Gaelic football, he was starting to weigh up his options, and soccer was no longer going to be his number one priority.

"Not getting off the bench in the Kennedy Cup left me feeling pretty down," the midfielder turned full-back explains. "If you come from outside Dublin and you want to make it, that is the best tournament to play at, but I didn't get a chance. Afterwards I decided I was going to concentrate on just hurling with my local team, Na Piarsaigh."

Then his mother intervened after hearing a radio advertisement for a Liverpool FC summer camp being held in Cork. "She suggested I went along and I agreed. But I didn't really think it would lead anywhere. For me it was just about the enjoyment, I didn't have any thoughts about getting spotted. Really it was just a chance to play soccer while there were no Gaelic games on."

Instead, some of Liverpool's scouts spotted O'Connor and a few weeks later he was invited to Kirkby for a trial. "I was lucky, very lucky," he laughs. "Jim Waldron and Stuart Gelling saw me play and it went from there. I was over the moon because I never expected it. The camp took place in June; around the end of July I was invited over. Then, from the end of September to the start of November, I was over and back every fortnight before I signed."

Going from almost giving up the game to suddenly becoming a Red is obviously a surreal leap, and O'Connor agrees. "My first game was against Wolves, then Man Utd.

Before that I'd been used to facing Blarney, Mallow and teams like that. My first start for Liverpool came in a game with AC Milan. I had to keep asking myself if it was real. Even now I still step back and wonder if I'm actually pulling on a Liverpool shirt."

As he says, the Ireland youth international has come a long way in a short space of time. Originally born in Jersey, his family moved between the Channel Island and Cork a few times before eventually settling in the city by the Lee. Growing up, he counted Rockmount – the club made famous by a certain Roy Keane – as one of those he played for. And despite wearing Liverpool Red, it's the Manchester United legend he names as his idol. O'Connor even took the brave step of chatting to Keane on Liverpool turf when the former Ireland skipper turned up at the Kirkby Academy to watch Sunderland's U18 side play. If the older Keano is his hero, it's another Irish legend that O'Connor is following in the footsteps of at the moment. Just like Ronnie Whelan before him, he's a United fan. Because of that, he's in a unique position when it comes to discussing the biggest rivalry in English football.

"You don't actually understand it properly until you move over here," he says. "Back in Ireland the banter between the different fans is always very friendly and light-hearted, whereas over here it has a bit more of an edge to it. That's completely understandable. As players we're obviously part of it too, so when it comes to playing against them I always want to win and I also have to say that the atmosphere at Old Trafford doesn't compare to Anfield."

Just like Whelan, and many other Irish youngsters who leave home early to pursue a soccer career, O'Connor found it tough to settle on the opposite side of the Irish Sea. "I thought it would be no problem and I never took my mam seriously when she suggested I'd miss home," he laughs. "But she was right, and the first six months were very tough. Eventually I got used to it. I went home quite a bit during the first year, but now it's not a problem. When we get some time off I pop over to Cork now and again, but I don't feel the need to do it as regularly anymore. Now I love it here. If I moved to another club I'd always come back to Liverpool on a regular basis because it's a great city."

When he does return to Leeside, he gets plenty of attention from his mates, who also can't believe the position he finds himself in. "They think I'm very lucky, but they make sure I'll never get bigheaded about it. They're still my friends and don't treat me any differently, thankfully. Also, I tell them that it is great but there are a lot of sacrifices involved too. People suggest all we have to do is kick a ball around but there's more to it than that. We work hard too and have to move away from home and go to

'When we get some time off I pop over to Cork now and again, but I don't feel the need to do it as regularly anymore. Now I love it here. If I moved to another club I'd always come back to Liverpool on a regular basis because it's a great city'

In action
against
the old
enemy –
United in
an Under-
18 clash

bed early all the time. For me I've had to give up sweets and chocolate which I love!"

Being at the club obviously has huge benefits, although it also brings with it one massive drawback. "I kept it quiet for a long time that I could get some tickets because I always remember [Roy] Keane complaining about it. I know he obviously got a lot more requests than I ever would, but I always thought it would be better if not too many people knew. My close friends do ask and I don't mind. It's always the big league games or Champions League ties people want to come over for."

If O'Connor does make the step up from the Academy to Melwood, and beyond, even more requests are sure to come flooding in, although he hasn't thought that far ahead. "I've been lucky enough to meet the likes of Ronnie (Whelan) and other Liverpool and Ireland legends," he explains. "I'm too young to remember them playing, but I know all about what they achieved and it would be great to follow in their footsteps. When people talk about stuff like that though, I can't help laughing. I'm still pretty young and I know just how tough it will be to make it here.

"To be honest, I don't know if my long-term future will be at Liverpool. Between the first team and reserve squad there are about 60 senior professionals at the club now, which is an awful lot. So for a young lad coming through to get a chance is rare. The other thing is the boss can always buy someone else. Anyone's dream would be to walk out

with 'YNWA' ringing in your ears, but at the same time I have to be realistic and I'll see where the next few years take me."

For someone so young, O'Connor's attitude is very mature and he feels that, whatever happens, he's already had a good grounding at LFC. "I've already worked with some great people like Dave Shannon, John Owens and Steve Heighway. They've really taught me the Liverpool way to play football; pass and move, and I love that. Steve was an absolutely brilliant coach, he was always tough and I didn't like him at first. But when I look back I have to say both him, and John, improved me an awful lot. If I ever did go on to make it in the game, I'd owe them so much. Also, they helped me settle and made it easier for me to become comfortable as a footballer. Even if I do move on, I'll still have the time at the club on my CV, which should stand to me."

And if soccer isn't to be his future, O'Connor has other sporting passions. "GAA will always be part of my life," he continues. "I always keep up to date with what's going on and if I'm back in Cork I'll watch any game from any age group. I love it.

"At the moment I obviously can't play no matter how much I want to because one bad knock - especially in hurling - could affect my chances here. But if I don't make it as a professional, playing GAA again would be a great upside to it."

'All the players in that Liverpool team were **absolutely outstanding**'

MARK LAWRENSON cost £900,000, but no one would deny that it was money well spent. Here he recalls the highs and lows of his Anfield career, and his subsequent moves through management and broadcasting

NOWADAYS Mark Lawrenson is a familiar face on TV, where he consistently displays what you might describe as a 'different' sense of humour. When you hear Lawro cracking jokes at the expense of himself, his studio colleagues and those in the modern game, it's easy to forget he was once one of the best defenders in the English top flight.

He initially sprung to attention as a youngster at Preston North End, and attracted interest from a host of clubs, including the Reds. "I don't know if it's true, but rumour has it that Liverpool bid £60,000 for me on deadline day in March 1977," he recalls. "I nearly went to Newcastle too, but ended up joining Brighton at the end of that season."

Becoming a Seagull rather than a Liverbird mightn't sound like the best scenario, although Lawrenson now views it as a blessing in disguise. "I wasn't anywhere near ready for anything like Liverpool so, in hindsight, it was a good move. Brighton had just been promoted to the old second division, and I was playing in the third division for Preston prior to that, so the step-up to the top league would have been immense.Thankfully, I went to Brighton instead, and within two years we had made our way up the leagues. For me it was a continuous and gradual rise rather than one almighty leap."

Lawrenson was an important part of that progress, and those at Anfield had kept a close eye on him. Everyone knew he would move on again at some stage, particularly with the financial problems at the Goldstone Ground, and when the time came at the end of the 1980/81 season, he had the pick of the country's biggest clubs.

"The day I signed for Liverpool, I also had the option of joining either Manchester United or Arsenal too. They weren't bad choices. Arsenal's boss was Terry Neill. He offered me less money than Brighton, where I was on a 10-year contract at the time. The wages weren't particularly attractive, and he was trying to sell the idea by showing me

the marble halls of Highbury, the underfloor heating and talking about the idea of playing with David O'Leary. But it simply wasn't an attractive proposition."

As Lawrenson says, it wasn't just the Gunners who were seeking his services. Ron Atkinson also wanted to take the versatile defender to Old Trafford. "Ron had signed Frank Stapleton and the deal went to a tribunal. Because of that he couldn't pay cash for me. Instead he wanted to offer Brighton some players. I said you better get on with it if you want to sort it because another club are also in for me. After all that, I met with Liverpool. Within about 20 minutes I'd agreed to go Anfield. They'd just won the European Cup in Paris and were obviously the best side around. I thought it wouldn't be a bad idea to go and play for them."

Bob Paisley obviously really wanted him and splashed out the considerable fee of £900,000 to get his man. Later, he outlined the reasons. "It was playing at the heart of Brighton's defence against Kenny Dalglish in March 1980 that he really caught my eye," the legendary manager explained. "Kenny is notoriously difficult to tackle. He is so clever and deceptive and uses his body to shield the ball from opposing defenders. And yet here was a 22-year-old, fresh out of the second division, winning the ball from him with sharp, clean challenges. I don't believe I have ever seen anybody who makes better tackles inside his own penalty area."

Some people might have been overawed by the task that lay ahead, but Lawrenson relished it. "Even in those days, the league was divided into three: the top, middle and bottom. I was going from the foot to the summit. But I was never intimidated," he states. "Of course you realise straight away the tradition and the history the club has. That really strikes you. However, I wasn't nervous because I knew some of the lads from the Ireland team and I'd played at Anfield already. Really it was all a fantastic new experience."

Lawrenson expected to wait for his chance with the firsts, as club tradition usually decreed for new arrivals. Instead he was chucked straight into the side and proved he could cope with the challenge, his versatility almost immediately coming to the fore. "The fact that I could operate as a left-back, right-back, centre-half or in midfield definitely gave me an advantage. When you've got a large squad, as we had, the ability to slot into different roles can help your

cause. Having said that, the management always told me they knew exactly where they wanted to play me: at centre-back. So filling different positions was fine by me."

He might have been a utility man at times, but it's his partnership with Alan Hansen at the heart of the defence – arguably one of the best we've ever had – that most people will fondly remember. "It wasn't something we really talked about that much," Lawrenson says. "It just worked. In one way it was a bit like Ian Rush and Kenny Dalglish, or John Toshack and Kevin Keegan. They just clicked straight away without too much effort, and so did we. It was easy to play with someone that good. Not just Al, but all the players in that team were absolutely outstanding. And when you work with better players you become better yourself."

By the end of his debut campaign at the club, Lawrenson had won a league medal, the first of five he would eventually claim. At the halfway stage of the season, Paisley's men appeared to be well off the pace before an incredible run took them to the top of the pile. And victory in the penultimate game would be enough to secure the championship. "I remember we beat Tottenham 3-1 at home," he says. "To win the title in this country is very difficult – it was over 42 games then – so that was very special."

What he doesn't mention from that win over the Londoners

is the role he played. As well as heading home an equaliser to cancel out Glenn Hoddle's opener, Lawrenson also set up Kenny Dalglish to make it 2-1. Ronnie Whelan added a third at the end to ensure the celebrations could begin.

When Lawrenson had arrived at the club in 1981, he'd just missed out on a European Cup victory. Three years later, he got his hands on 'old big ears' in the Eternal City. AS Roma's home advantage wasn't enough to prevent the Reds claiming our fourth continental crown. Following a 1-1 draw, Steve Nicol missed the first penalty before Phil Neal, Graeme Souness, Ian Rush and Alan Kennedy all converted theirs and Bruce Grobbelaar's jig distracted the Italians. Neither Hansen nor Lawrenson shot from 12 yards.

"We were in the centre circle arguing about who'd take the 10th and 11th," he replies. "If it had come to it, I think I would have been okay, or if the boss had wanted me to step up, I would have done so. At that stage of a game you just get on with it. You haven't got any choice."

Twelve months later, the holders were back in the final. Although, as we all know, events in Heysel before the game deemed the actual result irrelevant. Crowd trouble led to the death of 39 Juventus fans. In the end, the Old Lady took the trophy thanks to a 1-0 win. Few with Liverpool connections cared about the scoreline. During the build up to the game,

'We were in the centre circle arguing about who'd take the 10th and 11th. If it had come to it, I think I would have been okay'

Lawrenson, Nicol and Hansen do battle with Lineker and Sheedy in the 1986 FA Cup final (left). Below, Lawrenson shows off the trophy as the team parade through Liverpool

Lawrenson had been rated as doubtful owing to a shoulder problem, but it was eventually agreed that he was worth risking. Three minutes in, and his evening was over after the injury re-occurred.

"I was going to have an operation anyway afterwards so I played. But I ended up in hospital with some of the dead and the dying. It [the disaster] was very, very unfortunate, and I think one day the truth about what happened will come out. As a player you realised you just weren't in control of what was going on around you."

Those deaths affected everyone and even now still cause hurt. "It's a difficult subject," Lawrenson continues. "Even as a bunch of players we never really spoke about it afterwards. We came back and went to masses and services and then it was the summer holidays. I wouldn't say it was a taboo subject, but it was never really spoken about. A couple of years ago they did a documentary about it and I was interviewed. I actually found it very cathartic to talk about what happened. It was quite good in that sense. Even now, me and Al spend so much time together and we've still never really discussed it."

The 1984/85 season may have ended in tragedy and created headlines for all the wrong reasons, but thankfully attention was again turned to football in the season that followed. The league and FA Cup double was secured in spectacular style, with both trophies coming at the expense of our nearest rivals.

"To overtake Everton in the last week of the season, and then beat them in the cup final, was great. In all honesty, they could just have easily ended up with both. Obviously we were glad they didn't. In the end we just had that little bit of luck and managed

'I thought I still had a few years ahead of me. Then my Achilles went and I knew I was going to struggle to play again. Sometimes you just know'

to keep going a little bit longer. At Wembley, they were the better team for the first 60 minutes until we got it together and eventually swung the game in our favour."

While his club career was at its peak, on the international stage Lawrenson had been a Republic of Ireland regular since 1977, without ever enjoying any notable success. "I'd made my Irish debut against Poland on a Sunday at Tolka Park," he says. "The previous day I'd played for Preston and the following Tuesday I was back there for a match with Reading. It meant three games in four days, which would be unheard of now."

Talking a good game: Lawro has carved out a big reputation as a football pundit. He is pictured commentating at Euro 2008 with John Motson; and, above right, on the 'Football Focus' couch with Manish Bhasin, Motson and Tony Blair

Lawrenson's Irish qualification came from his mother's side, who all hailed from Dungarvan in County Waterford. "Alan Kelly (senior) was assistant manager at Preston, and he found out about that link," Lawro continues. "When you're in the middle of the old third division in front of crowds of 5,000 or 6,000, you do not hold any thoughts of playing international football I can assure you, so I was only delighted to say yes. We applied for a passport, got it straight away, and I was picked and played. It was as simple as that."

Pulling on a green shirt also helped Lawrenson boost his profile domestically and gain the attention of the Anfield scouts. "I think Liverpool signed me on the back of playing for Ireland, so it was a win-win situation. They obviously felt if I could do it at that level I was good enough."

If club success appeared to be a formality, the opposite was true when it came to reaching World Cups or European Championships. Eoin Hand's side narrowly missed out on a few occasions, and it's something Lawrenson has his own views on. "I think Eoin was a bit unlucky," he says. "We had some very dubious decisions that cost us dearly."

But he doesn't put the blame solely in the hands of the footballing gods or dodgy referees. "We were capable of beating anyone at home, and did so on plenty of occasions. If we had been a little bit better organised on our travels, we would definitely have reached something sooner."

Hand left his post without ever making it to a tournament. Then in 1986 the FAI took the brave decision to appoint Jack Charlton as their first-ever 'foreign' boss. The immediate aim was to put together a decent Euro '88 qualifying effort. Charlton set about doing exactly that in a group that also contained a Belgium side who had done well at the recent Mexico World Cup, plus Scotland, Bulgaria and Luxembourg. Along the way, Lawro popped up with the only goal during a crucial win against the Scots at Hampden Park. However, dropped points at home meant an unexpected Scotland win in Sofia was still needed to send Ireland to Germany, and their first-ever major tournament.

Unfortunately, by the time the plane for Euro '88 was being boarded, Lawrenson's career had cruelly and abruptly come to a halt. He was still only 30 at the time, and the news came as a huge shock to the fans, and manager Dalglish. "I thought I still had a few years ahead of me," he admits. "I was what you might call naturally fit. I didn't have to train particularly hard, I just ticked over and that was always enough, so I felt I would have lasted until the age of 34 or 35. Then my Achilles went and I knew I was going to struggle to play again, even though I did try to come back. Sometimes you just know."

Against Arsenal in January 1988 he left the park after 51 minutes and never lined up for the Reds again. "I went to see all sorts of different specialists. However, I knew in my mind that it wasn't going to happen for me, so I bowed out." Having won a host of honours at club level, playing in the European Championships would have been a fitting climax to Lawrenson's glittering career. But he's not bitter about what could have been. "I don't have any regrets because what will be will be. I never think 'if only'. I'm just not that

kind of person. It was one of those things. To eventually qualify for the Euros was fantastic in itself."

Instead of brooding and wondering about what he'd lost, the new retiree quickly moved into a different role. "The day after I announced my retirement I was the manager of Oxford United," he laughs. "It hadn't been planned for weeks or months in advance. I got a phone call the day I hung up my boots, went down to see them and got the job the very next day. It was that simple."

Unfortunately, his reign in the managerial chair didn't last too long. A dispute with the directors over the sale of future Red Dean Saunders led to Lawrenson being sacked. Spells as a player at Barnet, and coach at Tampa Bay Rowdies and Peterborough United, followed before he began to make his name as a pundit.

"I was lucky again. When I was living in the Oxford region I'd started working for a TV company. They came to interview me and offered me a job. From there, radio work followed, then Sky. In between I went to Newcastle as a defensive coach with Kevin Keegan before I got offered a BBC job."

Working in the media means he has covered both Ireland and England fixtures. On occasions he's used "we" when discussing the fortunes of each country, much to the annoyance of some viewers. There is a simple explanation for that slip of the tongue. "When you're at the BBC and covering the English national team, everyone refers to it as 'we'. That's purely because of the company. It wasn't because I'd suddenly decided I'm an Englishman. One or two people make an issue out of that, but such is life. If the two countries came face-to-face, I'd be shouting for Ireland every time," he concludes with a chuckle, as per usual.

'Liverpool is **huge** in Ireland and my move here **went down well** back home'

ROBBIE KEANE never doubted that one day he would play for his boyhood heroes, but his arrival at Anfield in the summer of 2008 was still a shock. Even though it didn't work out as well as he planned, he has no regrets about pulling on a red shirt

WHEN Robbie Keane joined us in July 2008 it was a sensational move and appeared to be the perfect match.

The boyhood Red was finally going to wear the Liverbird and hopefully form a fantastic partnership with Fernando Torres. If the fans were excited it was nothing compared to how the Dubliner felt.

"Liverpool and Man Utd are probably the two biggest teams in Ireland," he smiled.

"In my household and amongst my extended family everyone, including my brother, uncles and cousins, are all Liverpool supporters. The club is huge in Ireland and I think my move went down well back home.

"I'd been a fan all my life too, and when I was with Crumlin United I'd come over to watch Liverpool play a few times. Now I was joining the club. It was amazing."

Of course as a teenager the striker had an opportunity to move to Merseyside.

Keane celebrates his first goal for Liverpool, against PSV in the Champions League, in October, 2008

'When I was a kid it was all about Ian Rush and John Barnes –
Rush for his goals and Barnes for his silky skills. They were the two
players I really looked up to and wanted to be like'

Instead he opted for Wolverhampton Wanderers.

"I was maybe 14 or 15 when I came over to Liverpool on trial," Eire's all-time top scorer recalled. "That went well but I had a good feeling about Wolves. Being a Liverpool fan and having met all my heroes there, it was a difficult decision. I remember my mother, who didn't have a huge interest in football then, saying: 'don't sign for a team just because you support them. Make sure you go to the club that's right for you.' And, at that time, Wolves was the best option."

That choice might have been difficult but it proved to be correct. Aged 17 he made a goalscoring debut at Molineux on the first day of the 1997/98 season.

"If I'd signed for Liverpool I probably wouldn't have got that chance at that stage," he continued. "I knew at Wolves if I worked hard I would probably get an opportunity sooner. That was the main reason for my decision.

"Even though I was young, I wanted to play in the first team straight away. I was determined to do it. Thankfully I was able to pull on a red shirt in the end. I've no regrets about the choice I made back then."

Having impressed for Wolves, he moved to Coventry City and then, incredibly, on to Inter Milan. A change of management at the San Siro meant Keane's stay was short-lived, and a return to the Premier League appeared inevitable, with Gerard Houllier listed as one of those who was keen on securing his services.

"There was always talk about it and I think the club might have been interested around that time," he said. "But it never happened."

Instead Keane teamed up with David O'Leary at Leeds United, where he got the opportunity to work with one of his idols. "When I was a kid it was all about Ian Rush and John Barnes – Rush for his goals and Barnes for his silky skills. They were the two players I really looked up to and wanted to be like. I've met both of them and they're gentlemen.

"Playing with Robbie Fowler at Leeds was even more special. It was a real honour. When I was in my mid-teens he was THE man, and you could see all his ability when we trained together. Every day, left foot or right, he was the best finisher I've ever seen. Off the pitch he's a nice guy too, and when we worked together we'd chat about Liverpool and what was happening at the club."

While God eventually got the move to Anfield he craved, courtesy of a sensational return in January 2006, Keane had to wait a little longer. Instead, following some impressive displays at the 2002 World Cup, he exited Elland Road with White Hart Lane his next destination.

Clever play and some spectacular goals meant he quickly became a favourite of the Spurs crowd. Over six seasons he regularly topped the club's scoring chart, formed a superb partnership with Dimitar Berbatov and captained the side on numerous occasions during the absences of Ledley King.

Many felt Keane's chance to become a Red had passed him by at that stage, although he never thought that way.

"Even though I was pretty settled at Spurs I still believed I'd play for Liverpool one day," he explained. "I'd never given up on that and always hoped it might happen."

During the summer of 2008 the scenario became a reality, and Rafa Benitez brought Keane to Anfield.

'When I'm finished playing I don't want to look back on my career and say: 'If only',' was his take on the transfer.

"That's one of the biggest reasons why I knew I had to come to Liverpool; that and the fact that I've always been a Liverpool supporter."

The move was warmly received by one of his former teammates. "After the deal had been completed, Robbie (Fowler) was the first person to text me and say congratulations," he revealed.

Unfortunately, as we all know, Keane's time in L4 failed to follow the predicted script. The number seven didn't break his scoring duck for us until the start of October, during his 11th appearance in a Champions League clash with PSV Eindhoven at Anfield.

Everyone hoped that would be the start of a goal spree and he followed it up with another European strike during our 1-1 draw against Atletico Madrid later that month.

In November his first Premier League goals finally arrived – a brace in a comfortable 3-0 win over West Brom. Still though the doubts lingered, with Keane rarely playing a full 90 minutes. By late December his fortunes again appeared to be on the up. A stunning goal at the Emirates Stadium earned us a point and he grabbed two more in his next outing, a 3-0 win over Bolton Wanderers. Still rumours persisted during the January transfer window with Harry Redknapp obviously keen to take the attacker back to Tottenham. Few Reds believed the move would go through but on deadline day it finally did. Keane's Liverpool career was over.

"It's funny how football works sometimes and situations turn around very quickly. It was a difficult time for me at Liverpool, but there's no point in dwelling on it," he said after heading back to White Hart Lane. "It was a difficult decision to make to leave Tottenham. It proved not to be the right move."

Some have debated exactly why he didn't fit in to his new surroundings with Rafa offering the following assessment.

"I think Robbie played a lot of games here and for a lot of reasons together, he was not playing at the level he can," the Spaniard said. "We know he is a good player, he can play really well and hopefully he can do it at Tottenham.

"You can put a lot of things together to explain why he didn't do as well as we thought. The understanding with the other players, maybe the tactics of the other teams playing too deep and he didn't have much space, which is different to when he was playing at Tottenham.

"Liverpool is a different type of club, the expectation on him was high and everyone was talking about a partnership with Fernando Torres, maybe he had more pressure and it was more difficult for him to perform at the level he can achieve."

Keane made 28 appearances during his time on Merseyside, scoring seven goals.

It mightn't have gone exactly to plan for the Tallaght man but he lived his dream, even if it was only for the shortest of periods.

In the footsteps of legends: Number seven Keane and (inset below) Dalglish and Keegan with their Footballer of the Year trophies from the Football Writers' Association in 1983 and 1976 respectively

'It's funny how football works sometimes and situations turn around very quickly. It was a difficult time for me at Liverpool, but there's no point in dwelling on it. It was a difficult decision to make to leave Tottenham. It proved not to be the right move'

'Elisha Scott's **iconic image** deserves to be one of timeless **success**'

Journalist Gerry McGuinness reflects on the career of goalkeeper ELISHA SCOTT – Liverpool's longest-serving player, whose tussles with Dixie Dean were the stuff of legend on Merseyside

SOME people would have you believe that in 1912, the Titanic was Belfast's most famous export. Setting off from the River Lagan, the ship arrived safely at Southampton docks, where it was scheduled to depart on her maiden voyage across the Atlantic, omitting a stop at its registry port in Liverpool. Almost five months to the day that the Titanic left Belfast, one man made a more successful and fruitful departure from Irish shores and thankfully did make his scheduled stop on Merseyside. Elisha Scott was a 17-year-old rookie goalkeeper, less than six feet tall.

What the Belfast-born shot-stopper lacked in height, he more than made up for with agility and bravery. While the Titanic was being built in his hometown, Scott was building his own reputation as a junior, firstly with Linfield then Broadway United. Exactly which half of Merseyside he was going to represent was a matter for debate as his older brother Billy had just left Everton after eight years service and actually recommended young Elisha as his replacement.

Everton were discouraged by his youthfulness and declined but thankfully Liverpool manager Tom Watson and chairman John McKenna had no such qualms and Elisha became a Red. Scott went on to become the club's longest-serving player. He would undoubtedly have made more appearances than the 468 he did had it not been for the interruption of the First World War.

Even after the war, competition for the number one jersey at Anfield was fierce and required Scott to maintain his high level of professionalism and dedication to reclaim the honour from Arthur Riley either side of 1930.

The duels between the Reds stopper and Everton forward Dixie Dean were legendary on Merseyside, with stories regaled of how when they passed each other on the street and the Everton frontman nodded his head in acknowledgment, Scott leapt through a shop window to save an imaginary ball.

However, the year that Dean scored 60 league goals, the Belfast man watched both Merseyside derbies from the sidelines; in one of them, Dean scored a hat-trick. With the greatest respect to his replacement, had Scott played, the history books may tell a different story than they do today.

The brace of league titles that were won during his time at the club will forever be remembered in Liverpool folklore. Had it not been for his masterful efforts between the sticks, Liverpool's amazing roll of honour might be short of two English championships.

Proof of his personal contribution in the title-winning years of 1922 and 1923 are evident in the fact that the team's defensive record was the best in the league – a quality of worthy champions. Winning one league title is a sign of a good team, but retaining it displays the origins of a great one. Over a 42-game season, the Liverpool defence conceded just 36 goals in the first title-winning year and five fewer the year it was retained. Scott missed just three league games in the first title-winning season and was an ever-present the following year, underlining his importance to the developing Liverpool psyche.

The back-to-back successes of the early 1920s marked the first time the club had ever retained the crown as the best team in England, doubling our number of league crowns from two to four. This is a feat not to be scoffed at, as it wasn't until 1977 that the Reds achieved consecutive first-place finishes again.

Sadly, the era of success that followed the latter victories was not to be fulfilled in the 1920s, and the two league titles were Scott's last medals at the club. His continued determination, loyalty and skill gave him iconic status among his adoring fans.

Such was the bond that developed between the supporters and the Ulsterman that Scott was allowed to address the Anfield faithful from the director's box prior to his last game as an official Liverpool player. Although he

'Over a 42-game season, the Liverpool defence conceded just 36 goals in the first title-winning year and five fewer the year it was retained'

Safe hands: Elisha Scott pictured in 1925

didn't feature in the match, his pep talk to the crowd clearly worked as Liverpool beat Man City 3-2.

Pre-match speeches became natural to Scott, who returned to his hometown as player-manager with Belfast Celtic. His arrival heralded an unimaginable period of success. In the penultimate year of his playing career, the now 41-year-old tasted Gold Cup success, before ending his playing days a year later with his first Irish league win.

The high that ended his playing career continued into his management. Seven consecutive league titles, 10 in his 14-year stewardship, and a host of other cup successes make Scott one of the all-time great managers in Irish football history. Perhaps the only regret looking back on his career is that he never had the opportunity to manage at the club where he made his name.

Despite partition of Ireland, Scott was a man who cared little for the sectarian divide and demonstrated this through his performances with both club and country.

Record-holders at Liverpool are household names and legends. Ask who the Reds' all-time top goalscorer, league marksman or appearance-maker are, and fervent Reds will be falling over each other to spit out the names Rush, Hunt and Callaghan respectively.

Posing the question of who is LFC's longest-serving player might stump even the most passionate supporter. Elisha Scott gave 21 years and 52 days of his life to Liverpool Football Club, and deserves legendary status, not just in the era he played, but forevermore.

Whilst the Titanic stirred a legendary sensation in the era it was built, its iconic image is in its timeless failure. Elisha Scott stirred a legendary sensation in the same era and his iconic image deserves to be that of a timeless success.

Liverpool on tour

Over the next few pages, ROB GOWERS of the Liverpool Programme Collectors Club shares some of the memorabilia he has picked up over the years, while right, fellow collector GER SCULLY discusses how he built up his own admirable stash of treasure

AS a '60s child growing up in rural Cork, following The Reds was expected, but not the Anfield Reds, rather the Rebel Reds – Cork's hurling and football teams. We had one TV station, RTE, and my only contact with 'soccer' was through *Goal* and *Shoot!* magazine, and the hazy reception of BBC Radio 2. It was against this backdrop that I found myself rather unexpectedly having more than a passing interest in the fate of Liverpool. The fact that Steve Heighway was a pacy winger who just happened to play for the Republic sealed my allegiance to LFC forever.

Liverpool squad that beat Bohemians 4-1 in April 1904. Back row: James McLean, John Chadburn, Peter Platt, Joseph Hoare, Billy Dunlop. Middle row: Tom Watson (secretary – "manager"), Raisbeck (Alex's brother), Herbert Craik, Charlie Wilson, Maurice Parry, Alex Raisbeck, John Hughes, W Connell. Front row: Arthur Goddard, Fred Buck, Richard Morris, John Carlin, H. Nixon, Edgar Chadwick, Jack Cox, George Fleming.

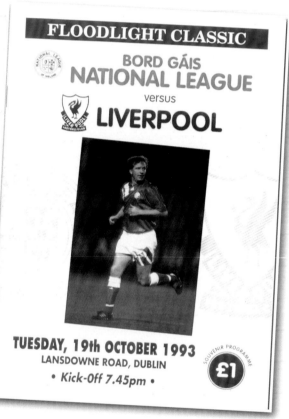

Bord Gais National League v Liverpool on Tuesday 19 October 1993. Attendance: 28,000. Liverpool won 2-1 with goals from Hutchison and an own goal by Coll. The Liverpool team was: Grobbelaar, Matteo, Bjørnebye, Ruddock, Piechnik, Nicol, Walters, Stewart, Fowler, Rush. Hutchison and Redknapp came on as subs.

Bass League Select v Liverpool on Wednesday 2 August 1978. Attendance: 25,000. Liverpool won 3-1 after goals from Souness (51), Jones (70) and Case (87). Liverpool team: Clemence, Jones, A Kennedy, Hansen, Thompson, Hughes, McDermott, Case, Heighway, Souness, Dalglish. Came on as sub: Fairclough.

Mementos from the Shelbourne friendlies in 1994 and 1995

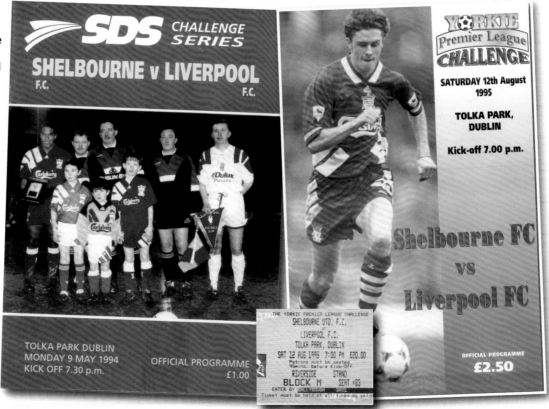

Just after the 1974 FA Cup final success, I saw an advert in *Shoot!* for the Manchester Programme Shop, and after persuading my mum to buy me a postal order, sent for the match programme from our Wembley encounter with Newcastle. Little did I know that this initial purchase would set me on course for a life-long collecting hobby.

I made my first excursion to the hallowed turf of Anfield on a rainy 22 March 1981. John Bailey headed in an own goal to secure a 1-0 derby win. That was to become the first of many, mostly successful trips to Anfield and further afield, as I followed the Reds on their trail to glory. It was on one of these trips that I met Seanie Walsh, secretary of the Waterford branch of the supporters' club. He encouraged me to set up an official club in Cork following an inaugural meeting on 5 May 1983, and through him I was introduced to Liverpool FC secretary Peter B Robinson. He had a great love for the Irish and he ensured that the newly formed Cork branch received an ample supply of tickets.

In 1986 Liverpool fulfilled their commitment to play an international XI managed by Jack Charlton in Flower Lodge, Cork. I travelled from Wembley on the team bus to Heathrow and got first-class treatment, even being allowed to carry the wooden box containing the FA Cup and the Canon League Trophy off the plane and onto the waiting coach. I was also handed the job of programme editor for the game. Anthony Dinan of the *Irish Examiner* ensured I was appointed official player liaison, stationed with the team in Jurys hotel looking after all the players' needs.

I had kept a scrapbook on the Reds since 1976 and I brought along my efforts from the '85/86 season in the hopes of getting them autographed. Kenny Dalglish readily

agreed to my request and he made sure that all the team signed it. After that I continued to collect programmes of matches I attended and met Keith Stanton who runs the New Liverpool Programme Collectors Club. I decided to collect home programmes back to 1959/60, and then collected 'aways' back to this season also. I quickly realised I was a 'completist collector', so I therefore began to collect home programmes back to 1946/47 and eventually relented to include 'aways'. Once I had completed the full set of competitive issues back to the war, I chose to focus on obtaining one home programme per season back to 1892, and I was fortunate to pick up all but three issues from the club's inaugural season in the Lancashire League in 1892, along with a club letterhead and season ticket.

The collecting bug continued to take hold and I focused on friendlies and Liverpool Senior Cup and Lancashire Cup issues, and expanded my focus to include first-day covers and trading cards. My collection also includes autographed items, videos, books, various club publications and replica shirts. I bid on and won a Billy Liddell 'Bukta' shirt from the 1950s at auction and then decided to include original player shirts, purchasing Phil Neal's European Cup final shirts from the 1978, 1984 and 1985 finals. I now have over 30 player shirts and tracksuits, the pride of which is Bill Shankly's tracksuit from 1973. Even now I get each season's programmes and add memorabilia through auctions and my daily visits to eBay.

My life is interwoven with the recent history of LFC. My mum jokes that "my religion runs in 11 Red shirts around Anfield", and I think she's not far wrong. It's in my blood, and for as long as I breathe I will forever be a Rebel Red!

OFFICIAL 25c PROGRAM

INTERNATIONAL SOCCER MATCH

LIVERPOOL
(Of the First Division English League)

VS.

IRISH INTERNATIONAL TEAM

A ticket and programme from Liverpool's game in Cork in 1986

| EBBETS FIELD | | THURSDAY NIGHT |
| BROOKLYN | | MAY 14, 1953 |

PHIL TAYLOR

Captain of the Liverpool team who has played for England several times in the international games and just completed 16 years service with his team in the right or left half back position on the line-up.

Liverpool v Irish International Team on Thursday 14 May 1953 at Ebbets Field in Brooklyn, New York. This match was played on the tour of the USA and Canada. Attendance: 10,072. Liverpool won 4-0, with two goals each from Bimpson and Liddell. Liverpool team: Ashcroft, Lambert, Spicer, Taylor, Hughes, Paisley, Payne, Smith, Bimpson (Moran), Jones, Liddell.

Kick-off 8:30 P. M.

Published by HARRY M. STEVENS, INC., 320 Fifth Avenue, New York

A signed menu from the post-match meal in Cork, 1986 (left); and a programme from the England v Ireland international at Anfield in 1959

Irish International XI v Liverpool on Friday 13 November 1981 at Tolka Park, Dublin. Liverpool won 1-0 after a goal by Johnston. Liverpool team: Grobbelaar, Nicol, A Kennedy, Hansen, Lawrenson, Johnston, Souness, Whelan, Sheedy, Johnson, Dalglish.

Ticket stubs (above and right), membership cards for the Cork Liverpool Supporters' Club (below right), and an Aer Lingus memento from Liverpool's game with Farenc-Varos in 1974

Limerick v Liverpool at Markets Field, 16 May 1962. Liverpool won 5-3. Goals by Callaghan, Lewis (2), St John and Melia. Liverpool team: Furnell, Moran, Byrne, Yeats, Leishman, A'Court, Melia, Milne, Callaghan, Lewis, St John.

League of Ireland Select v Liverpool at Dalymount Park, Dublin, on Friday 31 July 1970. Liverpool won 2-1 with goals from Graham and Thompson. Liverpool team: Clemence, Lawler, Yeats, Lloyd, Smith, Hughes, Callaghan, Thompson, Graham, Evans, Whitham.

Ulster United v Liverpool as part of the tour of the USA and Canada, 15 June 1948. Played at the Maple Leaf Stadium, attendance 8,000. Liverpool won 5-1; goals by Balmer (3), Liddell and Stubbins. Liverpool team: Sidlow, Lambert, Harley, Jones, Taylor, Hughes, Brierley, Balmer, Stubbins (Shannon), Fagan, Liddell.

Dundalk v Liverpool, 1982

Sixteen thousand people paid record gate receipts of £68,000 to see Liverpool end Dundalk's unbeaten home European record under Jim McLaughlin. Dundalk put up a good show, but they could not get to grips with the team who had won the European Cup three times in the previous five years. Liverpool played at their best, and if it were not for some resolute defending and great goalkeeping, the scoreline would have been much worse.

The speed of the Liverpool attacks provided a serious test for the Dundalk defence. The Reds got off to a great start after seven minutes. A move involving Rush, Hodgson and Dalglish ended with the ball being played into space for Ronnie Whelan – who had last played against Dundalk for Home Farm – who shot accurately past Blackmore from a tight angle.

The Dundalk full-backs were being given a torrid time by the Liverpool attack. Gregg made a mistake under pressure and Hodgson stole in, only to shoot wide in front of an empty goal. Liverpool were clearly intent on ending the tie as a contest as quickly as possible, and Blackmore had to be alert to save shots from Dalglish and Rush.

Dundalk rarely threatened Bruce Grobbelaar's goal. The one time they did get near the Liverpool area, Mick Fairclough set up Martin Lawlor, whose long-range shot went over the bar. After 29 minutes, Ian Rush and Hodgson set up Whelan to make it 2-0.

After Barry Kehoe tested Grobbelaar with a good long-range effort, Liverpool made it 3-0 after 32 minutes. A long ball by Kenny Dalglish was flicked on by Sammy Lee to Ian Rush, who finished superbly past Blackmore.

Ollie Ralph came on for Willie Crawley at the start of the second half, and very nearly pulled one back straight away. Grobbelaar came out of his box to intercept a long ball, but Ralph got there first and shot for goal. It looked like a goal all the way, but Alan Hansen somehow managed to clear the ball off the line and out for a corner via the crossbar.

On 55 minutes, Liverpool got their fourth when Alan Kennedy set up Hodgson to score from close range. In the closing minutes, Leo Flanagan got a consolation goal with a wonderful strike from a free-kick.

Taken from dundalkfc.com

The teams that night were:

Dundalk: Blackmore, Gregg, Dunning, McConville, Lawlor, Byrne, Flanagan, King, Kehoe, Fairclough, Crawley.

Subs: Ralph for Crawley, Archibold for Byrne.

Liverpool: Grobbelaar, Neal, Kennedy, Hansen, Thompson, Lee, Souness, Whelan, Dalglish, Hodgson, Rush.

'A move involving Rush, Hodgson and Dalglish ended with the ball being played into space for Ronnie Whelan – who had last played against Dundalk for Home Farm – who shot accurately past Blackmore from a tight angle'

Liverpool v Dundalk in the Fairs Cup, 16 September 1969, was a memorable occasion for several reasons. Liverpool ran out 10-0 winners, with goals by Alun Evans (1, 38), Chris Lawler (10), Tommy Smith (24, 67), Bobby Graham (36, 82), Alec Lindsay (56), Peter Thompson (69) and Ian Callaghan (76). Liverpool team: Clemence, Lawler, Strong, Smith, Yeats, Hughes, Callaghan, Graham, Lindsay, Evans, Thompson.

Alec Lindsay scored his first goal for LFC on his debut for the club, and it was also Gerard Houllier's first game at Anfield. He went on the Kop with Patrice Bergues: "I suppose going to the game with Patrice that day was a touch of destiny. Patrice had come over to spend a few days with me because I was here on my own, and so we decided to go and see Liverpool play Dundalk. What impressed me first of all was the atmosphere inside the stadium. We were on the Kop, and it was fantastic to see the unconditioned support of the fans. I was also impressed by the energy which was shown in the game, and the stamina of the players. I think 15 minutes before the end of the match the score was 8-0 and still Liverpool went looking for goals. In fact the score at half-time was 5-0. In France, if you are 5-0 up at half-time the game is over in the sense that you don't bother trying to increase your score. It's not like that in England."

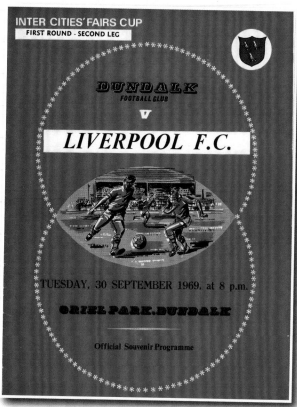

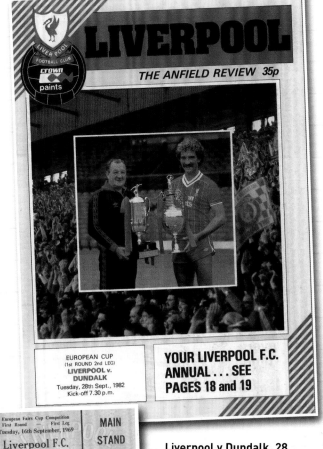

Dundalk v Liverpool at Oriel Park, 30 September 1969. Attendance: 6,000. Liverpool won 4-0, with goals from Thompson (13, 31), Graham (48) and Callaghan (81). Liverpool team: Clemence, Lawler, Strong, Smith, Lloyd, Hughes, Thompson (Callaghan 46), Evans, Graham (Hunt 58), St John, Boersma.

Liverpool v Dundalk, 28 September 1982, European Cup first round second leg. Liverpool won 1-0, the goal coming from Whelan in the 81st minute. Attendance: 12,021.

Testimonials

Billy Drennan's testimonial. Liverpool v Man Utd at Windsor Park, Belfast, 3 August 1983. Liverpool lost 4-3 despite goals from Rush (2) and Souness. Attendance: 30,000. Liverpool team: Grobbelaar, Neal, Kennedy, Hansen, Lawrenson, Lee, Souness, Johnston, Hodgson, Dalglish, Rush.

Windsor Park, Belfast
Wednesday August 3, 1983
Kick-off 7.30 p.m.

OFFICIAL SOUVENIR PROGRAMME 80p

Mementos from Ronnie Whelan's testimonial year and dinner (above), and a signed menu from Steve Heighway's testimonial dinner (right)

Monaghan man was first Liverpool FC manager

WHEN Liverpool FC won the European Champions League in dramatic style at the expense of AC Milan in Istanbul on Wednesday 25 May 2005 there was widespread euphoria among the legions of Liverpool supporters throughout Ireland, not least of all in Monaghan Town where there is a very active Liverpool Supporters' Club.

However, how many of the Monaghan revellers were aware that one of the founding fathers of the famous soccer club, and its first manager, was a North Monaghan man by the name of John McKenna?

He was born in 1855, the son of Patrick McKenna and Jane McCrudden, both of Drumcaw in the parish of Donagh, who were married in the Church of Ireland in Glaslough on 2 November 1850. The McCrudden family in fact still resides in that townland.

John McKenna, later known as 'Honest John', left Ireland as a 19-year-old youth to find employment in England. He began work as a message-boy for a grocery chain in Liverpool, but he also had a great interest in sport, particularly in rugby and rifle shooting. However, following many visits to the nearby Anfield grounds, home of Everton FC, he soon took a keen interest in soccer.

He never allowed sport to interfere with his strong religious beliefs, and became a very active worker in the local Anglican community. He never missed a Sunday service in Liverpool's Protestant cathedral. He became a great benefactor of the poor as part of his church work, and was a member of the West Derby Union, helping out with administrative duties for the several workhouses in the area.

Following a serious split at Anfield between the Everton club and their manager John Houlding, a new club was set up by Houlding, and McKenna threw his full weight behind it. Houlding, who was a major financier and businessman in Liverpool, became a close friend of McKenna and gave him the job of manager. The Monaghan man's vision and dynamism soon became inspirational, and his enthusiasm

'The Monaghan man's vision and dynamism soon became inspirational, and his enthusiasm proved infectious at the infant club, which would later go on to become one of the greatest in the world'

John McKenna: 'The many honours attained by Liverpool over the years owe their origins to a great Monaghan man'

proved infectious at the infant club, which would later go on to become one of the greatest in the world.

McKenna at first enlisted the services of many players from Scotland, and the first team he fielded contained not a single Englishman. That first outing was a 7-1 success over Rotherham, and it was followed by a series of victories that soon had huge crowds flocking into Anfield.

First Division status was eventually attained, although relegation followed later in 1895. Not only was McKenna a successful team manager, he was also a successful administrator. Now secretary/manager, he also built a new stand at the club, but the First World War intervened and fortunes dipped.

In 1915 he handed over the chairmanship of the club to WR Williams, but still remained in charge of team activities.

McKenna eventually left Anfield in 1922 after 30 years with the club. He had previously joined the Football Association Council in 1905 and was made president of the League in 1910, a position he held until 1935.

He died in March of the following year, aged 81. A commemorative plaque dedicated to him graces the entrance hall at Anfield, while a scroll and casket presented to him after a record 26 years as Football League president can also still be seen in the LFC Museum. The many honours attained by the club over the years owe their origins to a great Monaghan man.

SEAMUS McCLUSKEY's article first appeared in *Ireland's Own* magazine

'I'm **like a child.** When Liverpool score I go **crazy** and it's probably a little **embarrassing**'

Songwriter CHRIS DE BURGH's love of Liverpool – both the city and the club – began in the '60s and still dominates his life today. He even chartered a private jet to Istanbul and can be regularly found singing along to YNWA at Anfield

NOWADAYS, well-known celebrities aligning themselves with famous football teams is a common occurrence. Nearly every season someone from the world of film, TV or music suddenly declares their sudden, and previously unheard of, life-long support for a high-flying club. But in the case of Chris de Burgh, his love for Liverpool is nothing new.

The writer of 'Lady in Red' has been a fan of the famous shirt for decades, a fascination that was initially inspired by the Merseybeat era of the '60s. "During my teenage years, I always had a strong connection with the city because I was such a huge admirer of The Beatles and still am now," the successful solo artist says. "The whole scene around Liverpool was spectacular and obviously a major part of that was the football, with Bill Shankly, and later Bob Paisley, creating amazing teams.

"I was really drawn to it all, possibly because of the music and maybe because the city is commonly regarded as Ireland's second capital. I spent part of my childhood growing up in Wexford and Liverpool did resemble home in some ways. Another reason was some really good friends of mine lived in Liverpool and I'd go to stay with them on a regular basis. During those trips I'd spend time wandering around the streets and visiting the odd bar and restaurant, soaking in the atmosphere. I know it's a city that some people - particularly in the south of England - might look down upon, but it's got a heart that I haven't felt beating anywhere else in the world. It's a unique place with a great spirit."

De Burgh was reminded of that a few years ago when his son Michael embarked on a week of work experience at Anfield. "It was part of his schooling," de Burgh continues, "and he was based in the ticket office as far as I can remember. I travelled over with him and on the first day we were getting a taxi to the ground when the driver started chatting. During the conversation he asked Michael which team he supported. He's obviously a Red too so this guy said: 'I'll pick you up tomorrow and I'll have a special present for you'. I have to admit that at the time I was sceptical, but this man was as good as his word. The next morning at 10 past nine he handed Michael a training jersey signed by Steven Gerrard. And I was really moved by that gesture. I thought it summed up how a lot of people in Liverpool are, and it's a great quality. My son loved his time there."

That kindness is also something de Burgh believes is reflected at Anfield every season, particularly when former Reds return to their old stomping ground. "The respect the fans have for the players is amazing, especially when an old boy comes back with his new team. I've always been amazed by the reception they get. It's very rare for any of them not to receive a warm welcome, which you simply don't find at other stadiums. Anyone who doesn't must have been a bad character!

"I'll always remember when my friend Didi Hamann came on for Manchester City and he got an unbelievable ovation. Fernando Torres scored the winner that day but not even the roar for the goal was as loud. It was remarkable. So for me it's the whole picture: the city and the football team. It's something I've loved for a very long time, since Stevie Heighway was bombing up and down the wing right up to Istanbul and now."

Similar to the Reds, de Burgh has enjoyed success all over Europe, although the

'I simply live and breathe LFC. It's just my kind of team. I love the family atmosphere there and the way they look after the young supporters. Anfield is unique and that's why I like it so much'

price for selling so many records in so many countries is a hugely demanding schedule that takes him around the globe. With that in mind, he doesn't get to make the trip to L4 on a regular basis.

"Finding the time is almost impossible, especially during the early days of my career. At one stage I'd probably flown over our famous ground on hundreds of occasions but had never actually been there to watch the lads play. I'd always be away on tour or recording in the studio, so it just never happened. But I remember telling one of my closest friends that I would watch a Liverpool match at Anfield eventually, I was determined to do it. That was still the situation until about 10 or 15 years ago. Around then my sons, Michael and Hubie, started getting interested in football and I decided I'd take them to a game. The first time we went over we stayed with David Moores and his wife, who are firm friends of mine. My sons were shown all around Anfield and it was a magical weekend."

That visit obviously only increased the de Burgh household's appetite for more LFC action, and since then they've made the journey across the Irish Sea on a regular basis. "On another occasion I attended a Radio City charity auction and one of the lots was for two people to be matchday mascots. Naturally I immediately snapped it up for my boys and they absolutely loved it.

"To be honest, I'm like a child as far as Liverpool is concerned. When they score I go crazy and it's probably a little embarrassing. But if you can't be embarrassing in front of your family, then when can you be? I simply live and breathe LFC. It's just my kind of team. I love the family atmosphere there and the way they look after the young supporters. I've been to some other grounds and I was shocked by the corporate attitude. Anfield is unique and that's why I like it so much."

De Burgh's affection for our home is something that shines through when he speaks, and like the rest of us he hopes its character will be replicated in the new stadium at Stanley Park. "That's something that can't be lost when the move eventually happens. I've said to some of the people involved that they have to use an acoustic expert who knows exactly what's required. Reflected noise from the stands is vital. There are some grounds where that hasn't been incorporated and it's a shame. I've no doubt a bigger Kop will be an awesome sight, and if you can get the acoustics of the whole place perfect it'll be amazing."

De Burgh fans: Babbel, Henchoz and Owen

As the singer-songwriter mentions, he's a friend of David Moores and Didi, along with lots of other current and former Reds. It's one of the perks of his job, although even fame doesn't prevent him becoming star-struck when he bumps into those who've served the club through the years.

"I have my heroes and it's great to meet them," he smiles. "Obviously most of them are a lot younger than me, but they still seem familiar with my music which is a compliment. It's mainly come about because I've performed at the club Christmas party, and as a result of that I've managed to meet a lot of the guys. Didi has become a really good mate of mine. Him and Markus Babbel told me they were fans of my music when I first met them. Since then they've both been to some of my shows over in Germany, and when I played in Switzerland Stephane Henchoz came to watch. I've had a few interesting nights out with Didi, as you can probably imagine. He's a hell of a nice guy and I like him a lot. Sami Hyypia is another who I've been really impressed by. Any time I meet him he always has a kind word for my kids."

De Burgh – or one of his records to be exact – has also got a special place in the home of one of our former goalscorers. "Michael Owen once told me he had one of my signed albums in his house sat beside a matchball he'd received after scoring a hat-trick. That was brilliant to hear, it's a great honour. And I always got on very well with Gerard Houllier every time we met. I know some supporters have mixed emotions towards him but he's a great man who really cares for the club. Not too many of the footballers I've met have a bad attitude. There's only been one or two that I've got a bad vibe from and most of them quickly moved on. I think, even with all the changes in the modern game, the ethos of Liverpool weeds out the guys who don't really fit in. It's not just the supporters. I think to be a success at the club you have to understand the history and what it all means. And not every player gets that. Thankfully, the majority do."

Of the more modern crop of players, de Burgh also has his favourites, with obvious names at the head of the list. "Torres' first year was simply spectacular. His goalscoring and skill is there for all to see. But what really stands out for me is his attitude. When he's fouled you don't see him rolling around like a baby. There are other guys playing the game who start whimpering and crying. There's none of that with Torres, who gets hacked down as often as anyone else. But does he complain? No, he just shakes his head, gets up and carries on. And that's a fantastic attitude to have. I'm also a big fan

'Torres gets hacked down as often as anyone else. But does he complain? No, he just shakes his head, gets up and carries on. And that's a fantastic attitude to have'

of his Spanish colleague Pepe Reina. I think he's a top-class goalkeeper who understands the game really well. And then there's Stevie G! He really is just fantastic. Look at what he's done in the biggest games over the years."

Of all those massive occasions when the skipper's come up with the goods, there is one that still sits head and shoulders above the rest for de Burgh. "I don't want to sound boring because I know everybody says it, but Istanbul is my standout moment as a fan," he understandably states. "When Luis Garcia decisively, without doubt, scored that goal in the semi-final against Chelsea – none of the 'not over the line' rubbish – I was immediately on the phone trying to sort out a trip to the final."

You'd imagine securing flights and tickets would be no problem for someone of de Burgh's stature. That was far from the case. "My music has a strong following in Turkey and the hotels knew my name, but they just couldn't get me a room for that night. It was impossible."

Getting to Turkey also proved to be an organisational nightmare. "The next day I tried all the airlines and couldn't obtain any flights. For over a week I thought about it and contemplated different solutions. During those seven days the pressure was gradually building inside my own head and within my family. Obviously we all desperately wanted to go. So I contacted my promoter in Istanbul and told him the problem. Two days later he came back to me and said: 'I can get you a room in the Crown Plaza Holiday Inn about 50 miles from the city.'"

So was it a case of problem solved, albeit far from perfectly? "No, of course not. Instead of charging €100 a night they were looking for a thousand. That was obscene and I refused to pay it." Thankfully the promoter had also come up with a plan b. "The other option was a friend of his who had a boat with four cabins moored in the city.

Immediately I was sold on the idea," De Burgh laughs. "We overcame the flight problem by taking my private jet."

With all the arrangements in place, the de Burghs were bound for a boat on the banks of the Bosphorus. "The journey required a refuelling stop in Italy," he continues. "While there, the handling agent took us for lunch in one of his friend's restaurants. It only cost €20 per head and we ate and drank ourselves stupid. It's one of the best meals I've ever had. Then we got back on the plane, eventually landed in Turkey and got taken to the boat where we went for a night cruise. Next day we did a bit of sightseeing and then went to the match. All you could see was this massive red army making its way along what looked like a moonscape. And of course everyone knows what happened that night."

Many claim they still believed the Reds could secure our fifth European Cup despite the fact Kaka and co had run riot during the first half and we were three goals down at the interval. De Burgh is not one of those. "I remember looking around at half-time and there were so many people with their heads down and crying," he recalls.

"I was speaking to Didi a few weeks later and he said they could hear the AC Milan players celebrating, which must have been an awful feeling. In the stands, 'You'll Never Walk Alone' started echoing around. Naturally I joined in, but it wasn't because I thought the lads could come back. I honestly felt the deficit was irretrievable. In my mind it was a sort of 'thank you' to the team. 'It's been a brilliant journey, and, although the dream of winning the European Cup isn't going to come true, we'd like to say well done.

Thanks for some amazing nights on the way to the final.' Didi told me the players heard this down below and it was like something from an American movie. A defiant last stand against impossible odds, if you like. Of course it wasn't just the song, it was the players who did it. Didi came on and made a huge difference that day in what we all know was a sensational triumph."

Nobody could truly believe what had happened just before his or her eyes. Even watching it back now, it's still a slight surprise when we emerge victorious. And many Reds didn't know how to react. "What can you do in such circumstances?" he reflects. "My daughter Rosanna was standing on a seat shouting: 'I don't believe it, we've won the Champions League', and crying her eyes out. I think we all did the same. It eventually took us two hours to get out of the ground and it was around four in the morning when we got back to the boat. The whole thing was amazing from start to finish. For our family that was one of the best collective moments we've ever enjoyed. It's like a shining diamond in our memories."

Singing 'YNWA' in the Ataturk was a mixture of initially anticipation, then despair and later glorious ecstasy. A few months later, de Burgh was performing it again, although this time he wasn't part of the travelling Kop. "There was a gathering at the House of Commons to honour the team," he reveals. "I was recording in London at the time and got invited down. When I walked in, Gerry Marsden was there and I immediately spotted a piano in the room so I knew what was going to happen at some stage. Eventually Gerry

'Didi came on and made a huge difference that day in what we all know was a sensational triumph'

says: 'Come on, let's have a bash', and we ended up singing it together. As a Liverpool fan, and a musician, it doesn't come much better than that. It was my two greatest passions combined."

Having written hundreds of songs during his long career, de Burgh is something of an expert on the subject, and is a big admirer of our famous anthem, and not just because of his Liverpool allegiance. "As most people are aware, it was written · for the musical 'Carousel', and it's a very complicated piece of work. I've performed it on countless occasions and it's not easy. It switches key a lot throughout." With that, he proceeds to sing the chorus of 'You'll Never Walk Alone'. "It really is a beautiful piece of music," he eventually continues. So has the man who's registered number ones around the world ever contemplated penning his own football song? It's been a poisoned chalice for many acts, although it is a prospect he's tempted by.

"I've thought about it in the past," he admits. "I think it would be a similar experience to when I wrote a song about a horse winning the Kentucky derby. That was also very tricky. If I did I'd write more about the joy that football brings

rather than an individual team. When you think of the moment a goal goes in – particularly like in Istanbul or Stevie's equaliser in Cardiff – the emotion that's released by thousands, if not millions of people simultaneously, is extraordinary. Or Torres' goal sending the Spaniards wild after their Euro 2008 win, that's very much worthy of a song. I often say to my kids imagine this moment in every bar, home, restaurant and street in that country where people are going mad. I love the emotion involved, and for me that's what football's all about, millions of people going wild. I might get round to writing one some day."

As well as composing a football anthem, de Burgh also has one more football related ambition he'd like to fulfil. Like every fan, he'd like to play in front of the Kop, although in his case it's obviously a different kind of performance he's referring to. "A gig at Anfield would be the ultimate for me. I couldn't make it to the 2008 concert, and I heard Paul McCartney was spectacular. I wouldn't fill the ground myself, but I'd love to be involved in a big show there. I've played football stadiums on numerous occasions and it gives me an extra buzz. But nothing would compare to doing it at Anfield. That would be a dream come true."

'I'd **swap one of my All-Irelands** for a chance to play in the **Champions League final'**

Gaelic footballer COLM 'GOOCH' COOPER has supported Liverpool since he was a boy, but owing to work and sporting commitments he still hasn't made it to Anfield. Yet with a slight change of fate, he could have been playing there himself

AS one of the most talented Gaelic footballers the modern game has seen, nobody would expect Colm Cooper to be unsatisfied with his many sporting achievements.

A free-scoring forward, the man affectionately known as 'Gooch' won his first All-Ireland senior medal at the tender age of 21. Since then he's added numerous honours to his vast collection, although there is a particular title he'll never get his hands on. "I'd probably swap one of those All-

Irelands for a Champions League medal," he jokes. "Or maybe just the chance to play in the final. But I'll settle for watching Liverpool take part. That's good enough for me."

The man from the Dr Crokes club in Killarney is already a GAA legend, although his career could easily have taken an alternative route. "Like most kids I tried lots of different sports when I was growing up," he says. "Hurling was one of those, but when I was about eight or nine I needed a few stitches after an accident, so that was the end of that.

Instead, I played football and also soccer with Killarney Celtic. I was a midfielder or a striker, and spent most of my time trying to score goals. Soccer was great and all my friends were part of the team too so it was a major attraction for me. I kept at it until I was 17. Then, around that time, I had to decide between the two games."

With the benefit of hindsight, the choice he made was entirely correct. "It was a really tough call, but Gaelic took over. It became more serious and I just went with it. Thankfully it's worked out okay for me so I can have no complaints."

Cooper's soccer fascination didn't end there, though. Far from it. "By that stage I was already a huge Liverpool supporter. When I was growing up they were the team who everyone looked to. One of my brothers followed them so I took up that mantle as well. And I've been a die-hard fan ever since. I always keep up-to-date with rumours and the transfer market and everything else that's going on at the club. I want to know what's happening all the time. And I still get upset if the results don't go well."

Talk of the Reds naturally brings us around to Istanbul and Cooper can still clearly recall that night in May 2005. "Kerry had a game coming up and I remember rushing in from training. Unfortunately, by that stage we were already 1-0 down thanks to Paolo Maldini. After that it got worse before it got better. Even talking about it now is still fantastic."

So many years in Gaelic games means Cooper has nearly seen it all, including some momentous Istanbul-like comebacks. "I've been on both sides of it," he says, "having

big leads before losing and vice versa. With three points for a goal in Gaelic, it's probably more likely. Despite that, it's amazing when those kind of turnarounds actually occur.

"But you'd never imagine it happening in the Champions League final because it's such a high-profile game with top, top players involved. Thankfully the nature of sport means you never know what's in store, as we all saw that night. I'd love to have been there, and it's my dream to one day watch Liverpool in the final."

Before that, 'the Gooch' has more important LFC-related priorities. "I've still not been to Anfield," he confesses. "I was supposed to go over on a number of occasions. But owing to Gaelic football commitments and working in the bank it's always fallen through.

"I don't have much free time. If I do it's spent watching Liverpool or maybe playing golf now and again. I can only imagine what it will be like. I love listening to the Kop on TV, and I'd love to sit in that special stand. The passion of the fans is unique, and that's a really attractive quality for me."

With Cooper hailing from the Kingdom, it's obvious he knows all about knowledgeable and vocal support. "Definitely. I can see a lot of similarities between Kerry and Liverpool followers. Kerry are the most successful side in GAA history, and Liverpool are still the most successful team in England. I think Kerry people live for the game, and I'm sure it's the same on Merseyside. It's like a religion. I can totally understand why, and I love being part of both set-ups, as a player in one and a follower of the other."

If life had been different, that situation could have been reversed.

Cooper might have been running out in red on a regular basis rather than the famous green and gold. And he knows exactly who he'd like to have lined up alongside. "Steven Gerrard and Jamie Carragher are my two favourite players. I know they're local lads and it's expected, but you can see how much they love the club every time they take to the field. Stevie signing a long-term deal a few years ago was brilliant news, and I've kept an eye on Carragher since he broke into the first team.

"Originally some people didn't rate him, but he's improved so much and he's great to watch, especially in the big games when he always produces his best."

'Steven Gerrard and Jamie Carragher are my two favourite players. I know they're local lads and it's expected, but you can see how much they love the club every time they take to the field'

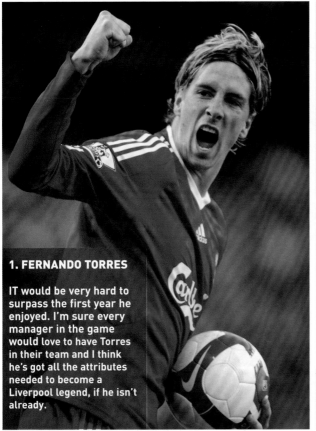

1. FERNANDO TORRES

IT would be very hard to surpass the first year he enjoyed. I'm sure every manager in the game would love to have Torres in their team and I think he's got all the attributes needed to become a Liverpool legend, if he isn't already.

2. ROBBIE FOWLER

THE local lad, and when I was growing up he was the main man. The fact that he was a Scouser obviously made him a crowd favourite, although just his goals alone would have guaranteed that. I remember being really excited when he and Steve McManaman burst onto the scene. The four-and-a-half-minute hat-trick against Arsenal was amazing. And for four or five years he was absolutely phenomenal. I was surprised to see Robbie return in January 2006. He obviously wasn't the same player, but that didn't matter. He was still a legend.

Gooch's top four Liverpool forwards

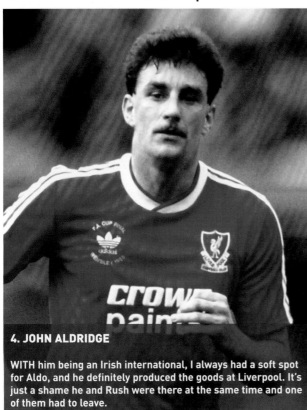

4. JOHN ALDRIDGE

WITH him being an Irish international, I always had a soft spot for Aldo, and he definitely produced the goods at Liverpool. It's just a shame he and Rush were there at the same time and one of them had to leave.

3. IAN RUSH

WHEN I was a kid, he seemed to score almost every week. To get two in the FA Cup final against Everton was amazing; to do it a second time was a fairytale. It doesn't really get much better than that. I've still got a video of the '89 final at home. We knew a few Everton supporters at school, so those goals were a great source of amusement for us.

'I recall **Macca's goals,** Molby and a girl throwing a drink over my mate ... not a **bad first trip'**

Radio One DJ and Channel Five presenter COLIN MURRAY was priced out of going to Anfield in his youth, but since his job first took him to our famous ground, he has never looked back. Here he shares memories of his favourite players and moments – and getting the red carpet treatment at Everton

I T'S 30 MAY 1984. Brucie's wobbler, the Romans defeated in the Eternal City. 'Old big ears' is ours again for an amazing fourth time in just eight seasons.

That night in Italy was memorable for so many reasons: Joe Fagan ending his first season with three trophies, Stevie Nicol missing his penalty, the joyous celebrations and those tracksuits. It's a great moment for every Red to recall, especially Colin Murray, for it was the first-ever Liverpool game the Northern Irelander watched.

"I've been told that I looked at the national team beating Spain in the 1982 World Cup. But I don't really remember that," he laughs. "The European Cup final is my first football memory. I probably had no concept of why it actually went to penalties because I was so young. But I do remember the

flares in the crowd and Bruce Grobbelaar doing his party piece."

Murray, a well-known voice on Radio One and now the face of football on Channel Five, had become a Liverpool fan because of a Shankly-esque figure in his neighbourhood. "My step-dad was a Spurs supporter, but there was an old Scottish guy who lived nearby and he was a massive Red," Murray explains. "He was a bit like Shanks and he had been a fan all his life. My mates and I would all go around his house and he'd tell us great stories about the club. We loved it and my fascination with the team grew from there. No matter what Irish league sides we followed, we all supported Liverpool because of his influence."

Of course there were other options available to the young

First memories: Brucie and the shoot-out in Rome, 1984

Macca magic: Celebrating one of his goals with Robbie Fowler and Mark Kennedy

Murray when it came to nailing his colours to the mast. "They always say Northern Ireland is split down the middle between United and Liverpool. United had George Best and Norman Whiteside and more recently David Healy, whereas Liverpool have the southern Ireland link through the likes of Ronnie Whelan, Steve Heighway and John Aldridge. You get a sprinkling of Arsenal because of Pat Jennings, Frank Stapleton, Liam Brady and Niall Quinn. And you see a little bit of Spurs in Northern Ireland too, also because of Jennings again, and Danny Blanchflower. But mainly it's Liverpool and United. In our area those allegiances were never drawn along religious lines. For example, two of my nephews went down the United route and my sister went for Liverpool. If it hadn't been for that old man I could have been a different kind of Red."

Having heard so much about the history of the club and witnessed our European Cup victory on TV, the next priority for the Ulsterman was a trip to Anfield. Unfortunately that wouldn't occur until nearly 15 years after the glory on the banks of the Tiber. "People talk about the modern game pricing normal fans out of it; when I was growing up I definitely couldn't afford to go," Murray reasons. "My family hardly ever went on holiday; I think our only foreign trip was

to France when we got ferries and drove all the way. Having enough cash to go to the match just wasn't realistic."

Eventually it would be his chosen profession that would lead to a maiden trip to our famous home. "I was doing a training scheme at the *Ulster Press* newspaper and a guy called Greg Harkin, who was a massive Red, took me and another guy to Anfield. I don't know why he chose us; thankfully he did."

Sheffield Wednesday were the opposition and they suffered a 4-1 defeat. "Steve McManaman scored a couple," Murray enthuses. "I don't think he even stopped to fix his hair that night. It was one of Jan Molby's last games, which I was so glad about because he was one of my favourite players. To actually see him play was amazing. I remember one of the lads upset some local girl afterwards and she chucked a drink over him. So McManaman's goals, Molby, and a girl throwing a drink over my mate were my main memories of the trip. Not a bad first time."

That visit was just the start for Murray. "I think when you go once it becomes a mecca and you want to go back again and again," he says. "I started earning my own cash around the age of 18 and would make three or four trips over to see them each season then. Around 1999 I started going a bit

'My family hardly ever went on holiday; I think our only foreign trip was to France when we drove all the way. Having enough cash to go to the match just wasn't realistic'

more. From 2001 it's varied depending on work.

"Between 2001 and 2004 I was doing daytime radio so I was making it to 30 or 40 games a year then. That was great. Now I'm working on Five Live on a Saturday morning and the show doesn't finish until midday. That rules out anywhere beyond Watford if it's a 3pm kick-off. The night-time radio show runs from Monday to Thursday and I have to take days off to present UEFA Cup football on Five. As a result of all that, Liverpool's European games are also out for me now. I find that bizarre because I hadn't missed a European match at home for years. I went to every one in 2004/05 and loads of UEFA Cup ties before that too. Since I moved to night it's been awful for me in terms of getting there. I'm probably making it to around 10 games a year at the moment."

Sometimes, though, not even huge work commitments can prevent him showing up to see his beloved Reds in action. "Me and three friends were all doing a job in Dundee on the day of the 2006 FA Cup final," he explains. "We paid £800 each to get a plane down and, as you know, it was well worth it."

If you ask any Red to name the best player from down through the years the usual names are quickly reeled off. Murray has a different take on the question. "I think the best and your favourite players are very different," he says. "For example, my first game, as I mentioned earlier, was the '84 European Cup final. If you go through that team, you can't look beyond Kenny Dalglish, Ian Rush or Alan Kennedy as the best players. However, I look at the side and my favourite players are Ronnie Whelan – I loved him – and Nicol. So for me the greatest aren't necessarily my favourites. If you were picking your greatest team you'd have to go by the stats, so Roger Hunt would be in there because he's our second top scorer. Whereas your favourite players are different."

So who makes Murray's personal list? "Molby – I just loved him," is the instant response. "I remember him playing in the Masters a few years ago. He came on and couldn't run. Instead, he just stood in the centre circle and set up three goals in the space of five minutes."

There's another magical Molby moment that stands out in Murray's mind. "During that first game I went to, he produced a pass from the corner of his own six-yard box to the edge of the other area. I just remember a gasp from the crowd in the Main Stand. You certainly didn't get anything

Class in the middle: Big Jan and Gary Mac

like that in Irish League football or from the Northern Ireland team. He's always been a hero to me."

Another midfield maestro is also part of Murray's chosen few. "Gary McAllister, definitely. I think he exemplified the passion you need to play for Liverpool Football Club. It was a surprise to us all when he arrived, and he was brilliant."

Since Murray became a regular in L4, two names have been on the team-sheet almost every week: Sami Hyypia and Jamie Carragher. "My favourite Sami moment was against Olympiakos in 2004," he laughs. "I remember right at the start they booted the ball towards Rivaldo and Sami just wiped him out, while at the same time he took the ball fairly. It was brilliant. Him and Carra were a fantastic central defensive partnership."

Reasons for admiring Carra are obvious, but Murray cites different factors for favouring the vice-skipper. "He's not just an amazing player but also someone who does so much work away from the spotlight to help great causes. Carra does it without fuss and of course his dad is a great character too. The story about the Champions League medal in a Tesco bag is the best one for me. Somebody asked Carra's dad if there was any chance of his son getting a look at the medal," Murray starts with a laugh. "Of course Philly said: 'Yeah, no problem.' A few days later, the guy rings and asks: 'Are you going to drop it around?' Philly says: 'I did, I put it though your letterbox in a Tesco bag.' It had been there for a few days and the guy hadn't seen it. I love Carra because you always get those sorts of stories about him or his dad."

Another player Murray admires is also famous for tales of his off-field escapades. "If I ever had to put six past or present Liverpool players around a table for a few drinks, Didi Hamann would be the first pick. I hosted a Gerard Houllier heart foundation dinner, and different squad members used to come along. You could tell that some absolutely hated it or didn't really know what was going on. Hamann always loved it. He was very funny and it was like being out with one of your mates. I've always felt, both as a player and a person, he's a top man."

All those Murray recommends are names from the modern era, so does he hold any of our older heroes in similar high regard? "I know I've gone for a lot of the guys who I've watched live," he admits. "If I was to name any

'Gary McAllister exemplified the passion you need to play for Liverpool Football Club. It was a surprise when he arrived, and he was brilliant'

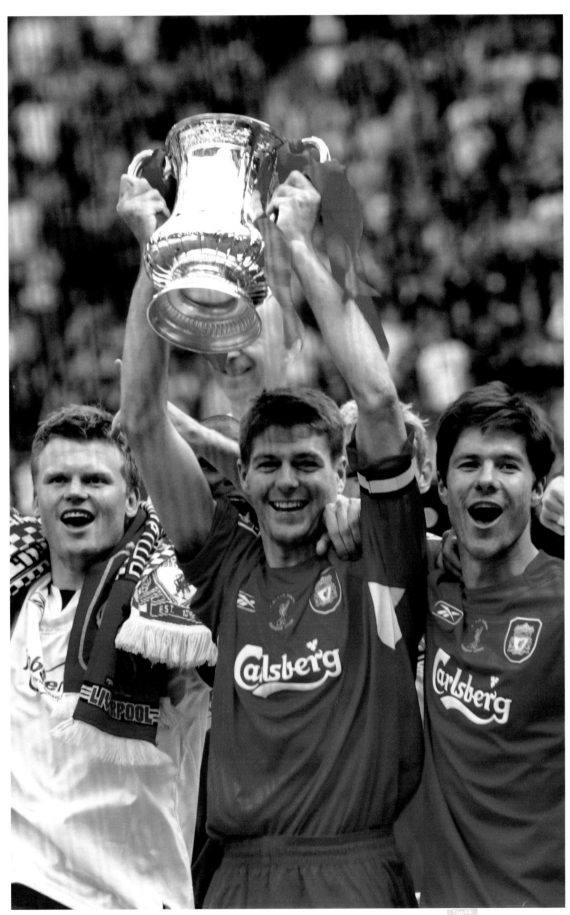

Well worth it: Murray and three friends paid £800 each to witness the win over West Ham in 2006

'If I ever had to put six past or present Liverpool players around a table for a few drinks, Didi Hamann would be the first pick'

others it would have to be Ian Rush, Robbie Fowler – even though I did see him play when he came back – Emlyn Hughes and Phil Neal. I loved him because he was a great player and for another reason too.

"We were taking part in a tournament and a lot of the ex-Liverpool players dropped out at late notice. Neal didn't and stepped in to give us an impromptu training session. It was amazing what he taught us so quickly. We were the oldest team and we were playing Derby County, who were the youngest. We went 3-0 down but managed to draw 3-3 thanks to Phil's management. He cared as much about beating Derby in a pro-celebrity competition as he did about winning the European Cup. It meant everything to him and that was just great to see."

While Neal played a part in our first four European Cup triumphs, it's the fifth which, unsurprisingly, Murray regards as his single best moment as a Red. "The whole experience of Istanbul, not just the game was absolutely amazing," he continues. "The people who organised it did an amazing job, especially when you compare it to Athens two years later.

"Turkey was a super 'old-school' fan day. For some reason it just felt like we were going to win. All the fans were sure, whereas in Athens that certainly wasn't the case. The other game I love was Juventus at home. Me and my mate Nick were sitting directly behind Luis Garcia's foot when that ball dropped in front of him. I'm sure we screamed 'hit it' about four or five times in that half-second it took him to do so. It meant quite a lot for obvious reasons, but as a game it was superb entertainment too. Of course the Chelsea matches are all special. As an adult, all the European adventures really stick out. I'll never forget those. I went to most of those games with my mates and that really makes it even

better for me."

European football has played a big part in Murray's LFC life, and also his professional life as the host of Channel Five's UEFA Cup coverage. The role has taken him to various grounds around England. In 2007/08 he spent a lot of time at Goodison Park when Everton reached the quarter-finals of the competition. With his allegiances to the club on the other side of Stanley Park well known, some stick from the Blue faithful could have been expected.

"I've only ever had one bad word actually said to me at Everton," he reveals. "And that was in the toilets. When I stood up to the person they quickly backed down. It is, without a shadow of a doubt, the friendliest venue where we do UEFA Cup football. There are other nice ones too, however Everton are tops. Hopefully they'll pardon the pun, but they do put out the red carpet for us. They're lovely people. Every time we turn up the security guards joke that I'm at the wrong stadium. It's very friendly and I really like the people. I cheered them on in that UEFA Cup campaign because they treated us so well."

While he might have initially made his name as a DJ, it's in sports presenting where Murray eventually sees himself operating. "I'm quite young for the TV job at the moment," he smiles. "All the bosses are 60 and the producers are 50, so I'm seen as the kid. I know I'm going to have to work hard. But I'm not doing this to get Gary Lineker's position. I'm doing it because it's a damn good job and it's challenging.

"People think you just sit around and talk about football all day: it's not that easy. With the commercial breaks we have, it sometimes means we're left with just 46 seconds to preview the second half of a game with Stan Collymore and Pat Nevin.

Hit it . . . ! Luis' famous goal against Juventus set us on the way in the first leg at Anfield

"I really enjoy it and I imagine I'll end up working in news and sport full-time some day.

"I don't want to be a grey-haired Radio One presenter. In fact, if I ended up working at Five Live when they move to Salford it would be great. I'd live in Chester and be able to go to Anfield every week.

"That would be the perfect job, being there, hopefully on the Kop, for every home game with the huge flag sweeping over us.

"For me, that's one of the best feelings in football."

'I got into Liverpool at exactly the **right time**'

"SIMPLY a great player who had everything and did it all with real style. Then he went on to manage the team and win the double in his first year. That was an amazing achievement."

There can only be one LFC legend in question as Dave Kelly tells us all about his love for the club and Kenny Dalglish in particular.

"Some people said he just carried on from where Bob Paisley and Joe Fagan had left off, but that's obviously not true. It was unbelievable to end up with the double when he was just starting out as a boss. And of course he also went on to win the Premier League title at Blackburn Rovers too. Again people took a swipe by saying it was just Jack Walker's money, but it's never that easy, as others have proved.

"I know he didn't have success as a manager at Newcastle or Celtic, but in my eyes he's still a legend. He'd definitely be up there as one of the top Liverpool players, and one of the biggest thrills I've ever had was getting to interview Kenny when he came to Dublin with Newcastle. Just chatting to him was great."

Kelly's honest enough to admit that he's been a Red since before The King inherited our famous number seven shirt from Kevin Keegan. "Yeah, my earliest memory is from 1977. Bob Paisley's side obviously won the European Cup and the League that year. But for some bizarre reason the FA Cup final defeat against Manchester United is clearer in my mind."

Naturally, like many Irish fans, there was one particular member of the line-up who drew Kelly towards Liverpool. "I think the important role Steve Heighway played is probably what really attracted me to the team. It was great to see an Irishman as part of a European Cup-winning side."

That continent-conquering group gave Kelly a close-up view of 'old big ears' in the summer of 1978. "Getting to see them play in Dublin was massive for me," the Bray man continues. "They came over to face a League of Ireland select side at Lansdowne Road and brought the European

FAVOURITE GOAL

❝ This isn't so obvious: Ronnie Whelan's equaliser against United in the 1985 FA Cup semi-final at Goodison Park. It came out of nothing and he just curled the ball into the top corner. Ronnie had a habit of scoring spectacular goals in big games, and seeing an Irishman do that meant a lot, especially the strikes against Spurs and United in the Milk Cup final at Wembley. ❞

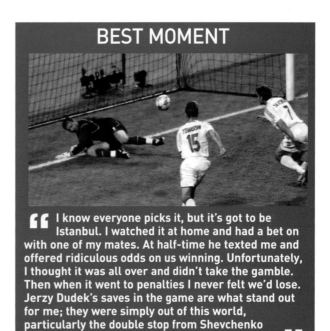

BEST MOMENT

❝ I know everyone picks it, but it's got to be Istanbul. I watched it at home and had a bet on with one of my mates. At half-time he texted me and offered ridiculous odds on us winning. Unfortunately, I thought it was all over and didn't take the gamble. Then when it went to penalties I never felt we'd lose. Jerzy Dudek's saves in the game are what stand out for me; they were simply out of this world, particularly the double stop from Shevchenko right at the end. ❞

Cup with them. It was great to see the trophy and such good players up close and personal.

"Looking back, I got into Liverpool at exactly the right time. Most Irish people tend to veer towards a team with an Irish player and I was no different. I'd always watch 'The Big Match' to see how Heighway was doing, and whenever Liverpool made a trip over – which they did quite often back then – I always tried to go along."

And it wasn't just watching football that became an obsession for Kelly. "I love collecting Liverpool programmes," he reveals. "I've probably got all the home programmes since the mid-'80s. And I'd have a few from before that too. It's a big interest of mine."

Now the players once profiled in those pages are work colleagues, and Kelly still has to pinch himself to believe it. "When I was growing up, if people had said you'll be interviewing the likes of Kenny, Ronnie Whelan and Mark Lawrenson, I would have just laughed. They were obviously great, great stars for Liverpool, so just to chat with them about football is special. At the same time, it's slightly surreal but I absolutely love it and I consider myself very lucky to be in such a position."

DAVE KELLY is a presenter on TV3 in Ireland

'I couldn't have asked for a **better** first game at **Anfield**'

Limerick hurler STEPHEN LUCEY's first memory of Liverpool is not a good one – Arsenal snatching the title from us in 1989. But his first night at Anfield brought sweet revenge

EVEN now, Michael Thomas' last-minute goal in 1989 is something every Red would rather forget. But, try as we might, it's engraved on our memory forever, and in the case of Stephen Lucey, the moment is even worse.

"Unfortunately it's one of the first matches I can actually clearly remember," the Croom and Limerick hurler says with anguish. "I would have been around eight or nine years old. One of my brothers followed Liverpool and my other brother followed Arsenal. I can still recall all of us in the living room watching it, and when Thomas scored my brother went absolutely nuts. I remember him grabbing me and jumping up and down celebrating. I think I spent most of the summer sulking over it."

Thankfully the 1988/89 season also contained much happier scenes for Lucey. "A few days before that I'd watched Liverpool defeat Everton in the FA Cup final at Wembley. Obviously I prefer to recall that game rather than the Arsenal result. It was a warm Saturday, and instead of watching the build-up to the match we spent the whole morning playing soccer and did so afterwards too. I think we all wanted to be John Aldridge and Ian Rush after watching both of them score in the 3-2 win."

Fast-forward nearly 19 years from that campaign and the Gunners again threatened to cause Lucey heartache. "2-1 up on the night and all set to go through," he laughs. "Then Theo Walcott took off on that run and Emmanuel Adebayor made it 2-2. Like most people, I thought we were going out. Then it all quickly turned again and we ended up winning 4-2. It was a real rollercoaster of emotions."

Everyone lucky enough to be inside the ground that evening still feels their pulse quicken when the Champions League quarter-final victory is mentioned. And, for obvious reasons, it means even more to Lucey. "I couldn't have asked for a better first game at Anfield," he explains. "Unfortunately, I played so much hurling and Gaelic football and did so much studying when I was growing up that I never had the opportunity to make the trip to Liverpool."

Lucey wasn't the only member of the Limerick hurling squad in the Kop on that never-to-be-forgotten night. "Donal O'Grady and Seanie O'Connor came with me," he continues. "It was everything I expected and a whole lot more. The whole night was special. We went for a few drinks in The Albert and The Park afterwards, and the place was buzzing. The stadium is similar to Croke Park in terms of the atmosphere around it. Croker is obviously bigger, but the match was special. If it had been 0-0, it might have been different. Thankfully, that wasn't the case."

While Lucey was fulfilling a lifelong ambition, one of his travelling colleagues probably felt a little out of place. "Seanie came along because there was a spare ticket. He's actually an Aston Villa fan and doesn't really have any allegiance to Liverpool. He's a bit crazy and during the middle of the game he started chanting: 'Villa, Villa.' We had to try and keep him quiet, which wasn't the easiest job."

That trip on 8 April 2008 might have been Lucey's first to L4, but it wasn't the first time he'd attended a Reds game. "Hopefully I'm a lucky charm for the lads because I

Not the best place to be: Half time in the Milan end in Istanbul. Top: The Kop party in Taksim Square

'When Xabi Alonso's equaliser went in, we were running up and down the stand in ecstasy'

managed to make it to Istanbul too," he laughs. Like everyone else he's got his own tale from that night. "We were some of the fortunate ones who actually got our hands on tickets. Unfortunately there was a mix-up and, as a result, we ended up in the middle of the Milan end."

Sitting amongst the travelling Kop in the Ataturk at the interval wasn't a pleasant experience, so we can only imagine what it felt like in the Italian section of the ground at that time. "It wasn't a great place to be," Lucey confirms. "I can still remember being surrounded by AC supporters and I was almost in tears. Obviously they thought it was game over, and you couldn't blame them."

Enduring Italian taunts wasn't the only cause for complaint Lucey had at that point. "Just as the half-time whistle went, lots of texts started arriving from my Manchester United-supporting mates back in Ireland. The trip cost us roughly €1,400, and they were kindly reminding us that we'd wasted our cash."

Obviously, by the end of the night that price tag proved to be a bargain as Lucey celebrated amongst the suddenly subdued Rossoneri contingent. "When Xabi Alonso's equaliser went in, we were running up and down the stand in ecstasy. I don't think that went down too well with those around us. But it was such a crazy situation that nobody really knew how to react. Afterwards we went to Taksim Square for a massive singsong and a celebration. Those were scenes that will stay with me for the rest of my life."

Even on the way back to Ireland the craziness didn't end. "People got on the wrong buses and the wrong planes," he continues. "Our flight was delayed by about 10 hours. It meant sleeping on the floor in the airport. I remember buying a shiny Liverpool tracksuit in one of the shops there just to kill some time – I still try to wear it whenever I watch a game on TV. Nobody minded all the delays because we'd just won the European Cup." Lucey's experiences of

watching the Reds live have been too few, and that's why he cherishes them so much.

In the future he hopes to make the trip across the Irish Sea on a more regular basis, although, with his demanding schedule as a GP, that can't be guaranteed. "It was tougher when I worked in the hospital," he says. "When I was doing a shift I'd be getting text messages from people to keep me updated on the scores. I'd also be timing my breaks to make sure I saw some of the game or hoping the nurses wouldn't ring when it was on. On other occasions I remember asking them to only buzz me at half-time or after the final whistle."

If practising medicine wasn't enough, Lucey obviously also has hurling commitments with his club and county. "Midweek training sessions mean missing Liverpool matches on a Tuesday or Wednesday night. But I'm always straight off the field to catch the last few minutes. At the weekends it's usually easier; I get to watch all the Saturday games. And I always make time to watch 'Match of the Day' or 'The Premiership', so I never miss any of the goals."

Naturally, how the Reds have fared leads to plenty of banter when Lucey next takes to the training pitch. Although one member of the Limerick panel is always guaranteed some stick, no matter how his side have done. "Amongst the lads there's a good mixture of allegiances to different soccer teams," he continues. "There's plenty of Liverpool and United. And then there's Dave Bulfin, the substitute goalkeeper, who supports Swindon Town. As you can probably imagine, he gets plenty of stick about it. I think he's got a valid excuse but I can't remember what it is."

Of course those efforts on the field are all geared towards attaining silverware and Lucey has already thought about that prospect. "Limerick winning an All-Ireland and then Liverpool claiming the league title would be the perfect year for me. If that ever happened I'd probably need 12 months off to celebrate. The party would be huge."

'Barnes was a **favourite** of mine. He was flawless'

Former Gaelic footballer turned pundit DARA O CINNEIDE tasted All-Ireland success at Kerry, but he's always had at least one eye focused on the exploits of his favourite soccer team across the Irish Sea

WHEN Steven Gerrard lifted 'old big ears' in 2005, it was obviously the culmination of a childhood dream. Born and bred in Liverpool, he was fulfilling the ambition of many a Scouser when he raised the trophy above his head after our dramatic penalty shoot-out victory against AC Milan. It was a special moment, even more so because very few sportsmen get to lead their local side to victory at such a high level.

Dara O Cinneide is one of those who's realised that ambition, as in 2004 he was Kerry captain when a 1-20 to 2-9 win over Mayo brought the Sam Maguire Cup back to the Kingdom after a four-year absence. And just like Stevie, he played a true skipper's role by notching eight of his side's 23-point tally that afternoon in Croke Park.

It was a moment O Cinneide had longed for while growing up in the home of Gaelic football, although there was another sport that also competed for his childhood affections. "When I was younger I used to follow Liverpool probably more than the Kerry team," he admits.

When you consider the status of Gaelic football's most successful side, and the immense pride Kerry people rightly have in the green and gold jersey, that comment is almost blasphemous. But for O Cinneide it was perfectly natural.

"You might only see Kerry on TV twice a year; in the All-Ireland semi-final and final when they made it that far," he reasons. "Kerry was, and still is, the home of Gaelic football. But even with that in mind there has always been a cosmopolitan interest in other sports such as soccer and rugby, even when those games weren't as fashionable as they are now.

"Towns like Tralee, Listowel and Killarney are big soccer strongholds, as much as Gaelic football. And there would be a lot of Liverpool fans in those areas. I guess it comes from the fact that soccer, and Liverpool in particular, was present almost all the time. The game got a lot more exposure than the Gaelic Athletic Association back then, and as a result I became hooked. I wasn't the only one; my brother is also a big fan and some of my neighbours were too. It was all about Liverpool."

That addiction went beyond simply watching games on the box. "We had the names of great players scribbled on our copy books and sports bags. And I used to buy *Roy of the Rovers*, *Shoot!* and *Match* every week in order to read all about the latest goings on in the English league. There were also Panini sticker albums, which we'd avidly collect and swap. I remember an occasion when I'd managed to obtain all but one sticker – Ronnie Whelan. No matter what I tried, I just couldn't get my hands on it."

The midfielder might have been a source of sticker-book frustration, but he was also one of the prime reasons for the corner-forward's infatuation with LFC.

"The first game I can remember was the 1982 Milk Cup final when I would have been around six or seven years old," he recalls. "Whelan was just emerging on the scene around that time and, being an Irishman, you associated with him. On the day he popped up with two goals, one very late on to take the game to extra-time and then another to put us 2-1 up."

Naturally a trip to Wembley wouldn't have been complete without the obligatory Ian Rush goal. The Welshman duly rounded off the victory in the 119th minute to ensure Bob Paisley's men retained the three-handled trophy. And if Whelan got O Cinneide into the Reds, it was our record goalscorer who fed his addiction.

"Around that time it was all about him and Kenny Dalglish. There was rarely a game where one or the other of them didn't find the net or do something special. Rush's double in the 1986 FA Cup final was particularly sweet because some of the other lads at school were Everton fans. That fact made the win even more enjoyable. So when he was sold to Juventus a year later I was really

LIVERPOOL
RONNIE WHELAN

Need! The elusive Ronnie Whelan Panini sticker

Role
model:
John
Barnes
was a
'world
beater'

disappointed. But, as with every team, the show went on."

Despite the absence of the Welsh goal machine, a glut of new arrivals would take up the mantle and provide O Cinneide and his pals with more great moments.

"John Aldridge, Peter Beardsley and John Barnes all seemed to come along at the same time, just after Rush had left, and that certainly made it a bit easier. Their team played some amazing football."

And it was our brilliant number 10 who really made an impact on the Kerryman. "Barnes was a huge favourite of mine. He was absolutely flawless. Nobody could stop him. It always seemed strange that he couldn't produce the same form for England. But when he pulled on a Liverpool jersey he was a world-beater."

With O Cinneide himself eventually ending up as a free-scoring corner-forward, it's no surprise that the players he looked towards weren't defensive-minded. But there was one man at the back who he did admire. "Defenders don't make the headlines too often, but I always had a lot of time for Alan Hansen. He was a real classy operator, and not many strikers got anything from him."

'Some of them just need to be touched and they hit the deck, which rarely happens in GAA. And guys like Souness, Hansen and Whelan wouldn't have done it in their day either!'

With O Cinneide currently working as a pundit on 'The Sunday Game' – the GAA equivalent of 'Match of the Day', you might say – maybe O Cinneide is attempting to model his own style on the BBC man?

Laughter is his first response to that suggestion before he goes on to explain: "I won't name any names, but I think there are some other lads in the studio who'd probably claim that title ahead of me. I've a long way to go before I reach Hansen's level."

While O Cinneide may be reluctant to accept those comparisons, his role in the media has enabled him to come face-to-face with another of our former famous Scots. "Graeme Souness does a lot of the soccer punditry on Irish TV, and he's always in and around the studios," he says. "I was introduced to him on one occasion and that was special. As a kid I never thought I'd get to meet any of those guys. He's a real Liverpool legend."

Unfortunately it was the departure of Souness's predecessor that O Cinneide remembers more vividly than the midfielder's playing days. "When Kenny quit as manager after the 4-4 FA Cup draw with Everton, that really hit me hard. It was a massive shock and I became a little disillusioned by it. I never thought he'd leave. I was 16 at the time and that moment probably made me realise there was more to sport than just going out on the field and kicking a ball."

By that stage the local version of football was already starting to occupy most of his time. "I never played soccer," he continues. "It just wasn't available to us. There was a huge following but it was never an option. Gaelic football was the only choice."

While starring for his local side An Gaeltacht, O Cinneide obviously impressed the county selectors and eventually got to fulfil his goal. "I wanted to wear the green and gold. That was the first priority. Then winning an All-Ireland was the next step. Thankfully, I was lucky enough to experience it; 2004 was a great year for the team and for me. It was an honour to work with such great players and coaches. Running out in front of huge crowds on the big stage was a massive buzz. It doesn't get any better."

Even with club and county Gaelic commitments, he still kept tabs on developments at Anfield. "I watched the great players like Robbie Fowler, Steve McManaman, Michael Owen, Jamie Carragher and Steven Gerrard emerging. In particular I remember travelling over for a game against Bolton when Owen was just coming through. There was a real buzz around the place about him and you could see exactly why as he scored the winner."

A few months later the young striker would go on to take France '98 by storm. And it wasn't just the youngster who made a lasting impression on O Cinneide.

"On every occasion I've been to Anfield - and it was the same that day - I've been hugely amazed by the volume and level of support. It's a unique place where you're surrounded by very genuine, die-hard fans and that is special. They seem to be more down-to-earth when you compare them to other supporters. I love the atmosphere, it's really very, very special and compares favourably to

Owen goal: Michael beats Bolton's Chris Fairclough to score the winner at Anfield in March 1998

'I remember travelling over for a game against Bolton when Owen was just coming through. There was a real buzz around the place about him and you could see exactly why as he scored the winner'

anything you'd encounter in GAA, rugby or any other sport."

That's quite a statement when you consider O Cinneide has played in the Gaelic game's best arenas and faced its most intimidating sight. "The Hill in full flow is special; it's unique in GAA circles. But it's very much a summer spectacle, whereas the Kop is present almost all year round. I get a lump in my throat when 'You'll Never Walk Alone' is being sung and all the scarves are being held aloft prior to kick-off. The genuine respect and tradition of the club is still there and that's a rare thing in modern-day soccer. I think anyone, from anywhere, no matter what their allegiance, couldn't fail to be impressed by the awesome sight."

Despite that genuine awe, there is a slight air of cynicism in the Raidio na Gaeltachta reporter's voice as he discusses the beautiful game. "Yeah, it's probably a combination of getting older and the way soccer's developed," he explains. "All my best memories of it are from my childhood. Now I don't watch it as much as I used to, although I do always

make time for Champions League games and big international tournaments. The antics of the players aren't something I find easy to handle either. Some of them just need to be touched and they hit the deck, which rarely happens in GAA. And guys like Souness, Hansen and Whelan wouldn't have done it in their day either!"

But even those feelings don't prevent O Cinneide rooting for the Reds whenever they go into action. "We all want to win the league," he says. "I'd never take anything for granted but I think we'll always do well in Europe, no matter what. It's what the club is built on. Over the last few seasons we've been one of the best sides in the Champions League and I expect that to continue for a long time. Two finals and a semi-final in four years is phenomenal when you consider the standard of competition. Now all that's missing is doing the same in the Premier League year in, year out. Putting together similar consistency over 38 games is the key. If they can it would be fantastic, almost as good as Kerry winning the All-Ireland."

Tiernan scores for the Liverpool
All-Star team in May 2008

'I don't know why but I texted **all my friends** and said: "You have to **believe..."'**

MOST of us can only ever dream about one day playing alongside our heroes. Receiving a pass from someone we've watched play in a Red shirt on hundreds of occasions, or celebrating with one of the club's best-ever strikers, are images that only ever appear in our minds.

For Tommy Tiernan those fantasies became reality in May 2008. The well-known comedian was part of the Liverpool All-Star line-up that went head-to-head with a similar Manchester United selection at Galway United's Terryland Park. It's a once-in-a-lifetime experience, and Tiernan even mentions it during his stand-up show.

But as if that cameo wasn't enough to make all of us green with envy, the Navan man went one better by also managing to get on the scoresheet in the 1-1 draw. Even now, the joy of that moment is still obvious when he recounts the strike – which he quite rightly cherishes and has even uploaded onto his website.

"It was a cracker with my left foot from just on the edge of the area," he chuckles. "The ball flew into the top corner. Normally in those kind of games they let people score but it definitely wasn't a soft effort." Anyone who watches the strike can't fail to agree with the description.

 Dreams became reality for comedian TOMMY TIERNAN when he got to play with some of his Liverpool heroes in 2008, and he's busy making sure that all five of his kids share his passion for the Reds

Tiernan himself has reviewed it so many times that he can recount the entire move from start to finish, not just the part he played. "Mike Marsh picked it up in the centre of the field and sprayed it out to David Fairclough on the left," he starts. "At this stage Fairclough's legs are well gone, but he just managed to lay it back to Marsh who found Aldo inside the box. Aldo tried to beat two defenders but fell over – he said later that he skipped past them – and the ball rolled to me from where I whacked it first time."

It's obviously something Tiernan still finds hard to believe, as his immediate celebration on the day indicated. "I just went insane," he confesses. "At first I didn't know what to do so I just started running like Usain Bolt and made my way over to my boys on the sideline.

'I got one of those hard kitchen chairs and plonked it five feet away from the TV, put on my hat and scarf and roared at the screen for the entire second half, through extra-time and the penalties'

Rome, sweet Rome: Emlyn Hughes lifts Liverpool's first European Cup in 1977 – one of Tiernan's first football memories

'When I was a kid and you supported Liverpool it was like God smiled on you every day because there was an endless procession of trophies'

"I don't think I've ever looked happier."

When he eventually returned to the pitch, all of his temporary teammates were on hand to congratulate him, although one of them had something different to say. "Aldo told me he was disappointed that I had run to my kids instead of him, as he'd done all the hard work for the goal. The lunacy of that statement only becomes apparent when you see the footage."

Finding the net in such spectacular fashion was far more than Tiernan ever expected. Just stepping out on the field would have been enough for him. "I hadn't actually played a game in such a long time so I decided the worst thing I could do was try too hard. Instead, I attempted to be graceful in everything I did. Playing with those legends like Phil Neal, David Fairclough, John Wark and Jimmy Case was incredible, especially Case. He was part of the first real Liverpool football memory I had, and to be running out beside him made it phenomenal."

As Tiernan says, Case holds a special place in his heart thanks to his goal in the 1977 FA Cup final. "United went 1-0 up and I remember some commentary that went: 'It's usually said Liverpool are at their most dangerous when they're coming from behind, let's find out.' That line always stuck in my mind. Then Steve Heighway had the ball on the left and he combined with Terry McDermott before Joey Jones knocked it into the box. It was too high for Kevin Keegan, but Case took it down, turned and banged it in. That's the first Liverpool goal I can recall."

Unfortunately, as we all know, United struck again through a Lou Macari shot that deflected off Jimmy Greenhoff, to take the victory. "That was a really tough afternoon," Tiernan continues, "but the following Wednesday more than made up for it when the Reds won our first European Cup against Borussia Monchengladbach."

Those few days were a sharp learning curve for the youngster, who was quickly discovering that the beautiful game could deflate you down to unprecedented levels before lifting you up again in no time at all.

"My family lived in Zambia for a while, and when I was growing up there the most famous team were a side called the Kabwe Warriors. I used to watch them and I can still remember one game when the opposition were awarded a penalty. They refused to take it until the Kabwe goalkeeper removed his lucky charm from the net. So in terms of soccer that was where I was coming from. Then, when we moved back to Ireland and Navan, my fascination with the game really started to take off and it was time to choose a team."

For a short while Tiernan did the unthinkable. "Yes, I supported United," he admits. "But I quickly decided it wasn't for me and changed after a day. That was the week of the '77 cup final, so after the defeat I might have been questioning my decision, although any doubts didn't last long."

From then on it's been the Merseyside Reds that have held Tiernan's affections, through the good times and the bad. "When I was a kid and you supported Liverpool it was

Tough afternoon: Jimmy Case scored the first Liverpool goal Tiernan can remember during the 1977 FA Cup final

More Milk Cup success in 1983: 'We seemed to win it every year when I was in secondary school'

like God smiled on you every day because there was an endless procession of trophies. For example, we seemed to win the Milk Cup every year when I was in secondary school.

"I remember fighting with people about whether or not Ronnie Whelan meant that goal against United at Wembley in '83. Of course I defended him to the hilt, but I still don't think he intended it. Apart from that trophy, everything else also seemed to arrive on a regular basis: league, FA Cup, European Cup. It just went on and on."

All of those triumphs were brilliant in different ways but none could eclipse the drama of Istanbul. Tiernan spent the night at home on his own in his living room, or at least the first half anyway. "I was on the couch watching Milan fire in those goals," he grimaces. "Then at the interval I decided to move to the kitchen where I could be closer to the TV."

While most of us felt the deficit would only increase during the second 45 minutes, the Navan man thought

differently. "I don't know why but I texted all my friends and said: 'You have to believe.' It didn't really make any sense, but in those situations you do what you think might work.

"After I'd done that, I got one of those hard kitchen chairs and plonked it five feet away from the TV, put on my hat and scarf and roared at the screen for the entire second half, through extra-time and the penalties. Thankfully, the events on the field were just as insane as those in my house."

Watching the Reds on the box is a regular tradition in the Tiernan household, and it comes with its own rituals.

"We managed to get a shirt signed by the entire Champions League-winning squad," Tommy explains, "and for the European nights we put it beside the TV, along with hats and scarves draped over it. Istanbul was terrific but it's better if we're all there, like the night of the 4-2 Arsenal game.

"When Theo Walcott went on that run and set up

'The seats we've had are just below the scoreboard and almost right beside the Kop. To sit there and get drawn into that well of passion is one of the richest experiences I've ever had. It's an honour'

Emmanuel Adebayor, my son Jake burst into tears. It was awful. He was so upset that he didn't see Ryan Babel earn the penalty seconds later. We're very serious about it all and I'm over the moon that my sons are also fans. It gives us something to do together."

Were the younger members of the clan tempted to follow in their father's footsteps and support the Red Devils, even if only for a day? "I wouldn't allow it, not even for 24 hours."

Being based in Galway or away on tour so often means Tommy usually has to make do with watching the Reds on TV, but he does get to Anfield whenever possible. "The first occasion was against Spurs a few years ago and I burst into tears because I was so happy to finally be there," he says. "It was just amazing. Since then we've managed to borrow a season ticket and been over loads of times and my boys absolutely love it.

"They're fanatics, particularly Jake who is a mine of information on the club. My partner Yvonne is very supportive and she comes over once a year too. Some of the seats we've had are just below the scoreboard and almost right beside the Kop. To sit there and get drawn into that well of passion is one of the richest experiences I've ever had. It's an honour."

Of course that giant passionate sea of Red is most famous for its anthem and Tiernan thinks that is the reason why the club is so special to so many people. "It's almost a religious fanaticism, like when you hear a hymn in a church and it resonates with you," he reasons. "It strikes a chord with me and as supporters we're almost disgusted by the fact that other clubs have the audacity to sing our song.

"We're not impressed with Celtic when they do it or – who's the other team? ('Feyenoord,' Jake shouts in the background) – or Feyenoord. They should come up with their own anthem. I think the club is defined by that song. It's not like supporting just any team. There is an extra element that 'You'll Never Walk Alone' brings. It's one of belief in each other and I think that's why I identify with Liverpool."

That identity is something that has spread to all parts of the globe including across the Irish Sea. Some people can't understand the fascination and Tiernan can see their argument. "In a way it makes no sense for people like us who live in Galway to associate so closely with a team based in England. But we do and that song is part of it. I guess that the tragedies at Heysel and Hillsborough also make the bond stronger. You just hope that the players share that same belief and passion. It's easy for them not to because they are very wealthy men and could be detached from the supporters. But when they go out on the field it's obvious if they care or not."

Despite his love for the Reds, Tiernan, probably like most fans, does have the odd moment of crisis. "I mentioned all the success we've enjoyed during my time as a fan, but there have also been some frustrating seasons. Periods when you know a manager's time is up are the worst. Everyone is aware that the position is unsalvageable but they keep hanging in there. That's when it gets bad. But I always support them no matter what. Once you're related

to someone, you're related, there's little you can do about it. Liverpool is like that too. It's a family."

As well as it being a family affair, Tiernan also gets a perverse pleasure from the whole process. "If it wasn't frustrating at times, it wouldn't be so fascinating," is his explanation. "If it were easy, not as many people would be so attracted to soccer. Sometimes it's a struggle, but we're there for better or worse. I know stuff like christenings, birthdays, weddings, etc are all important, but next after that is Liverpool. Yvonne wouldn't be as crazy about it as I am but she tries to understand."

Tommy's kids: Jake, Dylan, Eve, Isobel and Louis are all part of the Liverpool family and will continue to be as long as their dad has anything to do with it. Although, unlike the Reds, Tommy won't be looking for number six. "No, no, five is for keeps," is his final word on the matter. Spoken like a true Kopite.

Our Liverpool XI (2005-2008)

Reina   Carragher
Finnan   Agger Hyypia
Gerrard   Hamann   Babel
Garcia
Torres   Baros

Subs: Dudek, Cisse, Keane, Kuyt, Alonso, Crouch, Mascherano
Jake & Tommy

Jake's tactics

It's a 4-3-3, with Luis Garcia just behind the strikers. Ryan Babel and Steven Gerrard operate on the left and right, and I'm sure Fernando Torres and Milan Baros will get plenty of goals. The toughest decision was whether to go for Didi Hamann or Mascherano. In the end we went for Didi because of his experience.

Jake's favourite player (Undoubtedly influenced by his Dad): Kevin Keegan

'Seeing **the Kop** was like landing on another **planet**'

BERNARD O'BYRNE, former chief executive of the Football Association of Ireland, was reeled into supporting the Reds by Bill Shankly's mission statement and a close friend's trial at Melwood. Now a self-confessed 'football fanatic', he loves making regular visits to Anfield and hearing the Kop in full voice

BILL SHANKLY's stated aim to build Liverpool into 'a bastion of invincibility' obviously caught the eye of everyone on Merseyside. It also had a similar effect on the other side of the Irish Sea, particularly for one young Dubliner.

"His attitude seemed to embody a life lived for football. His passion seemed to just pour out of him and, for me, that was the initial hook," Bernard O'Byrne, former head of the Football Association of Ireland, recalls. "Of course at that time I was still a kid and now I've been a fan for over 40 years."

There is also another reason for O'Byrne's attachment to the Reds. "Back in those days a friend of mine had a three-week trial at Melwood. That really connected me to the club. The fact that a local lad from Inchicore could get a trial at Liverpool was just magic. I suppose at the time you probably have an idea about doing the same yourself, until you realise you can't even kick the ball out of your way! So ever since those days, it's always been Liverpool for me."

O'Byrne has spent the majority of his years involved in the beautiful game in one capacity or another until pretty recently. It was a commitment that meant he couldn't visit L4 as often as he would have liked. "When I was at the FAI, it was almost impossible," he explains. "And before that, when I played junior football, it was almost always on a Saturday so I never got the chance to go over. But it never lessened my passion; probably increased it if anything."

Now, working in a non-football-related post as chairman of the Mansfield Group means the Dubliner has a lot more free time. "In recent years I've been making the trip maybe seven or eight times a season, which isn't bad. When I go over with my daughter and wife or friends, it's a great treat."

Home from home: Irish fans see the sights ahead of the Euro 96 play-off at Anfield

'Back in those days a friend of mine had a three-week trial
at Melwood. That really connected me to the club. The fact that a local
lad from Inchicore could get a trial at Liverpool was just magic'

O'Byrne can still recall the first time he made the pilgrimage, and being blown away by what he witnessed. "It was a match against Spurs back in the mid-'80s. The atmosphere really shocked me. Straight away I was in awe of the place. Having been born a few hundred yards away from St Pats in Inchicore, I'd naturally gone there as a kid. But transporting yourself over to Anfield and looking at the Kop really was like landing on a different planet."

As well as sampling many great displays from the Reds down through the years, O'Byrne has also visited our sacred home as part of the Irish national team contingent. "I was actually on the team bus as part of the security set-up for the 1995 play-off game against Holland," he recalls.

It's a night that was filled with mixed emotions. "Football people know in their hearts how a game is going to go," he laments. "I felt it was one of the first times amongst the group that they knew they weren't going to win and wouldn't be going to Euro '96."

That 2-0 defeat at the feet of the Dutch was a watershed moment. "We knew it was the end of an era so it was a strange occasion," O'Byrne explains. "As we left the ground

afterwards, Jack Charlton walked down the bus and shook hands with all the players and staff, effectively saying goodbye. That scene in Liverpool really was a very, very emotional night, and it's one that I'll never forget as the atmosphere inside the stadium was special, especially seeing all those Irish fans on the Kop.

"During the Charlton era, four games stand out in my mind. Stuttgart '88 when we beat England; 1990 against Italy in the World Cup quarter-final in Rome; defeating Italy in New York; and then that night in Anfield. The fact that it was at that venue just added to it for me. For those four games to come along was incredible, and those scenes will probably never be repeated in Irish soccer. It was more than a match. It was the end of a great period. Because of those games, soccer really exploded in Ireland. A lot more kids started playing it and leagues were set up in counties where the game had never been that popular."

When asked to select his best ever Liverpool player O'Byrne needs just a second to come up with a name, excitment clearly in his voice.

"For me, there's no one that comes close to Kenny

A work
of art:
Kenny's
masterpiece
against
Bruges in
'78 sent
them wild in
Dublin (top).
Left: Paul
McGrath.
Main image:
The modern
day Kop

Dalglish. I compare it to conversations about the best-ever player for Ireland. Anybody who suggests it wasn't Paul McGrath is having a laugh. Really the only question is: who was the second best? When it comes to Liverpool, Kenny was number one, without any doubt."

O'Byrne's reasons are obvious, although there is one particular night that guaranteed the Scot a place in O'Byrne's affections forever. "Istanbul is up there as the best victory this club has ever had, but for me 1978 at Wembley isn't far behind it," he explains. "Kenny's finish against Bruges is still one of the most clinical I've ever seen in a high-pressure game. To hold your composure like that is rare. No doubt the vast majority of players would have opted for power in that position and probably hit the keeper with their shot. But Kenny executed it perfectly. It was almost art. I can still remember the manic celebrations in a

pub in Dublin. To do that in your first season is incredible, the perfect script, and it's for moments like that I hold Kenny in such high esteem."

O'Byrne has witnessed the game from various sides and, although he isn't involved now, he still spends most of his free time engrossed in the sport. "I do consider myself a football fanatic," he laughs, "even though I don't have any official connection with it anymore. Sometimes that's better. The only important thing is playing or being a supporter, everything else drains you. To me it can sap your energy and enthusiasm. I identify with following a team all around the country and the world.

"That's what I've done with Pats and Liverpool whenever I get the opportunity, and will continue to do so for many years to come. If you're not playing, that's the next best option and I love it."

'I compare it to conversations about the best-ever player for Ireland. Anybody who suggests it wasn't Paul McGrath is having a laugh. When it comes to Liverpool, Kenny was number one, without any doubt'

'I play **Gaelic** but get just as big a kick from **Reds**'

Mayo footballer CONOR MORTIMER says nothing can rival the high he gets when Liverpool score. Here he shares his greatest memories following the Reds, and his excitement for the future

I COULD score any goal or any point in any Gaelic football match including the All-Ireland final, but I still wouldn't get a buzz like I do when Liverpool hit the back of the net.

I've been a fan of the Reds all my life, for almost as long as I can remember. My brothers, Trevor and Kenneth, are also Reds and I think that's the reason I initially got into it. Where we're from in Mayo is a great breeding ground for Liverpool supporters, and there's a big group of us who all go on regular trips to Anfield together.

Even though I play Gaelic for the majority of the year, I prefer soccer, always have done and always will. I probably should have stayed playing the game, dedicated myself to it a bit more and maybe progressed, but there are hundreds of lads in Ireland with that complaint. Instead I get just as much of a kick from following Liverpool. When people ask me to pick my favourite game - or moment - one word is all that's needed to sum it up.

Istanbul. It still gives every Liverpool fan a special buzz.

I'm sure almost every Red would provide the same verdict; the 2005 Champions League final against AC Milan in Turkey will never be beaten. It's definitely my best memory. Nothing can ever top it; even winning the league, I'm not sure it would be so special. In many ways it was a strange game, initially a disaster that eventually became a very, very good night. If you wrote that script nobody would believe it. And to win the European Cup in such fashion was really special. There's probably no better way to do it. We were lucky enough to get tickets, and after celebrating out in Turkey we then went to Liverpool for a few days too. The party was amazing and I'll never forget the homecoming parade in the city.

Unfortunately, as we all know, 2007 wasn't so enjoyable. Myself and my brother Trevor didn't actually get our hands on the tickets until just before kick-off. My other brother Kenneth was also in the Olympic Stadium for our replay with the Rossoneri. At one stage we'd almost given up on getting in, and then we suddenly thought it was definitely going to be our night. Filippo Inzaghi had other ideas.

Bruno's finest hour: Cheyrou's Newcastle double in 2004

Going to big finals like that are obviously great but just as important were my first trips to Anfield. It's something you think about from a very young age, actually attending a game at the Reds' famous home. You imagine what it's going to look like and how it's going to sound. Will the Kop be such an awesome sight when it's up close and personal? Will 'You'll Never Walk Alone' send a shiver down my spine when it's belted out before the game starts? My expectations were huge – in such a situation they tend to be – and the reality usually never matches the hype.

Anfield exceeded them all, and by quite a distance. I think the fact that I'd never got the chance to make the journey across when I was a kid had really built it up for me. It was only when I could afford to do it myself that it actually happened. And it was well worth all those years of waiting.

The atmosphere is always buzzing and it probably eclipses anything you find in the Gaelic Athletic Association world. I've played in some good stadiums, but none of them compare to Anfield. I love the set-up. All the stands being so close to the pitch creates an intimidating arena and that's the way I like it. Croke Park is the best stadium in Ireland, but it's huge now and as a result a lot of the noise escapes.

My first visit to L4 was back in 2001/02 when Michael Owen scored two goals against West Ham in a 2-1 victory. It was special. Another great memory is the 2004 FA Cup win over Newcastle with the same scoreline. It was an evening game and the noise was spectacular. Then it got even louder when Bruno Cheyrou opened the scoring with something like less than two minutes on the clock. I don't think the crowd had even settled down when Laurent Robert equalised almost immediately. After that it developed into a real end-to-end encounter and Cheyrou got the second with a header at the Kop End from a Stevie G cross.

They're all great memories and I wouldn't miss those trips for anything. We probably fly over three or four times every season, whenever we get the chance. There are obviously lots of commitments when it comes to playing Gaelic with club and county, but I always ensure I find a couple of weekends to make the trip across. Right from the day the fixture list is released we're planning which games to attend. When we do there's always one man we hope isn't injured or suspended: Stevie.

In the last few years, people have constantly put forward Ronaldinho, Cristiano Ronaldo, Kaka and Lionel Messi as the best player in the world. But Stevie's got to be up there with all those guys. When the chips are down he usually comes up with the goods. Just look at the number of big games he's scored in. That's the sign of a real world-class talent and he's been doing it for a long time now. Nobody can question his ability or temperament. He does what a captain should by popping up when his team needs it most. He did it in Istanbul and he probably went one better in the 2006 FA Cup final against West Ham.

The game was over; we were dead and buried, then the ball dropped on the edge of the area. How many times do you see someone balloon the ball over the bar from that position, never mind the added pressure of the situation. But Stevie banged in a phenomenal strike. Everything about it was right: timing, technique, power and accuracy. I know extra-time and penalties were needed to eventually decide the outcome, but you could say that goal won the cup. To do it so late and in that manner was fabulous for us and absolutely devastated West Ham. They were never going to recover from conceding an equaliser at that stage.

In more recent years it's been our number nine that's attracted all the headlines and, like every Red, I always look forward to him performing. Some people suggested they were surprised by how well he did in his first season; I definitely wasn't. I always thought he'd score plenty of goals, although I'm not sure I would have predicted he'd end up with 33. My reason for having no doubts was the number of chances the team create in nearly every game, especially when Stevie's playing. Fernando Torres is the man to convert those opportunities. He also showed during the European Championships just how good he is at the highest level.

While those two may be seen as the star men they wouldn't be able to do so without their teammates, particularly Jamie Carragher and Javier Mascherano. I've really got a lot of time for those two guys.

They don't do anything flashy, but their roles are probably two of the most vital. The determination they possess is also something I admire. They refuse to lose, and that's the spirit you need to be a success at Liverpool. They've got it and that's why they have a special bond with the fans. Hopefully we'll be travelling over to watch them on many more occasions. Although I'm not sure we'll be lucky enough to see them score. That would be a perfect day.

'The atmosphere is always buzzing and it probably eclipses anything you find in the Gaelic Athletic Association world. I've played in some good stadiums, but none of them compare to Anfield'

World class: Nobody can question what Stevie brings to Liverpool

'To sit in the Kop and meet Mascherano would be my **perfect day**'

Rugby union star FELIPE CONTEPOMI, who plays for Leinster, has supported Liverpool since he was a little boy growing up in Argentina. Unsurprisingly, his favourite player is the engine at the heart of the Liverpool midfield: his countryman, Javier Mascherano

THE passion and intensity that Javier Mascherano brings to the field have made him a firm Kop favourite since he arrived on Merseyside in early 2007.

Almost directly across the Irish Sea, one of his fellow countrymen has made a similar impact in Dublin's fair city. Felipe Contepomi is one of the star names of the Leinster rugby union side, and he understands exactly what drives the Liverpool number 20.

"I don't know Javier personally," the out-half and centre told us when we caught up with him, "but I can empathise with the way he approaches football and the way he performs. He cares a lot about his team and is very passionate whenever he plays. I admire Mascherano because, naturally, it's always good to see a fellow Argentinian do well, and I love that style of footballer. His work-rate is phenomenal."

Contepomi was a member of the Leinster team that won the 2008 Magners League and also played a leading part in his national side's progression to the last four at the previous year's World Cup. But his sporting life could have been very, very different.

"I'm football mad," he reveals, "I always have been ever since I was a young boy growing up back in Argentina. There weren't as many satellite TV channels back then, so you couldn't watch all the matches like you can now. But I used to read as much as I could about the European game. And for some reason Liverpool were my team. I don't know why, I just identified with them. Back home I follow Independiente and, like Liverpool, they wear all Red, so that's probably the reason why I originally forged the bond."

As well as absorbing info on the European version of the beautiful game, Contepomi also spent plenty of time with his football boots on. "I played soccer until I was 18," he continues. "It was more of an enjoyable past-time with friends rather than a serious sport. I'd play rugby on Saturday and football on Sunday. Then rugby became a bit more important when I started lining out with my first division team and received a call-up to the national side. But football was always my first love. It's a religion for me. Whenever I get into a discussion on the game it can last for hours."

So would he rather be hitting the back of the net than dissecting the posts with precise penalties and conversions? "I'm pretty happy doing what I do," he laughs. "I'm lucky in that it's worked out well for me so far. I always joke that I'd love to be a footballer; if I had a second life that's what I'd want to come back as."

Contepomi's passion clearly burns brightly and has grown even more since he transferred to this part of the world, particularly his affection for all things LFC. "My love for Liverpool has probably increased since I moved to Ireland because there are so many supporters over here," he explains. "Dublin is obviously totally different from Argentina but it's very enjoyable. I've been here since 2003 and the people are very friendly. My wife and daughter like it a lot. Liverpool and Celtic seem to be the biggest teams around the area of the city where I live. The number of jerseys you see is unbelievable. Every day I see somebody in a Red shirt."

With Contepomi also holding down a job as a doctor alongside his Leinster duties, 90 minutes of the Reds in

Making a name for himself: Emiliano Insua shares his surname with Ruben Insua, a former top class midfielder

action allows him to take the rare opportunity to relax. "I am pretty busy most of the year," he explains. "With training, matches and working in the hospital I don't get much free time. So when Liverpool are playing, that gives me a chance to take it easy. I know a lot of fans have particular pubs where they go to for the game but I only do that on a rare occasion. I prefer to watch it at home."

And it's only natural that he pays particular attention to the displays of Mascherano. "He's a typical Argentine or Latin American player – he has that unique attitude. I remember when I was growing up we had a rule that if you were in the defensive midfield role the ball might pass or the man might pass, but never both together!" he laughs.

"That's the way Javier operates and he does it superbly. It emphasises the way a lot of Argentines think the game should be played. He obviously has plenty of skill but it's the way he tackles and harasses opponents that really stands out. In Argentina everyone – no matter what their allegiance – loves him. He played for River Plate but even if you're a Boca supporter you can't help admiring him. He never gives less than 100 per cent. Sometimes that gets out of control. But I think that fire is what gives him his edge; without it he wouldn't be as effective. I think most Argentinians have it inside them. As a result, we love players like that and he's probably the best example in the European game at the moment. Some other individuals – probably more skilful than Masc – are often questioned by the fans for their lack of effort and commitment. Joan Roman Riquelme is a prime example. For me, he's been one of the best offensive midfielders in the world, but Argentinian people mainly prefer Mascherano, even if he's not as naturally talented as Riquelme."

At the time of writing, Mascherano is the only Argentine featuring in the Liverpool first team on a regular basis, although another of their fellow countrymen in the shape of Emiliano Insua looks to have a bright future ahead.

The U20 World Champion left-back originally came to Anfield in 2007, and his name immediately struck a chord with Contepomi. "When Insua arrived I asked some friends back home for information about him," he explains. "A guy called Ruben Insua was one of my favourite players, one of the best Independiente had, a real top-class midfielder. So when I heard the name I immediately thought of him. Hopefully he can go on to become another first-team regular. If he did, it would be fantastic. You always need a few Argentinians in the side!"

While it's only natural for Contepomi to keep an eye on his countrymen's progress, there is one man who not even Mascherano can surpass in the eyes of the rugby star. "Obviously Fernando Torres has been unbelievable since he joined us, he's probably the best striker in Europe. But for me Steven Gerrard is still number one," he states emphatically. "I think he's the best in the world. Other people argue with me about it but I have no doubts. You

'The ball might pass or the man might pass but never both!' Masch tackles his international colleague Tevez

could put him anywhere on the field and I think he'd do a great job. The 2005 Champions League final is a great example of that. During extra-time he was operating as a right back and was superb. That was an incredible performance. And on the night he not only showed his quality as a player, but as a leader too by bringing his team back from what looked like being a heavy defeat."

Nearly every Red has a tale to tell about Istanbul and Contepomi is no different. "That's still my best memory as a Liverpool supporter," he beams. "I was on my way back to Argentina to play for the national side. It meant catching a connecting flight from Madrid, so I was in the airport when the final kicked off. Thankfully the flight was really late so I got to see all the game before I boarded the plane. It was a special night and it made my 12-hour journey a hell of a lot easier. Being in the air for that long is never good, but after watching Liverpool win the Champions League I could have stayed in the sky for a whole week!"

Naturally, Contepomi would liked to have been in Istanbul that night, but being unable to attend games is the price he pays for his profession. In fact, with the rugby and football seasons almost running parallel, it means he rarely gets the opportunity to see the Reds live.

"So far I've only managed to make it to one game," he admits. "It's very difficult to find a free weekend to make the journey. When I did go it was back in 2003, and I was still playing for Bristol. It was a 1-1 draw with Villa - Michael Owen and Dion Dublin scoring. But for me the result didn't really matter, it was more about the experience of going to Anfield. It was amazing. Ever since I was a kid I'd always wanted to attend a game there and - when I did - it was like a dream come true. Unfortunately I didn't get to sit in the Kop, it was the Main Stand. It was still fantastic, but hopefully next time it will be the Kop. To do that and meet Mascherano would be ideal."

'Hopefully Insua can go on to become a first-team regular. If he did, it would be fantastic. You always need a few Argentinians in the side!'

'It was **amazing** and something you never think you'll see'

RTE sports reporter EAMON HORAN couldn't get a ticket for the Champions League final in 2005, so instead he went to... Milan. Hardly the obvious choice, but he also avoids the obvious when choosing his favourite Liverpool players of all time

WHEN your team are taking part in a Champions League final 2,000 miles away, and your attempts to get there prove fruitless, what's the solution? Obviously for most Irish Reds, the best option would be to head for Merseyside, but Eamon Horan had other ideas when we reached our sixth European Cup final in 2005.

"It might sound a little bit strange but I went to Milan," the sports reporter explains. "Naturally I wanted to be in Turkey, but after trying various routes I had to admit defeat. It just wasn't happening so I abandoned the idea. I did consider going to Liverpool first, then I spotted some cheap flights to Milan and off I went."

It was obviously a slightly surreal experience but one that Horan wouldn't change. "I flew out on the morning of the match – I think it cost €30 return - and immediately started to sample the atmosphere," he continues. "Naturally, as you do everywhere you go, I bumped into a few Irish guys

who were on business. They also turned out to be Liverpool fans so we were in the same situation and had to keep very hush-hush about our loyalties."

We're all familiar with the half-time scenes of devastation amongst the travelling Kop in the Ataturk that night; what about the crowd in Milan? "They were all going nuts, as you would if your team was three goals ahead in a major final," Horan recalls. "Later on they were also going crazy but in a different manner and for a very different reason," he laughs. "Thankfully, I'm a small lad, so it was easy for me to go unnoticed in the crowd and quietly slip back to the hotel with a broad smile on my face. The distinct memory I have is of all these cars emerging on the streets with horns beeping and flags and banners hanging out the windows. It was Inter supporters celebrating as if they'd just won the cup themselves. A few of them even had Liverpool scarves waving over their heads!"

Like many Liverpool fans of a certain age, for Horan that night was the first 'real' experience of winning 'old big ears'. The wins in '77, '78, '81 and '84 were triumphs we'd heard of, read about or watched on VHS. In 2005, it was 'live', and for Horan it doesn't get any better than that.

"It was amazing and something you never think you'll see," he confesses. "I was born in 1975 and to be honest I started supporting Liverpool because they were a successful side. Most kids want to be associated with winners and I was no different. My best friend was a guy named Colin Quinn, and he picked Manchester United just to be different. That always led to a bit of banter between us. And he's given me plenty of stick over the years, but I've no regrets. I love Liverpool because it's such a spiritual and passionate club, and that'll never change. But those other European Cup wins came too early for me. That's why Istanbul was so good."

While that night in Turkey was the pinnacle for Horan, the first time he saw the Reds in action isn't so vivid. "I haven't got the best memory," he admits, "so I can't be completely certain, but I think the first-ever Liverpool game I watched would have been in 1986. I have hazy recollections of the double, but my first game would have been just before that. It was on 'Sports Stadium' on a Saturday, hosted by Brendan O'Reilly. And I think Liverpool were playing Watford. They produced some brilliant football and I think Paul Walsh popped up with a late winner."

As a result, the blond-haired frontman still holds a special place in Horan's list of LFC heroes. "Walsh was definitely one of them," he says of the man who joined us from Luton Town. "Because he looked like a rebel I thought he was great, him and Craig Johnston. There was a real novelty factor around an Australian playing soccer back then. It was very unusual. Those were the two that really stood out because I like flair players; the guys who can do something a little different. For some supporters Ian Rush is probably the main man from that side but for some reason I never really took to him. For me it was Walsh, Johnston and also Jan Molby. I thought he was fantastic too. I know everyone said he had so much time on the ball and it's true. He was a class apart."

Naturally being Irish there was another member of that side from the '80s that immediately drew Horan's gaze. "The first full game I remember was against Watford but I can recall Ronnie Whelan scoring in the Milk Cup final a few years before that," he says. "Jimmy Magee was commentating and I remember him saying something like: 'The Irishman scores.' As a kid I was so naïve that I thought it was absolutely amazing for someone from our country to

be playing and scoring at Wembley in a final."

Horan's job in the media means he comes into contact with a lot of Irish soccer stars. And, in 2001, he did exactly that while covering an Ireland game in Cyprus. "I think they sent me out to do it because it was a nothing match. I was in the middle of an interview with Roy Keane when Jason McAteer came along. For a laugh he decided to nudge me in the back and as a result I went flying straight into Keane, almost head-butting him. As you can imagine, he wasn't impressed. I'm not sure if that was the start of the feud between the two of them or not, but Keane definitely wasn't a happy man.

"That was pretty eventful compared to bumping into some of the other players. Obviously a lot of them do stuff with RTE so we'd see them in the studios. Graeme Souness is a popular guy around the building. I think some of the lads would like to tackle him in a five-a-side. If you did, you'd have to make a quick escape. Meeting those guys is one of the perks of the job but the former player I'd really love a chat with would be Bruce Grobbelaar because he's a bit of a character."

**Memories are made of this:
Liverpool's history relived on video**

Travelling is another advantage of Horan's occupation, although even when he's on another continent the Reds are never forgotten. "No matter where I end up I always keep an eye on the scores or what's happening," he explains. "Nowadays with the internet and satellite TV it's pretty easy. Although I remember spending a couple of summers on a J-1 visa in America in the mid-'90s when it was difficult to get any info on what was happening. Then I was at a party one night when this guy arrived wearing the brand new Liverpool away shirt. It was white and green with three black stripes at the bottom and we thought it was the coolest shirt ever. We all resolved that whatever cash we managed to save up would be used to buy that jersey when we got home."

The only problem for Eamon now is that his globetrotting has inadvertently directed his young son's loyalties towards another famous football team, rather than the Reds. "He's definitely going to be a Liverpool fan, that's for sure," Horan emphasises. "But right now he's got a fascination with River Plate in Argentina. My wife's sister lives there and we went to visit last year. I couldn't take him to a game because he wasn't old enough, so instead we went on a tour of the stadium and bought him the jersey. As a result he took a real shine to the colours and loves it. He wants to wear it all the time."

While Horan junior may have split loyalties at the moment, there can be no doubting his dad's allegiances. "I

Skippy and Walshie: Brought something a bit different to the side of the 1980s in their own unique way

'Because he (Paul Walsh) looked like a rebel I thought he was great, him and Craig Johnston. There was a real novelty factor around an Australian playing soccer back then. It was very unusual. Those were the two that really stood out because I like flair players'

first went to Anfield for a game against Newcastle a few years ago and I've been over plenty of times since," he confirms. "It's always a messy weekend but very enjoyable. "In that time we've seen some great matches and I think the only real disappointment was the 2008 Champions League semi-final when John Arne Riise scored that own goal. It was devastating."

You'd imagine working as a sports reporter would guarantee access to tickets for any game, but like the majority of fans, the Offaly man doesn't find it that easy. "It can be difficult at times. But a few of my friends usually get it sorted. As a result I've never had the pleasure of sitting in the Kop, I'm usually in with the prawn sandwich brigade!"

And if no tickets materialise, there's a last resort involving Eamon's brother Dermot, who's also a Red. "He's the

spitting image of Rafa Benitez, so much so that on a couple of our trips to Liverpool he's been mistaken for him," Horan laughs. "The only thing he's missing is the goatee. If he grows that, it'll be perfect. So our back-up plan is to pretend he's him and stroll in through the front door!"

We're not sure if Dermot would have the tactical nous to mastermind a Champions League triumph a la Rafa, but the brothers do have an ideal scenario in mind if we do make it to another European Cup final. "Milan again," Eamon chuckles.

"It would be perfect if we ended up against them for a third time. "I'd go straight over there to watch it in the main square, just like 2005, and I'd take my son with me. He'd love seeing all the Inter fans out celebrating when we win it!"

From Zanzibar to Istanbul

 Under normal circumstances, I would have been on my way to Istanbul for the 2005 Champions League final. Instead, on one of Liverpool's most historic European nights, I found myself in Africa, on the island of Zanzibar, relying on a TV in a bar that was 100 yards from my beach hut . . .

THE safari guide's face lit up as he mentioned 'the big five'. "Leopard, rhino, lion, elephant and buffalo are the top attractions in the Serengeti," he reliably informed us. Unfortunately, it was completing a different quintet that I had on my mind. It involved beating AC Milan and keeping the European Cup.

Back in January when we had initially booked our trip to Tanzania I informed my mate: "I'll have to cancel if the Reds make it to Istanbul." Being a Villa fan, he laughed at such a suggestion. And despite that terrific night against Olympiakos, I still didn't believe we could make it to our sixth final. But the Red Army were on the way to Turkey. That was where I should have been, but I couldn't afford to cancel our African adventure. As it turned out, we were on the island of Zanzibar on the night of the final. The tiny coastal village of Nungwi was our location.

Now my most pressing worry wasn't the threat of Kaka and co. We had to locate a TV that would be showing the game. One hundred yards from our beach hut stood a bar, and outside it a large sign declared: 'Champions League Final Tonight'. Panic over, I relaxed for the day.

The weather was getting stormy as we arrived in the pub later that evening and met up with some other tourists. Tim was an American guy who had "never watched a soccer match before". Despite this, he had still heard of the famous Liverpool FC. Somehow he was also aware of a London team that plays in blue. He couldn't understand how they could be Champions of England but not be in the Champions League final. Naturally, I took great pleasure in informing him that Chelski had already been eliminated on an unforgettable night in L4.

Of course the bar was packed with football-mad locals. We had seen numerous English jerseys on our travels in Tanzania. They mainly consisted of Arsenal, Man U and Liverpool. Strangely, we had also spotted a West Brom shirt in one village. As I kept reminding my mate, there had been no sightings of the increasingly rare Aston Villa colours.

With the time difference, there was a lot of confusion regarding kick off, but we eventually took our seats. Naturally I was asked for my prediction. I couldn't see us outplaying the Italians but felt we could sneak the game on penalties. "My head says 2-0 to Milan," was my first response. "And what about the rest of you?" my Villa mate asked. "Pool win on pens," I smiled.

Of course everyone knows how the first half progressed. My mate was laughing before he started feeling embarrassed for us, while I'm not sure our American friend realised the gravity of the 3-0 deficit. One of the locals had screamed in anguish each time the ball hit the back of Jerzy's net and was in tears at half-time. I wasn't far behind him.

I had to get out of the bar and made a quick trip to the bathroom, where I tried to convince myself that we could turn it around. We'd been two down at Fulham and came back to win. But that was against Zat Knight and Moritz Volz, not Paolo Maldini, Cafu and Jaap Stam.

'There is no picture on the screen. The TV has gone dead. People are shouting at the barman. He glances at the screen before turning back towards the unhappy customers ...'

CAUTION !
DO NOT GET OUT OF THE CAMPSITE
ANIMAL MAY ATTACT HUMAN BEING

AC Milan

25.05.05

Liverpool

Island exile: I would rather have been in Taksim Square, Istanbul than in a beach hut in Zanzibar

THEM SCOUSERS
AGAIN

AC Milan
25.05.05
Liverpool

'The barman unplugs the TV and immediately plugs it in again. Unsurprisingly, that fails to solve the problem. Then he gets up on the low thatched roof and starts moving the satellite dish; still no effect. This is getting ridiculous'

From the toilet door I could see our nearby beach hut. If I sneaked back to it I could just go to bed and forget all about this nightmare. I could read the horrible match reports on the internet tomorrow. I still don't know why, but I decided against it and went back to watch our pain continue.

"Crespo will probably get a hat-trick," were the first words from my Villa mate when I returned. "If we can get a consolation I'll be happy," I replied. Three consolations later and we're into extra-time. I've already been jumping around celebrating each goal. Our American friend is looking at me like I'm an escaped mental patient.

My Villa mate is suddenly supporting us. I'm biting my nails while we attempt to hang on. As the ball comes back off Jerzy and Andriy Shevchenko moves in for the kill, I turn away. In my own mind I think: "We gave it our best shot." Unbelievably, the big Pole somehow keeps it out. So we're into penalties. Rafa can be seen walking around the centre circle giving instructions, while the fans are easily out-singing their Milan rivals.

As I order another local beer the singing stops. In fact there is no picture on the screen. The TV has gone dead. People are shouting at the barman. He glances at the screen before turning back towards the unhappy customers. Then he produces the biggest remote control I've ever seen and points it at the TV in an extremely confident manner. Nothing happens.

I can imagine Rafa has decided the penalty takers by now. Surely Carra will be stepping up after the way he buried his spot-kick in the shootout against Birmingham. Djibril Cisse is probably a good bet too.

After that I'm not too confident. Xabi Alonso has already missed one tonight (although he did convert the rebound), while Stevie has never been the best from the spot. The customers are now getting restless. The barman unplugs the TV and immediately plugs it in again. Unsurprisingly, that fails to solve the problem. Then he gets up on the low thatched roof and starts moving the satellite dish; still no effect. This is getting ridiculous. Suddenly, from nowhere, one of the locals produces a mobile phone and dials a number before listening intently to the person on the other end of the line. "Miss two, miss two penalties," he shouts.

"Who? Who's missed two?" we shout back. But he still doesn't give us an answer. I've got my head in my hands as I imagine Dida denying Stevie and Jamie. "One nil, one nil to Liverpool," our man with the mobile screams. "Yes!" I shout, but I still don't believe it. Then there is a flicker of green on the screen as the TV comes back to life. A red shirt runs up and coolly slots the ball past Dida. It's Djib. He's scored. 2-0 to us.

I'm up and down like a jack in the box as Vladimir Smicer, Kaka, and Jon Dahl Tomasson all convert their kicks. Then, unbelievably, John Arne Riise misses by trying to place the ball in the corner. The man with the

Meanwhile, back in Istanbul . . . Jerzy is mobbed as the fans salute the famous win

hardest shot in England and he sidefoots it. That defies belief. Up steps Shevchenko. The best striker in Europe, if not the world. But he looks nervous as he glances at the ref and then starts his run.

Jerzy, all is forgiven! The howlers against United that gifted Diego Forlan his goals, your flapping at crosses and general shakiness is all forgotten in an instant. I'm running around the pub screaming.

I share high fives and hugs with my new Tanzanian friends.

When I got back home my brother summed it up best by saying: "You've spent three years living in Liverpool, and on their greatest night you were on a beach in Africa!"

The wildlife had probably never seen anything like it but I didn't care. The cup was ours for keeps.

'Aldo only played for us for two seasons but left a lifetime of memories'

EVERYONE loves Aldo. DAVE RANDLES, a writer for the club's official weekly LFC Magazine, sums up why the fans identify so much with Ireland's favourite Scouser

HAD I been blessed with the ability to play international football, then John Aldridge would have had a large say in where my allegiance lay. My affection for Aldo first emerged through my support of Liverpool FC, but was consolidated via an inadvertent result of my family tree.

You see, like pretty much most Republic of Ireland teams, our clan are a bit of a mixed bag. With Scouse grandparents of Scottish and Welsh descendancy on one side, and a Nigerian grandfather who was married to a dear lady from Cork on the other, I've never felt particularly English. Therefore, as the Republic of Liverpool is yet to be granted independent status, and because Scotland and Wales are eternally woeful, I always knew my international future lay in green. That left me with a simple choice between the Super Eagles or Eire.

In truth, with no internet and only your basic TV channels – just the three until I was eight years old – I didn't get to see much of Nigeria as a kid and probably couldn't even locate it on a map, let alone name five of their players. With my Englishness in tatters, plus the fact it simply felt wrong to feign interest in a team captained by Bryan Robson, I decided I would play for Ireland when I grew up.

Wine (Blue Nun), women (not nuns), song and a large dose of reality eventually put paid to my World Cup ambitions, and instead I sought solace through those who could play out my dreams. It was obviously the Liverpool lads who attracted most of my attention: Whelan, Lawrenson, Houghton, Staunton, Babb...I'd even wish Mark Kennedy well despite the fact he was never cut out to wear the Liverbird upon his chest.

Of all our Irish Reds, there was one who stood head and

shoulders above the rest. Aldo. Like me, he qualified through birthright on his grandmother's side, and sounds about as Irish as Jack Charlton. Aldridge only played for Liverpool for two seasons but made such an impact he left a lifetime of memories. We can talk all day about the goals for club and country, and, yes, that penalty miss in '88, but it's the other things that also made an impression on me. The boots and shirt into The Kop after coming off the bench to score a penalty in the 9-0 win over Crystal Palace, his last game at Anfield; the full-blooded and foul-mouthed tirade at the fourth official in that infamous touchline spat at the 1994 World Cup; seeing him hoisted on the shoulders of Liverpool fans and carried through the Sabiha Gokcen Airport after Istanbul, arms aloft, laughing and singing along with them.

These are all classic Aldo moments that have served to endear him more to those on both sides of the Irish Sea. Then, of course, there was Hillsborough. "I was the Liverpool player furthest away from the Leppings Lane terrace," said Aldridge, recalling the fateful events of a day on which he would probably have been with the fans had he not been on the pitch. He was the furthest away from the supporters only by distance. In every other way, Aldridge was the closest.

"I knew people on the Leppings Lane End," he later said. "Fun-loving Liverpool fans. My friends." Like all the Liverpool players, he attended countless funerals and made too many hospital visits to recall; anything to try and undo what could never be undone. But the image that sticks with me most is of Aldridge at the Shankly Gates on the morning of 16 April 1989, the grief written on his face as he attempted to dodge the press and cameras. Despite his elevated status from Kop to pitch, this was Aldridge as a

'Although he hung up his international boots over a decade ago, he is still eulogised in Ireland, where he is treated like a returning prodigal son whenever he goes back'

150

One of us:
Aldo provides Steve
McMahon with
refreshment, 1988

Liverpool fan again, wishing to pay his respects in private. It was the genuine response of a man who knew what it meant to support and then play for Liverpool Football Club, something that came naturally to him on both fronts.

He had to learn and adapt to the idiosyncrasies involved in representing the Republic of Ireland, just as he did as the first non-Basque to play for Real Sociedad. When he arrived in San Sebastian, they didn't want him there. By the time he decided to come home, they didn't want him to leave. I know people who shared a pint with Aldridge in his formative years at Newport County, and they too speak highly of him.

Although he hung up his international boots over a decade ago, he is still eulogised in Ireland, where he is treated like a returning prodigal son whenever he goes back. As a player, he was class. As a man, he's as genuine as they come. As a football fan, he's a Kopite. Try and get him on the phone for an interview and he's a pain in the arse, but that's only the mere matter of work.

Just as Aldo is proud to say he is 'Irish', Ireland can be proud to say he is theirs.

'That first trip was **amazing.** The noise, the colours, the singing: it was **mind-blowing'**

IT'S never been easier for Irish Liverpool fans to travel over to see a game at Anfield than it is today.

I get on a plane and I can be at the stadium in little more than an hour, and if needs be I can get home again just as quickly.

It's something we all take for granted these days but it's vastly different from the way things used to be.

When my father and his mates travelled across to Liverpool in the '50s and early '60s, they would have to travel on a cattle boat from Dublin.

The cattle would be boarded first, so they got all the best seats, and the people would squeeze on later. The boat would then go across to Holyhead, where the cattle would be offloaded and then it would head to Liverpool.

Depending on conditions, this trip could sometimes take up to 12 hours, but the ship would normally arrive in Liverpool at about 7am.

By the time I travelled across to see my first game at Anfield as an eight-year-old in 1973, things had improved.

There were no cattle involved in the trip anymore, and we would catch the 10pm ferry on Friday night, which would travel directly to Liverpool and would arrive there at between 5 and 6am the next morning.

This would obviously leave you with a lot of time to fill before kick-off, but fortunately I had an aunt who lived in the city and we would hole up at her place for a few hours before and after the game, and then catch another night ferry which would get us back into Dublin in the early hours of Sunday morning.

This may seem a long and arduous journey by today's standards, but I made many such trips throughout the '70s and into the '80s, and they were great craic.

The humour and camaraderie on the crossing, coupled with the magic of seeing the Reds in action, made it all worthwhile, and I wouldn't have missed it for the world.

That first trip was an amazing experience for me. The noise, the colours, the singing, the chanting: it was simply mind-blowing, and I've been addicted to the Reds ever since. The real icing on the cake was that we got a 2-1 victory over Ipswich on the day, with our goals being scored by Kevin Keegan and my big Liverpool hero of those days, Steve Heighway. Indeed, Heighway was a big hero to most Irish Liverpool fans at that time.

He was one of the best players in the great Liverpool sides of the '70s, but as an Irish international player born in Dublin, it felt like we had one of our own playing for the Mighty Reds, and we were damn proud of it.

He was the only Irish player to play for the club in the '70s, but the '80s turned out to be a golden era for Reds who wore the Green.

Ronnie Whelan and Mark Lawrenson made their Liverpool debuts in 1981, and both went on to become two of the finest players to ever don a Red or Green shirt. Michael Robinson came along for a couple of seasons in 1983, and Jim Beglin in 1984, but a leg-breaking challenge involving Everton's Gary Stevens would eventually end his career at the age of 27.

Ray Houghton and John Aldridge arrived in 1987 and fortunately both qualified to play for Ireland through their ancestry. Steve Staunton played his first game for Liverpool in 1988. The club eventually sold him far too early, but he went on to win a record number of international caps for Ireland. All of those players enjoyed great success at club level with Liverpool in the '80s and, with the exception of Robinson and Beglin, all played a big part in getting Ireland through to at least one of our first two major finals, Euro 1988 in Germany and the World Cup finals in Italia 1990.

'The humour and camaraderie on the crossing, coupled with the magic of seeing the Reds in action, made it all worthwhile, and I wouldn't have missed it for the world'

Steve Heighway was Gerry Ormonde's hero in the '70s

The '80s really was a great decade for Irish Reds. The '90s weren't so productive. Jason McAteer was probably the best of the Liverpool players in that decade to make it as an Irish international. There were also players like Phil Babb and Mark Kennedy, but let's not go there!

Steve Finnan was our "Mr Consistency" at right-back who did us proud and gave the club great service, and when he departed another Irishman in the shape of Robbie Keane came along to wear the Red shirt, although he didn't stay too long.

These players played a small but significant part in the Liverpool sides I've watched over the years, and having a few fellow countrymen playing in the team certainly helped to strengthen our connection with the club. But it is on the terraces where the Irish have really made their presence felt. There are probably as many social reasons as there are football reasons why there is such a strong bond between the Irish and the Scousers, but it's always been there and it's still as strong as ever.

From those packed cattle boats of the past, through to the packed planes of today, we have crossed the Irish Sea in our droves to add our voices to the Kop.

Wherever the Liverpool team is battling it out on the pitch, you can be sure to find a healthy amount of Irish voices mixed in with the Scouse, cheering them on. I think we can even take credit for adding one of our own songs to the Kop's bumper collection with 'The Fields of Athenry' a.k.a 'The Fields of Anfield Road'.

It's this combination of Scouse and Irish that ensures that, even if our team may struggle on the pitch, up in the stands our supporters are simply unbeatable!

GERRY ORMONDE is the writer and editor of Kopblog, winner of the 2008 Best Football Blog award in the Football Pools Fanzine Awards.

'My dad taught me to enjoy a good game, and also to **love the Reds**'

PETER SWEENEY, a journalist for the Irish Daily Star, was brought up as a Liverpool fan by his dad, and fostered on TV highlights of European triumphs. In recent years he has been able to afford to cross the water to follow the Reds, and his experiences include one rather memorable trip to Ewood Park...

MY support for Liverpool FC goes back pretty much as far as I can remember. There was always sport on television in the house I grew up in, and if there was ever football on, I would sit down with my dad and watch it.

He always taught me to enjoy a good game, but he also taught me to love the Reds. My dad came to Dublin in the mid-1960s when Ireland was a very different country, and shortly after he arrived in the capital – moving with his brother and mother after they sold the small family farm in Co Mayo – they got their first television.

And on that television he started to watch football from England. The player that caught his eye was the great Stevie Heighway raiding down the wing for the Reds, even if in those days it looked like he was wearing grey.

His love affair with Liverpool dates back that far, and he used to travel over to England on the ferry once in a while – a big deal back in those days when people generally only left Ireland to emigrate – with my uncle to catch a game.

He always recalls to me how surprised he was on his first visit at how "small the pitch looked" because where he grew up – the rural west of Ireland – there were only Gaelic pitches, which are roughly twice the size of the paddock at Anfield. My mother had – and still has – relations in Salford, Manchester, who, of course, were United fans. She always cheered them on, but nothing was going to come between me and my obsession with the Reds.

One of my earlier memories of watching Liverpool was the 1984 European Cup final against Roma in Rome on the television in my parents' front room. I was only six then, but I can still vividly remember the penalty shoot-out that won the club's fourth European title.

Growing up in the early '80s in Ireland, there were three teams for a young lad to support – Liverpool, Manchester United and Everton, though there was always a smattering of Leeds, Spurs and Arsenal followers too. Games in the playground or on the green were always divided along those lines and I used to flit between playing as King Kenny – one of my absolute heroes growing up and still someone I would love to meet in my current incarnation as a sports reporter – Ronnie Whelan (because he was from Dublin, as well as being a brilliant player) and Bruce Grobbelaar.

I was never much usé as a player, though I was fast enough to get away with certain things down the flanks, and I often ended up between the jumpers. But this was never a problem because that meant I got to pull on the gloves (woolly, not goalkeeper) and pretend to be Brucie. Grobbelaar was an intriguing character in a team full of real personalities, and I loved nothing more than dragging down my mates right in front of goal on purpose – even when I didn't have to – so I had the chance to face the spot kick.

This meant I was able to recreate the famous trick that he pulled off in the penalty shoot-out against Roma. Those wobbly legs helped to win Liverpool the '84 European Cup, though it usually didn't do too much to put the lads off when we were down at the end of the road after school. Maybe they'd seen it once too often.

When I was about 10 years old I got a present for a birthday or Christmas, I'm not sure which, that's still on the go to this day. Back then, replica gear was something pretty far-fetched – particularly in recession-hit Ireland – but there was a thriving market in souvenir products that weren't entirely licensed, and I doubt whether the club ever saw any of the profits. It was a leather kitbag with LIVERPOOL emblazoned in big writing down one side with a Liverbird and a player on top. I used it every day as a school bag until I moved on to secondary and it wasn't big enough to fit all my books.

After that, my Dad took possession of it, and nearly 20 years later he still brings his lunch off to the building site every day in that trusty bag. I'm hoping that it will see him to retirement in a few years' time.

Another treasured possession that I still have is a copy of the 1986 FA Cup final programme, the day Liverpool completed the double against Everton. A team picture from that programme hung on the back of my bedroom door for many years, and I used to love reading and re-reading the

Brucie bonus: One of Peter Sweeney's childhood idols, Bruce Grobbelaar

Owen scores in the 1-1 draw at Ewood Park, Nov 2001

player profiles. I was particularly proud that Mark Lawrenson, an Irish international, was still – at that point – the most expensive player at Liverpool, having cost the grand total of £900,000. That's not bad money for a high-quality centre-half – just contrast that with the amount paid for another Irish international stopper, Phil Babb.

I used to follow Liverpool on television – Elton Welsby was a regular in our front room – and in the papers, and I think it was this that inspired me to become a journalist. That is, once I realised that I wasn't ever going to score the winner in a cup final. Back in those days, I even used to root for Emlyn Hughes' team on BBC's 'Question of Sport' because he had been a Liverpool captain. It probably helped that old Crazy Horse was hilarious and was always laughing madly while Bill Beaumont usually just looked confused and cauliflower-eared on the other side of David Coleman.

Many summers I'd go to watch the visiting superstars playing League of Ireland part-timers in pre-season warm-ups at falling-down grounds around Dublin, but because money was pretty tight when I was growing up, it wasn't until I was earning my own wages that I was able to travel to see Liverpool. I used to go once or twice a year, as often as I could as a struggling freelancer at the time, but for some endlessly frustrating reason, I spent a lot of time and money before I actually saw them winning a game! The usual result was a deflating 1-1.

I was devastated when my best friend, at the time recently qualified as a doctor, told me that he was leaving Ireland to practice medicine in England, but the mood brightened considerably when he told me that he'd gotten himself a job in a hospital in Liverpool. Better than that, he was going out with a girl – who later became his wife – who has a cousin who remains a Premier League footballer (I'd better not say with which club), so tickets were no longer too much hassle to come by.

The first time I went to visit my mate he was supposed to meet me at the airport, but because he had a big one the night before, he wasn't that long in bed and there was no one to greet me on arrival. This was a major problem because I had no idea where he lived, his phone wasn't being answered and we had to get ourselves up the road to Ewood Park, where Liverpool were playing Blackburn Rovers that afternoon. Eventually I got hold of his mam in Ireland, and she gave me the address. The taxi driver who took me there, I later learned, was called Eddie, and his head was completely bald, but he had a handlebar moustache that he grew all the way back to his ears.

"Alright la, over for the football?" he asked. When I replied in the affirmative he enquired: "Red or a blue la?" "Red," says I, and we spent the next 20 minutes discussing how Phil Thompson, who was temporarily in charge at that time, could pick Emile Heskey ahead of Robbie Fowler any day of the week. Better yet, he was heading up to the match in his cab with a few of his friends and he offered to bring me and my best buddy all the way to Blackburn and back in return for just a few quid in diesel money!

We got to my mate's digs and after I dragged him out of the cot and got him out to the taxi, there were a few awkward seconds of silence as the two men – Eddie and my friend – shared a brief second of recognition.

My friend – and you'll see now why I'm not using his name either – issued a heartfelt and pretty sheepish apology and an explanation about how under-the-weather he was on the way home the night before after a tough shift at the Razz. It was a bumpy journey, apparently, and Eddie had taken a few of the roundabouts a bit sharpish too.

It turns out that my man had spent most of the journey back to Fazakerley with his head hanging out the side of Eddie's cab, unloading the contents of his stomach. A few extra quid was offered to pay for the washing of the vehicle, our chauffeur was sweet again and the lift was back on.

It was the start of a great day, but it was just a shame that my wait to see Liverpool winning a competitive match went on for a little while longer – they drew one-all.

'I just can't bear to throw away **any** Liverpool shirt'

EVER since he was a very young boy, James Hayden can recall always being decked out in a Liverpool shirt.

Hayden, who works as a journalist with the *Tipperary Star* newspaper in the heart of Ireland, has been a Liverpool supporter since as far back as he can remember, and over the past 25-odd years has collected every outfield Liverpool jersey.

"I can vividly remember when I first got a Liverpool shirt. It was an old Umbro yellow away strip with the thin red stripes, and I can remember it was a hand-me-down from my cousin," James explains. "He was a couple of years older than me and a mad Liverpool fan, and I can remember wearing it and never wanting to take it off."

All throughout his school years at Nenagh CBS, Hayden proudly donned a Liverpool shirt for PE classes or when he was lining out for training with his local soccer team, Nenagh AFC.

"To be fair my mother always allowed me to buy the Liverpool home and away shirts all through primary school with pocket money I had saved up, and if I was short she always chipped in with the balance."

With a younger brother who somehow managed to support Everton instead of Liverpool, James had no one to hand his old shirts on to, so he put them in the attic for safe keeping.

"My brother Thomas started following Everton partly because he just wanted to annoy me and partly because he hated me taunting him about Liverpool's success. As far as I was concerned, he had wandered over to the dark side, and I can remember the classic 1986 FA Cup final between the sides and we actually ended up re-enacting the game over and over again on the back lawn. My mother used to ask why I was keeping my old shirts and I used to always come up with some reason."

Today, the lifelong Liverpool fan has a room in his house in the rural Irish countryside dedicated to the Reds.

"My wife kind of understands it, but I'd say when she saw all the framed shirts going up on the wall she thought to herself: 'What have I got myself into here?'

"Over the past number of years, though, she has come to accept the fact that I just can't bear to throw away any Liverpool shirt. At this stage I can confidently say I have every home and away Liverpool shirt for the past 30 years.

"My favourite, though, is the specially commissioned shirt that was released prior to the 2005 Champions League final. It takes pride of place in my Liverpool room together with a fully intact unused ticket and programme from the final. I still have that first shirt that was handed

down to me by my cousin and it also ranks up there very highly as one of my favourites," James says.

Other items in his collection include two framed Hitachi-sponsored Liverpool shirts (both home and away), together with shorts and an authentic replica shirt from 1977, manufactured prior to the final in Rome. Also afforded pride of place are the Crown Paints and Candy shirts from the late '80s and early '90s.

With regards to travelling across the water to support the Reds, James explains that he tries to make it over to Anfield at least twice during a season but, with work constraints, he often finds it quite difficult to make it, and has to settle for watching the game on TV. "The last game I was at was the 2008 Merseyside derby at Anfield, and I thoroughly enjoyed the trip, and the fact we won 1-0 was the icing on the cake.

"Just being at Anfield makes the hairs on the back of my neck stand up. Being a sports journalist, it's hard to get away from covering events here at home at weekends, but whenever I can organise it, I make it across the Irish Sea."

Not satisfied with his ever-growing collection of shirts, James also collects programmes and memorabilia, and has all five original programmes from the Reds' European Cup triumphs as well as an authentic autographed picture signed by the great Steve Gerrard – a present from his wife, Mary, two years ago.

"Many of my friends who see the room are genuinely taken aback, but my wife's friends think I'm absolutely bonkers and have warned that I may, in time, be forced to turn the room into a nursery or bedroom.

"All I can say is that any child that has the privilege of gazing at Liverpool shirts throughout their formative years will not stray from their one true calling – to support the mighty Reds!"

JAMES HAYDEN works for the
Tipperary Star newspaper

Heighway taking on Newcastle United's Frank Clark in the 1974 FA Cup final

'I **loved** Heighway back then. He was **everything** I aspired to be'

IT'S 1975, I'm 17-years-old and the careers teacher has just told me I'm looking at good enough A-level grades to go to university.

I tell him the only person in the history of our family who's been (my brother) dropped out after a month because he felt more at home in a leper colony, so I'm not sure it's for me.

He motions for me to shut it, drops a dusty box containing every university prospectus in Britain, and waddles off to sentence some other poor sod to a life in Barclays Bank.

I start to delve. I'm not inspired. The covers either contain shots of bespectacled 20-somethings musing outside redbrick buildings or teenagers sat on grassy knolls smiling at each other like actors in a condom advert.

And then the cover of Warwick University's booklet leaps out at me. There, in full balletic flow, leaving a Coventry full-back on his behind, with massive sideys, a superhero spring in his heel and a Liver Bird on his chest, is the university's most famous graduate, Stevie Heighway. And my future was decided.

I loved Heighway back then. He was everything I aspired to be. Not only was he Liverpool's number nine, who could skin opponents at will, and a good-looking git who had his name sung by the Kop to a Deep Purple classic ('Black Night'), but he was also an Englishman playing for Ireland.

I know that as a baby he spent five minutes in Dublin, but he was brought up over here, sounded English and – if he'd wanted to – probably could have been wasted by Alf Ramsey the way Peter Thompson had been.

But he chose Ireland, and I loved him for that. Just as I was to love John Aldridge and Jason McAteer, a pair of Scousers who remembered the green blood that flowed to their heart and did the decent thing when the Mother Country called.

Like many Scousers, I am part-Irish. I was born in Liverpool, but my nana was from Dublin. She it was who filled me with tales about the Easter Rising and the Black and Tans.

She it was who lied to me about being named after the last Irish king Brian Boru, and told me that what was bred in the bone comes out in the marrow (she also said: "Put a divil on horseback and he'll ride to hell", and I never understood that either).

And the more I grew to loathe the English football team, its followers and their national anthem, the more I knew what country I most identified with. And it wasn't the ones singing about the Queen.

So I both admired and envied Heighway for choosing Ireland, especially in those pre-Jack Charlton days when they were far from world-beaters. But then I'd been hooked on Heighway since that first season when his explosive impact had Kopites drooling and outsiders offering serious comparisons with George Best.

He really came into his own on 21 November 1970, my second day as a teenager, and first game on the Kop after serving my apprenticeship on the Anfield Road.

Everton were champions and playing like it. The Horse (Joe Royle) and the Rat (Alan Whittle) had put them 2-0 up with 20 minutes to go.

Misery stared me in the face and a surrounding knot of Evertonians were chortling their Blue heads off.

When Stevie Heighway jinked inside and let one rip towards the near post, leaving Gordon West stranded, a human wave lifted me and nearly unhinged my neck from my spine.

When Heighway crossed six minutes later and Toshack soared above Brian Labone to plant the equaliser in the top corner, I flew a full 30 feet down the terrace and was thrown

Heighway brought through McManaman and Carra during his time at the Academy

back like whiplash.

And when Heighway crossed again to Toshack's head and Chris Lawler met the knockdown with a volley that won the game, I went under like a dog in a lake tied to an old bed.

I was sucked up, heaved back, tossed into the air, and when I hit the deck I was minus one patent-leather Chelsea boot and my money.

I walked the seven miles back home to Huyton, a grin splitting my face and the concrete splitting my sole, re-living those Heighway surges, thinking: "We haven't just found the new Best here, we've found the new Pele."

OK he didn't quite live up to that company, but what great service he gave to Liverpool. In arguably the two most emphatic cup final victories in Liverpool history (the 1974 FA Cup final and 1977 European Cup final), Heighway was pivotal, scoring against Newcastle at Wembley and making two of the goals in Rome.

Then there was his beaut in the 1971 final that made Bob Wilson look like a bevvied pensioner, and had us dreaming of glory until Charlie George broke our hearts.

As academy director he brought through the likes of Michael Owen, Robbie Fowler, Steve McManaman, Jamie Carragher and Steven Gerrard, as well as winning the FA Youth Cup three times.

Which is why Stevie Heighway, the only man apart from Errol Flynn who could get away with a moustache, I salute you.

For being on the wing when we had dreams and songs to sing. And for choosing to bring glory to the Fields of Athenry.

Brian Reade's book *43 Years with the Same Bird – A Liverpudlian Love Affair* is in the shops now. He also writes a regular column for the *Daily Mirror*

'When Stevie Heighway jinked inside and let one rip towards the near post, leaving Gordon West stranded, a human wave lifted me and nearly unhinged my neck from my spine'

'The landscape of Merseyside's **footballing future** could have been **very different**'

WILLIAM HUGHES, a journalist for Sport Media, shows how with a twist of fate, Kevin Sheedy could have muscled out Ronnie Whelan

BUT for an untimely injury, the Liverpool side of the '80s and early '90s could have had a totally different shift to the left. When Ray Kennedy was sidelined, Kevin Sheedy looked like being next in line. The promising midfielder had been snapped up for a six-figure fee from Hereford United in 1978, and had shown signs of his potential during League Cup ties against Exeter City and Middlesbrough in 1981/82. He also provided a glimpse of his eye for goal in those fixtures, scoring in both ties.

But Sheedy was struggling with an injury himself. And so his housemate and future Republic of Ireland team-mate Ronnie Whelan was given an opportunity to stake his claim. The fact that Whelan was still an integral part of the Liverpool midfield more than a decade later tells its own story. Sheedy went on to win the hearts of the Irish footballing public when he scored the nation's first World Cup goal against England at Italia '90. And yet just as he would ultimately slip from Liverpool's grasp, he could easily have got away from the Republic.

Born in the ancient market town of Builth Wells, he might have pinned his colours to the Welsh mast had they paid any interest in him. Their failure to do so saw him pledge his international future to the Republic. By the time he won his first senior cap, he was establishing himself as one of the stars of the Merseyside football scene. Sadly for Liverpool fans, it was on the other side of Stanley Park.

With Whelan by now a regular fixture at Anfield, Sheedy had taken the plunge to join Everton when Howard Kendall came calling in 1982. Sheedy had taken his time in agreeing to join Everton and the move had initially been put on hold when Kendall wouldn't agree to his terms. Had he not changed his mind, the landscape of Merseyside's footballing future could have been very different.

The last few years have seen a dearth of quality left-sided midfielders, as various English national team coaches will vouch for. It has also been a problem position for Rafa Benitez to fill. While the Spaniard will be hoping his compatriot Albert Riera will finally provide the solution, it reiterates how fortunate Liverpool were to find themselves blessed with talents such as Whelan and Sheedy in the early '80s.

Sheedy quickly became a favourite at Goodison, with his 'wand-like' left foot helping him to become one of the best exponents of set-plays in the game. The special service it provided to strikers was lapped up by Graeme Sharp and Andy Gray, and later, while on national service, Niall Quinn and Tony Cascarino.

He also rubbed the Reds' noses in it from time to time. Although injury prevented him from appearing in Everton's FA Cup success in 1984, he was a prominent figure in the club's 1985 League championship season. That year, he also played a key role in the Blues' only European triumph, scoring in the European Cup Winners' Cup final victory over Rapid Vienna in Rotterdam.

In 1986/87, he moved into a central midfield position, and in that role he helped the Toffees relegate Liverpool to second spot in the final Division One reckoning. That season also saw one of the incidents for which he will be best remembered: flicking a V-sign at the Kop after firing a trademark free-kick past Mike Hooper in the derby.

Speaking about the incident in an interview a few years ago, Sheedy admitted there may have been a hint of frustration about his time at Liverpool, and it had come out in his reaction. When he was brought before the FA to explain himself, however, he claimed to have been raising

'Sheedy was struggling with an injury. And so his housemate Ronnie Whelan was given an opportunity to stake his claim'

one finger to indicate he had scored the goal!

At international level, Sheedy will always be remembered as a part of the team in the Republic's greatest footballing era to date. Having helped them qualify for their first major tournament, Euro '88, he played in all three matches in Germany as Jack Charlton's side narrowly failed to make the semi-finals. Two years later, Ireland lit up the World Cup finals in Italy, and Sheedy wrote his name in the record books as the scorer of the nation's first goal in the tournament. Gary Lineker had given England an early lead in the game in Cagliari, but Sheedy struck with 17 minutes remaining to provide the catalyst for a memorable run. He

later said it was the most special goal of his career.

After draws with Egypt and Holland, the Republic went through to the last 16 on the drawing of lots, with Holland the unlucky losers having to face Germany. Everyone remembers David O'Leary's winning spot-kick in the penalty shoot-out with Romania, but it was Sheedy who calmly slotted home the first to put the Irish on their way to a place in the last eight. In nine years of playing for the Republic, Sheedy won 46 caps, netting nine goals along the way. Many of those came alongside his former housemate Whelan and yet, if it hadn't been for a twist of fate, their futures could have mapped out so very differently.

'The **only reason** I got through that tough time was the run to **Istanbul**'

GROWING up in Dublin in the 1980s, there was a choice for every young football fan to make, and that was between supporting Manchester United or Liverpool.

My decision was basically made for me because my older brother was a Liverpool fan and I pretty much copied everything that he did – incidentally, he changed to Man U not long after, but by then I was making my own decisions and stuck with my Reds. I may not have realised it at the time, but I would come to believe that supporting Liverpool was a destiny for me.

Supporting the Reds during the mid-1980s wasn't difficult at all given the success we had, and I lived for my yearly trip to Anfield.

I saw Liverpool win many games, but the one that started to guide me towards a career in football was when I attended the Reds' defeat to Genoa in the UEFA Cup.

I was hoping to witness a famous Liverpool comeback in Europe as we were 2-0 down from the first leg, but instead I learned about the character of the Kop.

A goal from Carlos Aguilera meant that Liverpool faced an uphill struggle, and although Rushie did equalise, Aguilera ensured that we went out of the competition early.

Normally that would have been enough to send me into depression, but the reaction of the crowd to Aguilera's first goal will forever live in my memory.

The stadium went silent for all of 30 seconds before the Kop took a deep breath and reached full voice to get behind the team again.

More seasoned Kop veterans may tell you there was nothing special about the atmosphere that night, but to me it was mesmerising. We were down and out but the crowd never stopped getting behind the team.

When the final whistle went, the Kop proceeded to chant "Genoa, Genoa" and give the winning side a warm send off after what is surely one of their most famous victories.

I remember asking my football coach why the Liverpool fans would do this and not go home with their heads down like I did in the streets of Coolock after a defeat. He told me that it was because Liverpool fans were very fair and the most knowledgeable in the game – something I would hear Graham Taylor echo after a similar ovation when his Watford side shocked the Reds at Anfield years later.

It was then that I made it my mission to become the most knowledgeable fan possible, something that would be crucial as I started on my journey to become a football pundit in the United States.

It is a career that would never have gotten off the ground but for the second reason that proved to me that it was my destiny to support Liverpool Football Club.

Many Liverpool fans will remember 9 March 2005 as the date Liverpool won in Leverkusen to start our magical run to Istanbul, but for me it was the day my marriage officially fell apart. I wasn't too upset about that but it left my status in America vulnerable so I was forced to come home to Ireland and re-apply for a work permit so I could continue my career in the States.

It was a difficult few months for me, and my mam and dad struggled to get me out of my room for anything other than those memorable Liverpool games.

I remember coming downstairs to watch Liverpool take on and beat Juventus and Chelsea, with Liverpool belittling their underdog tag.

I remember thinking that my chances of returning to the US were a long shot, just like Liverpool's chances of winning the Champions League, but as long as the Reds kept winning then hope for my own future remained.

When Liverpool reached the final, many of my family decided to go to a local bar to watch the game, but there was only one place I was going to watch it: my living room. The same living room where I had watched Liverpool beat Roma for the European title 21 years earlier.

'Many Liverpool fans will remember 9 March 2005 as the date Liverpool won in Leverkusen to start our magical run to Istanbul, but for me it was the day my marriage officially fell apart. It was a difficult few months for me, and my mam and dad struggled to get me out of my room for anything other than those memorable Liverpool games'

Keith Costigan remembers the win over Bayer Leverkusen in 2005 for personal reasons

The first half was an absolute blur, and would have only helped to reinforce my feeling sorry for myself had I not seen the tremendous response from our fans.

Not for the first time in my life, I watched my side stare defeat in the face only for our fans to rally like no other side's would. Just like that game against Genoa, the fans were not going to let an impossible situation see them give up hope, and it is something I had to apply to my own life.

It may sound corny but in that instant I knew that even if I couldn't go back to the US, everything would work out for the best. The Liverpool comeback in the second half only enforced my new belief that any situation can be overcome, and I spent the next few weeks enjoying my time back in Ireland before my visa interview – although the new Chelsea fans that had popped up since I left disturbed me.

I eventually got the green light to return to America and resume my career but I am positive the only reason I got through that tough time was the amazing run to Istanbul.

It may have been a coincidence that Liverpool picked the same year I had my struggles and returned to Dublin to awaken in Europe, but to me it was destiny and the reason I was always meant to support the club in the first place.

KEITH COSTIGAN is a California-based Kopite who originally hails from Dublin. He works for Fox Sports and writes for *The Kop* magazine.

A taste of the red and white stuff

WHEN the Reds play, there are exiled fans all over the world doing whatever they can to keep up to date with the action. In Ireland, it's no different. Rival fans stand shoulder to shoulder, pints in hand, glued to the big screen. JOHN HYNES travelled from Merseyside to Liffeyside to sample the experience of the biggest game of all – Liverpool v Manchester United...

EVERY Irish Red would love to be sat in the middle of the Kop whenever we face our biggest rivals.

Of course that's not possible, and only the lucky few can be there when 'You'll Never Walk Alone' rings out around Anfield prior to kick-off. For those without a ticket, the next best alternative is heading to the local pub to watch the 90+ minutes unfold on the big screen, and that's exactly what we did in September 2007.

The only difference was, with me being based in Liverpool, getting to a real Irish watering hole required a flight from Merseyside to Liffeyside. It's the reverse of the journey most Reds in the Emerald Isle make on a regular basis, a fact that was slowly sinking in as I stood in the queue at John Lennon Airport 24 hours before our clash with Manchester United.

Small groups of supporters clad in Red were making their way through the building, obviously here for the following day's 12:45pm fixture. There were also one or two white shirts with AIG on the front, but they were mainly in the minority. While the Manc supporter with 'Rooney' on his back was guaranteed a freezing welcome from both sides of the 2008 Capital of Culture.

When we land at Dublin Airport 50 minutes later, it's a similar scene. Once more there are Liverpool and Manchester United shirts dotted about, some of whom would probably be lucky enough to sample the big game atmosphere the next day. The Irish Independent immediately catches my eye as they tip United by suggesting 'it is hard not to see Ferguson's men once again opening up a sharp division in class'.

The Indo goes on to describe the game as 'an intriguing battle'. That's always the case, and this is definitely the most high-profile fixture during the early weeks of 2008/09.

Venue: Rody Bolands bar, Rathmines, Dublin, 13.09.08

Occasion: Liverpool v Man Utd, Barclays Premier League 2008/09, Anfield

However, there is little sign of that the next morning as we take the city's fairly new mode of transport, the sleek and shiny Luas tram, into town. A lone United shirt in the same carriage is the only evidence of what's about to unfold. Then we spot two red jerseys walking side by side; one of the good Red persuasion, the other has 'Berbatov' adorned across the back. This is definitely a sight we wouldn't witness on Scotty Road.

Shortly afterwards, a boy with 'Gerrard 8' on also goes past, although it's probably a safe bet he'll be watching the TV at home rather than in the pub.

With it being an early kick-off, my United-supporting mates have no problem gaining a good vantage point and we ready ourselves for what I'm hoping will be our first home league win against the Red Devils since 2001.

All around us there are small groups huddled at various tables. And each contingent appears to contain both Man U and Liverpool supporters. When 'You'll Never Walk Alone' is aired, there's no real singing of our famous anthem by those in attendance, while at the same time the United fans don't boo, as they traditionally would if at Anfield. Just before kick-off there are shouts of "come on reds" from various parts of the pub. Which 'reds' they are urging on isn't entirely clear.

That only becomes obvious less than three minutes in when Dimitar Berbatov's dangerous low ball across the box brings audible intakes of breath from Irish Kopites, while United fans are urging someone to get on the end of it.

Unfortunately, as we all know, Carlos Tevez does exactly that to dispatch a crisp finish into Pepe Reina's net.

All around us there is the sight of people at the same table reacting in entirely opposite ways. Some are on their feet celebrating, fists punching the air a la Tiger Woods. Others, obviously Liverpool fans, remain seated, head in hands, swearing, while glaring at their suddenly joyous friends. If you wanted to sum up the power of football to bring out different

Friends
and rivals:
A Dublin
street,
Saturday
afternoon
and the
city is split

Fighting talk by Benitez sets tone for Liverpool

emotions in people it's here right in front of us. For some it's ecstasy, for others – stood less than a foot away - it's pure agony.

These people are clearly mates who, prior to 12:45pm, had been chatting and having a laugh. Now they are almost polar opposites and will be for most of the next two hours. Sky Sports would love 'the sheer drama of it all'. You can imagine Jim White stressing just how good it is over and over again.

It's the worst possible start and, as Alex Ferguson's men spend the opening quarter pinging the ball about, all kind of nightmare scenarios are running through my mind.

'The United fans remain seated and silent. Our first league goal against the Mancs since 2004 is an own goal, just like the last one. Grown men hug each other and jump around. Bemused girlfriends look on...'

Those around us with Old Trafford allegiances are clearly loving it, hoping our worst fears are about to become a reality. Frustration is already starting to creep in amongst the Irish-based Anfielders, as a roar of "come on Carragher, get 'em going" clearly illustrates.

Then it looks like a quick equaliser is certain. Edwin van der Sar flaps at Fabio Auerlio's in-swinging corner and the ball drops to Dirk Kuyt, less than six yards from goal. Some Liverpool fans are already on their feet, urging him to smash it in.

This time it's the turn of the United contingent to hold their collective breath. "How the hell has he not scored that?" tells us that Dirk hasn't done it - we can't see the screen because bodies are in the way. "Bloody handball on the line," someone else replies. (Replays later indicate it clearly wasn't.)

Suddenly there is a feeling that the Reds aren't out of this yet. New boy Albert Riera is starting to enjoy some decent moments. The Spaniard is answering the United fan near us who previously asked: "Who's he?" We're enjoying a bit of possession and then a leveller comes, almost out of nothing. Xabi Alonso's shot - or is it a cross? - causes an unreasonable amount of panic in the area.

Van der Sar again looks uncertain as he races off his line. A weak punch only deflects the ball onto Wes Brown before it trickles back towards the empty net.

You wouldn't see the likes of it in pub football, but none of the Liverpool lads care. The United fans remain seated and silent. Our first league goal against the Mancs since 2004 is an own goal, just like the last one.

That fact matters little as grown men hug each other and jump around.

Bemused girlfriends look on. Some are wearing Liverpool shirts, although they clearly haven't gathered just how significant the moment we've just witnessed actually is. All the opposition fans offer is a shake of the head. "Now let's go and win it," shouts one Kopite. It's amazing what a goal can do for your spirits.

Half-time arrives without any further scoring. The whistle brings a rush to the bar, toilet and smoking room, although not in that particular order.

Again, now that on-field hostilities have temporarily ceased for quarter of an hour, Reds and reds chat as they wait for a drink or drag on a cigarette.

We obviously can't see it from the other side of the Irish Sea, but I'm pretty sure the same scenario isn't unfolding in the Annie Road End right now.

Glasses refilled, bladders temporarily emptied and nicotine craving sated for another while, everyone reconvenes on their stool as Alonso and Robbie Keane kick-start the second half.

Obviously with this being the Irish capital, the new number seven is held in high esteem, and whenever he picks up possession, there is a buzz of anticipation as people are willing him to do well. Unfortunately it's not happening for the Ireland captain, who somehow mis-kicks in front of goal on more than one occasion.

Still, his busy and industrious running is helping to put the opposition under pressure and setting a pattern all over the pitch. The champions can't relax for a second as Keane, Kuyt and in particular Javier Mascherano constantly harass them.

Having finally scored in this fixture, and not allowed United too many opportunities, the momentum is definitely with us. Fergie's men are there for the taking, if only we can step it up. At the same time, those around us obviously sense this too, as they begin to urge Rafa to introduce "Stevie and Torres". In the end, the boss only opts for one of his aces, with the skipper replacing Yossi Benayoun.

On the other side of this Dublin-based Liverpool-Manchester divide, there are clearly some worried faces.

Rafa's on the sideline again. This time Riera, who's done quite well, makes his way off to be replaced by Ryan Babel. Almost simultaneously, a man in a Liverpool shirt gets up from his seat and makes his way towards the toilets.

The Dutch supersub of course goes on to make a telling impact, while one of United's replacements also makes a major contribution to the decisive goal of the day. What Ryan Giggs is doing, only he knows. "Will you get rid of it!" comes a shout from the crowd. Too late. Mascherano pounces and takes the ball away, allowing Kuyt to arrive in the box.

"Give it, give it!" is the shout, from the back of the pub.

Our day: Edwin Van der Sar and Wes Brown chat about the mix-up (top) while Rafa and Robbie get involved

SCANLITE
LIVERPOOL 2
Man. Utd. 1

Who he's supposed to pick out isn't immediately clear. Thankfully the number 18 has a good idea and squares it to his compatriot. Babel bounces the ball high into the net. All around us Liverpool fans are bouncing too, and for once it's not in honour of Fernando Torres. Again the Tiger air-punch is on display, and it's not the United fans executing it this time. Some Liverpool supporters share high fives, while the guy who had just disappeared into the gents runs out to discover what he's missed.

There's a slight look of anguish on his face, although that quickly becomes a smile when he watches the replay.

"If you go back in there, we might score another one," one of those at his table instantly jokes.

The game resumes and straight away people are on their feet again, unlike Keane or Nemanja Vidic. "He should be off for that," more than one Red suggests after the defender upends the Dubliner almost straight from the restart. "Not a chance, it's only a booking," is

the response from the United contingent. Eventually, when those in the pub, the stands and on the pitch calm down, Howard Webb issues a yellow card.

In the closing minutes, we could just as easily be at Anfield as nerves set in amongst the 'home' support. On each occasion United pump the ball towards the box, there is a nervous silence followed by a relieved roar when the danger is cleared. There's also some worry when Mascherano picks up a knock and remains on the turf, although that tension is punctured by the fact each and every LFC fan is urging him to stay down and use up some valuable seconds. In the end, United don't find their usual late strike. The only real drama of the last few minutes involves Vidic again.

This time it is a red card after a 'challenge' on Xabi Alonso that would have been more at home in Croke Park. As the centre-half exits the screen, there is a joyous chant of "cheerio". Victory is close, so close. With only seconds remaining, two more football shirts enter

the pub, one Manchester City, who is clearly delighted to see the other Manc team trailing. He's accompanied by a Sunderland fan, although his feelings regarding this result are less obvious.

Then the final whistle goes and again the Irish Liverpudlians are on their feet celebrating. United fans only glance at the floor and then look at their mates, some of whom are trying not to rub it in. Others are doing the opposite, and who can blame them.

Even on this side of the water, the wait for a home win in this particular fixture has been tough to endure. While Richard Keys, Jamie Redknapp, Dion Dublin and Graeme Souness pick the bones from a hugely entertaining encounter, the supporters in the pub do exactly the same.

There's heated debate and joyous celebrations, but no more than that: all the passion and the knowledge, without so much seriousness. If only it was like that in every place after every game, whatever the result.

'The final whistle goes and the Irish Liverpudlians are on their feet. United fans only glance at the floor and then look at their mates, some of whom are trying not to rub it in. Others are doing the opposite'

'Had Anfield had a roof, it would have **been raised**'

Liverpoolfc.tv's PAUL HASSALL recalls the special night a Kop legend said an emotional farewell to the club he loved

Signing in: Aldo on the Kop, January 1987

AS a youngster the first thing I noticed about John Aldridge was that he was a dead-ringer for Ian Rush – the second was that he could finish like him, too. So much so, that a rumour doing the rounds at the time suggested that Juventus were beginning to think they had been sold the wrong player.

Such a tale may suggest Rushie didn't enjoy the best of times with the Old Lady, but in truth, it simply served to show how good a goalscorer John William Aldridge was. The mere mention of his name immediately conjures up images of the mouthwatering triumvirate he formed alongside John Barnes and Peter Beardsley during the all-conquering 1987/88 season. He was part of a side that played football at its most sublime, and while the aforementioned duo would so often be the architects behind Liverpool's goals, Aldo would usually be the beneficiary.

Such prowess in front of goal undoubtedly leads to adulation from the Kop – but it was different with Aldridge. There was a class and humility about the man, and his decision to commit to an international career with the Republic of Ireland prior to his arrival at Anfield did little to affect the supporters' love for one of their own. That in itself perhaps shows the seamless bond between Liverpool and Ireland, a relationship that has a deep-rooted past.

Aldo may well have been a born 'n' bred Scouser, but he was fiercely proud of his Irish heritage, and showed the same passion for his adopted country as he did while bearing a Liverbird upon his chest. Never was this more noticeable than in the 1994 World Cup finals when he memorably showed his anger after an official delayed his appearance as a substitute in a group clash against Mexico. Jack Charlton's side were trailing 2-0 at the time, and Aldo's commitment to the cause was there for all to see. When he did finally enter proceedings, he duly notched a goal, and although Ireland lost the match 2-1, the incident further enhanced his position as a hero back in Eire.

Such an honest, human reaction was just another reason behind the fans' adulation, and this was evident in his Anfield swansong - my abiding memory of the 'Irish' Kopite. The return of the prodigal son, Ian Rush, was restricting his appearances for the Reds, and Aldo knew his time at Liverpool was up. On the eve of the clash with Crystal Palace in September 1989, he was all set for a move to Spanish side Real Sociedad – but was named as a substitute against the First Division's newcomers.

It proved to be a very special night for both Aldridge and Liverpool as they put Steve Coppell's side to the sword with an emphatic 9-0 victory. The match provided a montage of great goals, but there was no doubt as to what most of the 35,779 privileged fans inside Anfield felt was the highlight of the night. With Liverpool leading by a 5-0 scoreline, they continued to attack at will and were eventually awarded a spot-kick in front of the Kop.

The crowd had already been clamouring for Aldo's arrival, and at this point the chants reached fever pitch. Kenny Dalglish duly obliged by sending the striker on in place of the superb Beardsley. Had Anfield had a roof, it would surely have been raised, such was the level of noise – but it was nothing compared to the cheers that greeted the striker as he coolly dispatched the spot-kick to put the Reds 6-0 up. At the final whistle, a visibly emotional Aldo ran towards the Kop and stripped down to his shorts to provide some lucky fans with a memento of a short, but truly great, Anfield career.

Final goal: Aldo steps up to score from the spot in his memorable farewell game

Below: A cutting from the Liverpool Echo the day after

'They continued to attack and were awarded a spot-kick in front of the Kop. The crowd had already been clamouring for Aldo's arrival, and at this point the chants reached fever pitch. Kenny Dalglish duly obliged by sending the striker on in place of the superb Beardsley . . .'

THAT 'ALDO NICELY!

King John is spot on as Reds' Roy of the Rovers says goodbye!

by Ken Rogers

ROY OF THE ROVERS is alive and well and heading for Spain, under the alias of John Aldridge.
Like the comic strip hero who always comes out on top, the man Liverpool are

PUTTING HIS SHIRT ON IT . . . John Aldridge is congratulated by a dazed Perry Suckling, as the Liverpool hero races to toss his shirt into the Kop.

171

First visit to Anfield: The 2-0 win over Arsenal in 1996

'We were **gobsmacked** by

MONDAY night football on Sky Sports, 19 August 1996. This is it. Liverpool v Arsenal at Anfield in the Premiership and I have finally arrived. A Liverpool fan since watching them lose the 1985 FA Cup semi-final against bitter rivals Manchester United, the Arsenal game was my first trip to Anfield and, immediately, I was hooked.

I've been back numerous times since, and as a regular traveller, I like to get over to the famous old ground at least seven or eight times a season. In recent years, I've watched the Reds away from home at venues such as Goodison Park and White Hart Lane, while the Stade Velodrome in Marseille has been visited twice.

I'll never forget my first experience of Anfield. A ferry trip from Dun Laoghaire to Holyhead in the small hours of the morning was followed by a coach transfer to Liverpool. With three of my childhood friends, we sank several bottles of beer en route and we were simply gobsmacked by the fervour and passion of the locals as we sampled the pre-match atmosphere in The Park pub behind the Kop End. The 'badge man' Pete Sampara was present, and as banners hung from the walls, we felt very much at home.

It's sometimes difficult to explain to people in Ireland how an English football team can have such a hold over you, but Liverpool is very much an obsession of mine. Perhaps it has something to do with the fact that League of Ireland

football is quite poor in comparison, but there's also the fact that Scousers are generally a friendly bunch and the atmosphere at Anfield on matchdays is second to none.

There's nothing that can compare with a European night, and I've been lucky to have attended quite a few games and seen some of Europe's best teams up close and personal – Roma, Barcelona, Benfica, Porto, Arsenal and...erm... Chelsea. For circumstances outside of my control, I was unable to make it to Istanbul in 2005, and it ranks as the single biggest regret of my life. I watched the game with a mate of mine in Cork and I was elated at the final whistle, while also cursing the fact that I couldn't be there. I made it to Athens in 2007, but unfortunately Milan got their revenge for that defeat from two years before.

Premier League matches that spring to mind are the 2-0 and 3-1 victories over Manchester United earlier in the decade, while I was also lucky enough to be present for the 2-1 win in 2008. I've been at Merseyside derbies home and away and seen the following Premier League teams live against Liverpool: Middlesbrough, Aston Villa, Manchester City, Tottenham, Blackburn, Arsenal, Chelsea, West Brom, West Ham and Newcastle.

I always enjoy the visit of Newcastle because their fans bring a special atmosphere. I was present for the 4-3 victory some years back (the year Fowler scored the late winner), while another standout memory is Xabi Alonso's goal from

Home from home: The Park pub, behind the Kop end. Opposite page: Steven Gerrard and Michael Owen help us beat United

the **passion** of the locals'

the halfway line! The Arsenal visit back in 1996, when Steve McManaman scored both goals, opened the floodgates to many more visits to watch Liverpool. Of course, the financial strain can be huge, and I envy the supporters based in the city who can stroll down to the game on a matchday.

A typical visit for me might begin with a 5am start to make the two-hour journey from Tipperary to Dublin to catch a 9am flight to Merseyside. The same trip is made home later that night once the game is over but more often that not, the trip has been worthwhile.

There have been some horror shows of course, most notably home defeats against Manchester United, along with Everton some years back when I travelled with some bluenoses and they were on the right end of the result as Kevin Campbell netted at the Kop End. That was the game where Steve Staunton ended up between the sticks when Sander Westerveld got involved in fisticuffs with Francis Jeffers. Other horrors include a 1-0 home defeat against Birmingham City, when Darren Anderton scored; and there have been other frustrating results along the way.

The ultimate dream of course is to witness the lads winning the Premier League. I grew up at a time when Liverpool collected trophies at will, and it must be said that the last decade or so has sometimes made for painful viewing, save for the highs of Cardiff in 2001 and Istanbul in '05.

I look forward to many, many years supporting the Reds at home and abroad, and so far, it's been an absolute privilege. I must admit to some poor decision-making when choosing my shirt numbers down through the years, however. Rob Jones was one of the earliest ones before shin splints ended his career, while other 'greats' such as Ziege, Kewell and Sissoko have adorned various home and away tops. When some of my mates spot who I have put on the back of my shirts, they shudder at the long-term prospects of the players in the question, but I think I've played it safe this time with 'Mascherano 20', my favourite Liverpool player! For me, there's no greater feeling than pulling on that Red shirt at some ungodly hour in the morning before getting into my car for the trip to Dublin and on to Liverpool.

Ryanair have made it easy to get across to Anfield, and over the years I've seen some great goals go in at the Anfield Road and Kop Ends. The Kop is the place to be for me, and the passion evoked in blocks 304, 305 and 306 is sensational. There's nothing more frightening for opposition teams than that roar.

Jackie Cahill is a freelance Gaelic Games reporter. He is also the author of two books: *Passion and Pride – the Davy Fitzgerald Story* and *Final Whistle – the Paddy Russell Story*

'I recall 'Stan's' face after **Thomas** scored. **I cried**'

Sport Media journalist SIMON HUGHES felt a kinship with Steve Staunton as soon as he saw him in the World Cup, and he still regrets the fact that 'Stan', as he is known, spent his best years away from Liverpool

L IKE me, Steve Staunton was ginger and ugly. We were also both as slow as Jan Molby after a heavy night on the Benylin. Therefore, my desire to mimic him on the schoolyard was very understandable.

I first remember watching Staunton breeze down the left wing at Italia '90. He was playing in the emerald green of Ireland against the greyish white of England. The game was in Cagliari, Sardinia. The pitch had been scorched by the midday sun and sodden by afternoon rain. I was six years old, Liverpool-born of Dundalk decent (Staunton of course played for Dundalk) and I found myself willing on Jack Charlton's men. The shirts of the Irish players reflected off the floodlights and that dazzled me. For some reason, I already knew Staunton was a Liverpool player. My earliest football memory was watching us lose to Arsenal in the 1989 title decider. I vaguely recall Staunton's face at the final whistle, moments after Michael Thomas scored. Empathising with his disappointment, I cried.

Maybe I also liked him because I had just started to play Sunday league football. Even though I was more in the Niall Quinn mould and loved scoring goals, maybe the flame-locked full-back gave me hope that one day it would be me stooping to head home one of his crosses. I liked the way he was totally one-footed. Although I only used my left for standing, I admired his cultured (aren't they all?) left boot.

Back then, he played at left-back or in midfield, but was equally adept at both. He attacked at will, and that excited me. At the beginning of the World Cup, I asked my dad who would win it. He said Brazil, so I watched them intently as they tore past Sweden in their opening game. Careca and Romario were the stars, but Branco, the rubber-faced left-back caught my eye with his marauding forward runs and a foot like a traction engine, as Alan Partridge later put it.

I tuned into every game from there on (school permitting), trying to cobble together some kind of World Cup XI, like some of the other kids in my class. By the final round of opening group games there were lots of Italians, even though they were playing poorly. My team went: Zenga

'To my relief, Stan returned to Anfield in 1998. But Villa had seen his best years and he was almost 30'

(owing to his exotic-sounding surname), Bergomi, Branco (of course), Baresi, Massing (for turning Caniggia into a hamburger), Donadoni, Valderrama, Matthaus, Scifo, Schillaci (thanks to Barry Davies who described him romantically as "the man with those Sicilian eyes"), and Omam-Biyik (Milla was yet to make an impact). No Argentinians were selected because I hated them. Dad had told me about Maradona and his handball, and I have always disliked people who have personally profited at the expense of others.

But then Group F began and nothing had prepared me for Staunton. I didn't dislike England and desperately wanted them to win the whole shebang later on (I was six, remember), but tonight I was Irish. We all know about Charlton's tactics. Every Irishman who got the ball, you could tell what he was thinking like he was shouting it through a megaphone: "How far can I kick the thing this time?" 'Floodlight height', as Pete Davies later put it in his book *All Played Out*.

Any amount of English quality was abruptly terminated by another train crash of a tackle. And that night Staunton did tackle, taking Chris Waddle and John Barnes, at the risk of being sacrilegious (this is England, though), completely out of the game. I also enjoyed watching him link up with the classy Kevin Sheedy, who later scored the equaliser. "Who's he?" I asked my Dad. "He plays for Everton, but used to play for Liverpool and never got his game," he responded. "Why did we let him go?" I thought.

The Irish progressed to the quarter-finals without winning a single game. They drew again against Egypt, Holland and Romania (beating them on penalties on the only occasion when I would rejoice at the skills of David O'Leary), before losing narrowly to the Italian hosts in Rome. Packie Bonner was at fault for the goal, but Staunton was peerless, especially against Roberto Donadoni, who I earlier earmarked for greatness by including him in my XI.

I couldn't wait for the following season. Liverpool were champions and were expected to lift the title again. Staunton was an integral part of Kenny Dalglish's team and his versatility suggested he could have been the left-footed answer to Steve Nicol (another ginge). Two summers later, though, Staunton was no longer a Liverpool player. Graeme Souness had taken over by then, and one of his first acts was to sell Staunton and Ray Houghton. I hated him deeply for that. It was a disgrace that two players of their undoubted ability were jettisoned for lesser beings. All I need to say is "Istvan Kozma".

The next time I saw Staunton, he was playing for Aston Villa in the semi-final of the League Cup at Prenton Park against Tranmere. Although the Wirral side won the first leg, Staunton was instrumental in the return match as they won through on penalties. Liverpool had long since started their decline, but even Tranmere had gone further than them in a competition that the Reds had won more times than any other club in England.

Now Staunton was winning it with another team (against Man United), and it stank. To my relief, Stan returned to Anfield in 1998. But Villa had seen his best years and he was almost 30 by now. Stan Staunton became Stan Boardman. His pace now was truly gone, and an ignominious end came when he was forced to play in goal for the final 10 minutes of a lost derby after Francis Jeffers had started a punch-up with Sander Westerveld and the pair had been sent off.

Watching Staunton prance about in front of the Anfield Road was a sad sight, and his Liverpool exit seemed ominous, especially with Gerard Houllier reshaping the squad. After a loan spell at Crystal Palace, he came back to Liverpool for one final substitute appearance against Olympiakos in Athens. He hit the bar, too, but the fact he had replaced error-addict Djimi Traore at half-time says it all, really, about how far he had fallen.

Committed: Staunton battles with Jamie Carragher against Valencia in 1998 (right) and shows bravery as he goes in head-first against Everton's Ibrahima Bakayoko

'Dalglish was **special**. There was something **timeless** about Kenny'

From an early age, Irish Independent journalist DION FANNING was captivated by Kenny Dalglish, and he used to mimic his hero when playing football with friends. Here he remembers King Kenny with affection – from the highs of European and league trophies to the lows of Hillsborough and resignation

THE first thing I remember learning about Kenny Dalglish was that he had "the biggest backside in football". I must have read this in *Shoot!* because it was my only source of football knowledge in the days when I wanted to play like Kenny Dalglish.

It has taken me a long time simply not to want to be Kenny Dalglish. His game, *Shoot!* told me, was all about holding off the defenders, and I learned that he was the best at turning and getting a shot in when his marker thought every angle was cut off. I would replicate this on the grass where we played every evening, jutting my arse out in an attempt to make it the biggest backside around when that seemed like a desirable objective. I would then spread my arms wide in what I believed was the manner of Kenny Dalglish. Then I would swivel and shoot into the frame of the swings, which were our goalposts.

In three-and-in, the game we played, this is a deeply unsatisfactory style of play for everyone, but mainly for your opponents, other seven-year-old boys who aren't obsessed with Kenny Dalglish or his backside. They are expecting shots and crazy, 40-yard dribbles, but that was not what I, or I imagined Kenny, was about. I would repeatedly go through the shielding of the ball thing as I inched it closer to the goal where the whole back-to-goal-turn-then-shoot manoeuvre would be rolled out once again.

Sometimes I would be through on goal and then decide to practise turning like Kenny, so I would wait and let the defender get goalside again before, to much derision and weariness, roll out the whole production, the arms, the arse, the turn. (I used to do something similar when I played cricket in the summer, but then, with a little less taste, I wanted to emulate the notoriously dull English opening batsman, Chris Tavare. For what now seems like hours, I would simply block during games of beach cricket and just when the bowler, usually my father, was getting weary, I would glance a ball down the leg side for an easy single while, all across the beach, fielders groaned. I think my childhood damaged others a lot more than it damaged me.)

But before I knew about Dalglish's backside, I knew about his face. When I was about five, my mother wrote to Liverpool for me and in return they sent a price list of what was available in their shop. I can still remember the excitement of that letter arriving, with some sort of club frank on it. I remember wanting a Liverpool watch but there was some problem with the Liverpool watch, it didn't arrive or they wouldn't send it to Ireland, but they did send a selection of black and white photos which I put all over my bedroom wall. Kenny was there, of course, but also Steve Heighway, Terry McDermott and Phil Neal.

They stayed on my wall for years, surrounding a dartboard so that many of them were pockmarked to the point of disfigurement, although at that age I saw nothing symbolic in throwing a dart at a player's head. But I did know that I didn't want Kenny disfigured so I kept him far away from even the most wayward shot.

Dalglish was always to be protected in my world. He had a special authority, and it is strange to think that he was the roughly the same age when he signed for Liverpool in 1977 as Robbie Keane was when he signed in the summer of 2008. Of course, it's not strange; I'm older than Robbie Keane so he is just a boy. But there was something timeless about Kenny. He was 26 when he arrived at Liverpool, an age that I am tempted to say seemed ancient to me then but, actually, had no meaning at all. I had no comprehension of what it was to be 26 rather than 22, 35 rather than 30. I'm not sure I do today.

But Kenny just arrived with time-capsuled presence. His celebration was iconic because, like all great artists, he kept it simple. And his football was beautiful.

I went to Anfield for the first time in 1982. My father and I caught the boat from the North Wall on a Friday night and arrived seven hours later in Liverpool at about 6.30 in the morning. We were heading back that night, so time, it's safe to say, was on our side.

On top of
the world:
Kenny
celebrates
with 'Old
Big Ears' in
1978

Later, I would spend many more dawns at Liverpool having arrived by boat after all-night sailings, but I didn't have the same methods of killing time when I was 10 that I would acquire later.

We had travelled to see Liverpool play Luton. The game finished 3-3, I know who scored because I've looked it up, but all I remember of the day was being transfixed by the Kop and the way the hands on the terrace moved at times I couldn't predict. I didn't take my eyes off it.

Later that day, we met Bruce Grobbelaar in the St George's Hotel and then we caught the boat home and I struggled but failed to stay awake to watch the highlights, but all I thought of was the Kop.

It was a few years before I went back to Liverpool, but from then on we started to go every year, and every trip affected me in the same way. I could remember incidents in the game, but more than anything I was infected by the need to belong to the spirit, the unity that rose from the Kop.

When you are young you think nothing will ever change, and as you reach adolescence, secure in the knowledge that nothing will ever change, you decide that everything will have to be changed by you. In football terms, I lived in a

world where Liverpool would always win when they had to and Kenny was the godhead.

The World Cups in '82 and '86 introduced us to players who seemed to be able to do things we had never seen before, and for a while my shielding technique was replaced by the backheels of Zico and Eder from the Brazil side of '82. But I never disputed Dalglish's place at the head of the thing I worshipped. For me, he was the best because he seemed to score goals when required or be involved as Liverpool were always winning, but, most importantly, because he was there.

I read a quote from Kenny in *Shoot!* one week. "If I score and we lose, I'm fed up. If I don't and we win, I'm happy." I considered it a profound philosophy (perhaps the exact opposite of Aldo's), even if it may be more challenging and controversial in the modern game than it was then. The 'we' too seemed self-explanatory. Kenny belonged to Liverpool, there was no question of any other loyalties.

A few years later, I read the story of a Scotland squad meeting before they played Ireland, and the manager, Andy Roxburgh, asked the Scottish players at Celtic, Manchester United and Liverpool to talk about the Irish players at those

'For me, Kenny was the best because he seemed to score goals when required or be involved as Liverpool were always winning, but, most importantly, because he was there'

clubs. So Gordon Strachan started off, telling everything he knew about Kevin Moran, Paul McGrath and Frank Stapleton. Then Roy Aitken filled them in on Mick McCarthy, Chris Morris and Packie Bonner.

Finally, Roxburgh turned to Dalglish for the skinny on Whelan, Houghton and Aldridge. "Kenny, can you tell me about the Irish players at Liverpool?" Kenny paused and was said to have replied, "I don't have anything to say about the Liverpool players who play for Ireland."

I was reminded of that story when I read about a text exchange with Dalglish after Jamie Carragher missed a penalty for England in the 2006 World Cup. Dalglish sent his commiserations. "At least it wasn't for LFC," Carragher responded. Dalglish, I'm sure, was proud.

As I knew Liverpool were always going to be winning, I drifted away for a couple of years. By 1984, I was devouring music, everything and anything, with none of the filters that develop later to separate cool from uncool or even good from bad. In 1985, I took the day off school to see Frankie Goes to Hollywood play in Dublin. They weren't on until the evening but my oldest friend Dominique (who never had any interest in football, referring once to the kit as 'uniforms') and I queued from the morning to get a place at the front of the stage (that was also the first night I drank – whiskey and coke on the way home, a good springboard for a 12-year-old, but that's another story).

Part of the appeal to me was that Frankie were from Liverpool, even if their only connection with football

seemed to be that Holly Johnson fell asleep when his father took him to Anfield. But I still felt as if they belonged to the tribe with whom I had aligned myself.

Later that year, I was playing football on my road when a friend shouted out that there was a riot on TV. Heysel was happening and I sat and watched the strange violence from supporters I didn't think were capable of things like that, preceding a match of which I was only dimly aware. In the aftermath, I was drawn back into football. Kenny was now in charge, I had kind of assumed he always was, and, driven by a younger brother whose obsession was even greater than my own, I didn't take victory for granted anymore.

There were more trips to Anfield, the most memorable being the derby win in November '87, a game of seek and destroy which Liverpool won memorably, and the noise from the Kop suggested that every person standing there had some personal need for victory, which, of course, they did.

And then came Hillsborough. Years later, as a journalist, I would occasionally be required to take an objective assessment of the facts (this happens much less frequently than some imagine) regarding Dalglish in management. To be honest, when Kenny was boring them at Newcastle and doing a pretty hopeless job at Celtic, I couldn't move past the godhead. Hillsborough, to me, defined the man, and if parvenus like Newcastle weren't happy with Kenny and wanted 'sexy football' instead, well, screw them.

When Liverpool trounced Newcastle just after they'd fired Dalglish and replaced him with the sibilant and sexifying

Grieving: Kenny with his wife and daughter at the Hillsborough memorial service in 1989

Lows and
highs:
Kenny in
1991, just
before his
resignation,
and in 1989
(far right)

Gullit, I rejoiced at the sounds from the travelling fans. "You can stick your sexy football up your arse", and, more poignantly, "Dalglish, Dalglish". If Hillsborough haunted Kenny, he possessed Liverpool from that time as well.

Nothing else mattered except the way he behaved and held the club and the city together, which, typically, he didn't think was remarkable at all. To him, it was his duty and that was what made him great: he perceived duty as giving everything – his talent, his personality and the love of his family for their adopted city – towards a cause.

He did, and his wife Marina did that, and I remember the picture of his son Paul standing on the Kop wearing a Juventus jersey (that had a poignancy, too) shortly afterwards. I no longer wanted to rebel, I wanted to belong. Hillsborough showed, in the most impossibly painful, tragic way, how important belonging is in Liverpool. Kenny had understood and appreciated that from the moment he arrived. He belonged to these people, I think that is what

'I believed his reasons and thought there was nothing more important than that, nothing as overwhelming as trying to win for a football club that you loved, a city you belonged to and 96 you couldn't stop grieving for'

he believed, and whatever they required from him, he would do.

Looking back, February 1991 doesn't seem very distant from April 1989, but at the time it seemed like an age. Now it seems painfully obvious that a man who gave everything for a club and a city might be at the point of collapse 18 months later, but then people insisted there had to be more. I was never interested.

My mother told me that Kenny had quit on a Friday lunchtime. I was 19, old enough to care less but I couldn't think about anything else. I went and met my brother after school and told him, and then we tried to devour all the information, demonstrating a need for 24-hour news that preceded its arrival. All I felt was sadness. The 4-4 Merseyside derby was being suggested as the trigger for his downfall.

The shots of him haunted and alone in the dug-out suggested a man at the end, but they only suggested that afterwards. At the time, it seemed normal. Kenny always exuded a sense of solitude. It was what made his wit, his smile and his gifts so exciting: they were coming from the place where all great artists go, and they always have to go there alone. But Hillsborough took him somewhere else and that sadness never left him. I think he would have found it a betrayal of the families if it had.

There were always people who wanted to engage in debate, question the timing of his decision and the other usual stuff. I couldn't even debate. I believed his reasons and thought there was nothing more important than that, nothing as overwhelming as trying to win for a football club that you loved, a city you belonged to and 96 you couldn't stop grieving for.

Rumours and conspiracies usually hint at something more profound or deeper than the official reasons, but in this case they were all trivialities. The most obvious explanation was also the most earth-shatteringly true.

For a couple of years, I used to think Dalglish would come back, but he never did. It would be corny to say he never left, but it felt true on that bizarre day when he came to Anfield and won the league with Blackburn. Kenny was home and was smiling. Liverpool had won, Blackburn had won, it seemed like everyone had won. Naturally, on that day, Kenny wasn't fed up. And when Kenny smiled, nobody who cared about Liverpool could be fed up.

'No one lacks the **passion**

WESTPORT, County Mayo. Its name gets straight to the point: a port on the west coast of Ireland, 30 miles north of Galway.

A scenic town, Westport boasts the feel of a provincial French village, with winding avenues and shops arcing up hills.

Old buildings with unusually colourful façades – yellow, lime, orange, deep red, bright blue – belie their age yet retain their charm.

The town somehow manages to be both sleepy and vibrant; relaxed and busy. It has a quaint feel, but also modern amenities and trendy internet café bars. It's rustic without being an anachronism.

It is late August 2005, and the Westport Supporters' Club is meeting on the 10th anniversary of its formation. More than 100 members are present, here to sample the European Super Cup final on a big screen with a pint of the black stuff, three months after gathering to witness the greatest night in their football-watching lives.

For good measure, a re-run of the Istanbul final is also on the agenda; not that memories need refreshing. I am present as guest of honour, following the recent release of my first book.

There are a lot of Irish stereotypes around, but one that is deservedly true relates to an innate friendliness. It's also true that the country has a high proportion of Liverpool fans.

As in the Far East and Australia, the following for English football seems to have arisen decades ago owing to a lack of any meaningful kind of professional domestic league.

Liverpool were high-profile during the '60s and '70s, and the city is a short ferry ride away from Ireland's east coast, so the attraction, as it is with Manchester United, is fairly logical.

The Westport Supporters' Club was formed in 1995, after a gang of Reds met up in the local pub; a loose gathering quickly became an official collective.

At half-time, with the Reds trailing to CSKA Moscow in Monaco, I get talking to Peter Flynn, the club's treasurer and the man who has organised tonight's event.

With genial face and gentle manner, he stands fractionally taller than Steven Gerrard in a picture I am shown of the two: Peter presenting the Liverpool captain with Westport's 2004 Player of the Season award.

Also in the picture is Christy Moran, a small man in his late 40s with a slightly lazy eye but a sharp mind regarding Liverpool.

The chairman of the supporters' club and I had managed a brief chat earlier in the evening, when he spoke 10 to the dozen about the Reds, with an almost religious fervour. The man is an intense fan. I sense that if cut, he would bleed red with microscopic white Liverpool crests.

Peter tells me more about how their supporters' club came into existence. "The formation coincided with a time when the country as a whole was emerging from a long period of depression, when jobs and cash were very scarce.

"At present we have a hardcore group of about 60 people with about another 50–100 who tend to change over time. Many of our new supporters are parents who decide to take little Mary or Johnny to their first Liverpool game and we are more than happy to assist if at all possible.

"Ultimately, these kids are the next generation of Reds supporters, and if we can help to keep the Liverpool legacy alive then we feel we are playing our part, even if it is only a

First trip: Carra's first goal in 1997 and (right) lifting the Super Cup in 2005

required to be a **true Red'**

minor contribution.

"The first official trip to Liverpool was organised at the start of the 1996/97 season after we got confirmation from LFC that we would receive an allocation of 30 tickets for the home game against Villa in January 1997."

There was another first that day: a full league debut in midfield for Jamie Carragher, who marked the occasion with a goal. Little did the Westport boys know they were witnessing something that would prove about as frequent as Halley's comet.

"For nearly all of us that travelled over in January it was a first time ever to see the Reds live. It was also a time before low-fare airlines, so the only option for people was to travel by boat to England.

"Our travels started Friday morning at 7.25am when we got a train to Dublin, which took just under four hours. From the train station in Dublin we then had to make our way to Dun Laoghaire to catch the ferry at 2pm.

"We got into Holyhead just before 5pm and two trains later we finally arrived in Liverpool, roughly 12 hours after leaving Westport.

"It was my first time ever seeing Liverpool playing in the flesh, and my first experience of Anfield.

"Even after multiple visits since then, the memory of seeing what looked like a green carpet and hearing 'You'll Never Walk Alone' at the beginning of the game will always remain with me. The journey back on the Sunday followed the same route as getting there, and although it took us over 24 hours coming and going, it was worth every minute just to be there. Since then, 30 to 40 of us travel over two or three times a year, with a few of us also trying to get to a European game whenever possible. Thankfully, with

Ryanair and Knock Airport we can now get to Liverpool in about three hours." So why Liverpool?

"I have been supporting the Reds since the age of four when my friend and neighbour Paul O'Grady and I used to think we were Kevin Keegan and Stevie Heighway! Back in the early '70s in Westport, we had one TV Channel (RTE), which only showed events like the FA Cup final and European Cup. To follow Liverpool it was the newspaper, *Shoot!* magazine or BBC Radio, which had a brutal reception most of the time! That said, I can especially remember tuning into mid-week games against Wolves, Derby, St Etienne, Borussia Monchengladbach, to name but a few. I hadn't a clue at the time where any of them were from, but it didn't matter once we got the result. We only hit the big time in the mid-'80s when the west of Ireland finally got BBC and 'Match of the Day'. I fully sympathise with locals not getting tickets, but knowing the gang from our fan club in Westport, there is no one lacking the knowledge, passion and voice required to be a true Red.

"I suppose not surprisingly since Liverpool won the Champions League in 2005, getting tickets via the Official Supporters' Club is getting harder and harder."

As in Istanbul, the game in Monaco goes to extra-time, with Djibril Cisse having got the Reds back in the game in the second half of normal time.

This time penalties aren't required, as Cisse again, and then Luis Garcia, wrap up a 3-1 victory, and the Super Cup is Liverpool's. Irish eyes are smiling.

PAUL TOMKINS writes for liverpoolfc.tv and has published several books on Liverpool FC

The Westport LFC Supporters' Club celebrate their 10th anniversary in the Wyatt Hotel, with the FAI Junior Cup and the Mayo Super League Cup. Paul Tomkins is third from left in the right-hand picture. *Photos by Frank Dolan*

'John Lennon Airport may change its motto to 'Above us only **Kopites**"

 Fans from across the Irish Sea have been instrumental in creating the legendary Anfield atmosphere, says CHRIS McLOUGHLIN, journalist with *The Kop* magazine

L IVERPOOL don't have any local supporters anymore. All real Scouse football fans follow Everton, and the ones who do still support the Reds do so from the comfort of their armchair or the pub. There, they reminisce about the days when 50,000 locals used to sing Beatles songs on the Kop when the Reds won The Title every year and the only out-of-towners were in the away end.

Complete rubbish, yes, but a taunt with a spiky edge that has been used to cut Scouse Kopites deep for quite some time now. Liverpool is the Catalonia of England. Merseysiders have always had a strong local identity, and in many ways, like the Catalans in Spain, feel isolated from the rest of the country. Take a trip to one of our museums if you want the full history lesson, but Liverpool has always been a city that looks after itself. The question of whether Liverpool should break away from the rest of the country to become a self-governing city is one that has been treated extremely seriously on Merseyside, and the Kop's "we're not English, we are Scouse" chant is sung with feeling.

Liverpudlians are proud of their city and their football club. So when rival fans suggest there is a lack of Scousers at Anfield, it strikes a raw nerve. Unquestionably there are fewer Scousers who get to see Liverpool at Anfield than 20-30 years ago, for a number of reasons. A combination of all-ticket matches, all-seater stadiums and Liverpool's global attraction means tickets for most Premier League and Champions League matches are like gold dust. That's without mentioning the prices, Fan Cards, Official Membership Schemes and the growth in corporate tickets.

Quite simply, more people from all over the world want to see Liverpool and, thanks to technology and improved transport links, it's far easier to get to Anfield these days. Back in the '70s and '80s, if you queued up long enough outside the Kop you would get in. But things have changed, and the thousands who used to leave their homes after 'Football Focus' or 'Saint & Greavsie' and pay on the turnstile are the ones who feel particularly hard done by.

Somewhat inevitably, out-of-towners (or 'Woollybacks' as they are known by many Scousers) are an easy target for those frustrated by the way football has developed over the past 15 years or so. The taunts from other clubs' fans questioning the local supporters' loyalty add to the problem. But let's be realistic. The majority of Scousers do not have a problem with out-of-towners and welcome them with open arms. As Gerry Marsden once sang: "We don't care what your name is boy, we'll never turn you away." It's the day-trippers that upset Scousers. Stand next to any fanzine seller outside Anfield on a matchday and you'll see them coming a mile off. "Is that the programme you're selling? Which end is the Kop? Do you know where the shop is?"

The match itself is a 90-minute inconvenience for some, who are more bothered about getting out of Anfield without getting their Steven Gerrard photos crushed than contributing to the atmosphere. Then when the 5-0 win that was promised in the museum before the game doesn't materialise, they give the players stick before phoning a national radio station on their way home to slag off the current team scapegoat. Then it's a case of telling their mates the next time they see them that they've sat on the famous Kop (although a load of people tried to wreck it by standing up whenever things got exciting).

The problem is that 'fans' like this don't know the history and traditions of the club, and don't even try to learn about them. This kind of 'new age' fan gives out-of-towners a bad name because they become tarred with the same brush. A great example of it happened when Robbie Keane scored his first goal for Liverpool at Anfield against PSV Eindhoven. "Keano, Keano," came the shout from the Main Stand. Seconds later, to the tune of 'Let It Be', the Kop responded directly. "Robbie Keane, Robbie Keane, Robbie Keane, Robbie Keane, his name's not f*****g Keano, Robbie Keane."

Singing "Keano" was a big a no-no if you're a Liverpool supporter, but there are a lot of Reds who don't understand it. They are the ones that cause the ill-feeling because when you are passionate and dedicated to something like Liverpool FC, seeing others jump on the bandwagon without even trying to gain a proper understanding of the Kop's traditions and history is quite offensive.

This issue of out-of-towners v Scousers has cropped up repeatedly in *The Kop*, so let's put the record straight. Out-of-towners and daytrippers are not the same thing.

Flying the flag: Scouse fans head out of the airport – while Irish Reds head in

Daytrippers can come from anywhere, Liverpool included, but won't necessarily come back. They can take it or leave it. It's a fashion, not a drug, and when something better comes along they'll move on. It's like watching Wimbledon for a fortnight but never going to another tournament. Some people wrongly label these types as out-of-towners.

True Kopites can't live without their fill of LFC, wherever they come from. The adrenaline rush of seeing the Reds live has to be satisfied, whatever the cost. From my experience there are Irish Reds who fall into both categories. I like to think the eejits are outnumbered by those who know their Kozmas from their Kvarmes, but those well-travelled Irish Reds I know tell me it varies from game to game. The dedication of those who spend the season personally financing Michael O'Leary and Stelios Haji-Ioannou for 90 minutes of football at whatever un-Godly time Sky or Setanta make us play deserve much credit.

John Lennon International Airport does so well out of Liverpool's travelling brigade from Ireland that it's thinking of changing its motto to "Above us only Kopites". And, as you'd fully expect, Irish Kopites never shy away from helping to create the Anfield atmosphere – the sound of Liverpool chants containing a distinct Irish twang is not uncommon. Indeed, there is evidence to suggest that the unique atmosphere for which the Spion Kop became world famous in the 1960s had a huge Irish influence behind it.

Scousers were arguably the out-of-towners by the end of the 1840s, and when the Kop used to hold 28,000 in the glory days of the 1960s, it's a fair bet that a substantial number of those who stood on it were of Irish descent. In 2004 I compiled a book (*Oh I Am a Liverpudlian and I Come From the Spion Kop*) to commemorate the 10th anniversary of the Spion Kop's last stand. In it, author Alan Edge, who wrote the excellent *Faith of our Fathers*, discussed how the singing started at Anfield in the first place. As the Mersey Sound resonated around the world, the full throttle of 28,000 of its own kind promptly amplified it. Cocooned and isolated in a way you could never get today, the patrons of the Kop simply did what came naturally to them, and swayed and sang along heartily with the pre-match Tannoy. Not many Kopites at the time were strangers to belting out a communal tune from the comfort of their own alehouses on a Saturday night. The Kop simply became a giant extension of that concept. Now where do you suppose that 'Liverpool Irish pub sing-song culture' came from? With that kind of history behind us, it's sad that there are divisions between some Scousers and Irish Reds.

Education is the key to narrowing the gap. Out-of-towners, whether from Ireland or elsewhere, should not be branded as inferior to local Kopites because they aren't from Liverpool. By the same token, those from outside Merseyside should not think of all Scousers as out-of-town-haters (because that is not the case for the majority), nor slag off our city (which is more commonly heard than you might imagine). There will always be divisions between people from different places, as I'm sure everyone in the Republic of Ireland and Northern Ireland can appreciate.

At Anfield, though, when all of us shout for the same cause, there is no reason for any divisions. That will only happen if everyone works together to educate the day-trippers who don't understand what supporting Liverpool Football Club is all about.

We are the Irish, the Irish **Kopites**

From ferries across the Irish Sea to flights packed full of travelling Kopites, Irish Reds have stopped at nothing to follow Liverpool through the wind and rain over the years. Here are some of your stories and pictures showing what the club means to you . . .

With tickets like gold dust, 'two Irishmen came with nothing and got it all'

IT takes a certain type of person to be a Liverpool supporter and fit in with the Liverpool way. For generations, Irishmen have eagerly adapted to this role. The link between the Irish and Liverpool is a longstanding, irremovable bond. It is a relationship that goes beyond scratching the surface. We're proud to call ourselves adopted scousers – Irish Reds.

As an Irishman studying in Liverpool at the time of the Istanbul final, the homecoming parade in the city is an image that will forever live in my memory. Two years on, student days over, I had returned from my adopted city to the one I grew up in – Belfast. There was a sense of deja vu for all Reds, however, as the semi-final once again threw up the prospect of Abramovich's Chelsea. It was a game not to miss.

Such was the clamour for tickets, the fancard used for the previous round was no longer an option – I had no match ticket. To soften the blow, a fellow Irish friend from Tipperary was in the same boat. This felt like an advantage, as we could cover twice the ground, ask twice as many people and, if all else failed, return to The Stanley to watch the action in each other's company.

This is not an unusual position for travelling Reds to find themselves in. Outside the stadium that night there were many faces as forlorn and hopeful as ours. Whatever size the new stadium will be, the demand will always exceed the supply, and hopefully in the future Liverpool FC will grace many more European semi-finals to prove that very point.

Arriving the day before the game, I was determined that nothing would be left to chance in the hunt for that elusive ticket. Back in Aigburth, 1 May 2007 was a gloriously sunny day. I was entrusted with the house keys as those with more demanding workloads or less imaginative self-diagnosis skills went to work. Aware that my only responsibility prior to an early arrival at the ground was letting my fellow ticket hunter Jimmy into the house in the afternoon, I put the phone on the charger upstairs and headed outside to drink a cup of tea and bask in the Merseyside sunshine.

In a split moment, my late morning paradise crumbled around me. Frequent visitors to Liverpool will know that even on mild days, a sharp wind can soon develop, and so it did, slamming the back door, which had no outside handle. Instant panic set in. As luck would have it, the keys for the front door were in the pocket of my jeans. Roaming the back alley behind the house, unable to contact anyone, I attempted to climb the greaseproof gate, but my lack of experience in such circumstances told as I slid back down on the same side I had started. It became apparent that the only solution was to break one of the small glass panes on the back door and force the handle down from the inside.

Dry mouth developing, I went back to the gate for one last attempt. Seeing two women getting into a car on the far side of the street, I shouted out, handed over the keys and invited one of the ladies to go in the front door, through the house and open the back door for me. I can only assume she put her own fears to one side owing to the desperation and anguish in my voice. Back inside, a sense of bewilderment at what had just happened had to be put to one side; I was ready for Jimmy to arrive. This was going to be a memorable trip no matter what. The atmosphere was building throughout the town. A good old singalong outside the Law Courts in the afternoon was getting everybody psyched up. Messrs Hicks and Gillett were given a rapturous reception on their departure from the establishment opposite. Outside the stadium, it was down to the business of ticket-hunting. Taking up a position out the back of the Kop, hopes seemed to be gradually fading.

You could hear the atmosphere building. Songs were in full flow, and from our position outside we heard the stadium announcement confirm there was just 15 minutes to kick-off. With all hope running out, a shout from Jimmy to signal he had a seller sent the heart beating into overdrive. A fellow Irishman, as casual and calm as anyone we'd met that day explained that two lads from Ireland couldn't make the trip and so the tickets were spare.

Agger steers in Gerrard's free-kick at Anfield in the Champions League semi-final second leg in 2007

'Linford Christie in his prime couldn't have caught up with us; the world's strongest man couldn't have wrestled the tickets from our grasp...'

It felt like this man had been sent from Shankly in the heavens above. With a quick exchange of notes, a hug and a great deal of thanks, two young Irishmen went sprinting out onto Walton Breck Road, around behind the Centenary Stand and down towards the Anfield Road end. Linford Christie in his prime couldn't have caught up with us; the world's strongest man couldn't have wrestled the tickets from our grasp. The buzz in the neck, back and legs comes rushing back even today just thinking about that moment. Perhaps it is because what followed later in the evening, including the drama of penalties in front of us in the Anfield Road stand that makes it all the sweeter, but it's a moment that will forever stay in the memory. Two Irishmen came with nothing and got it all.

GERRY MCGUINNESS
Templepatrick, County Antrim, Northern Ireland

Blank cheques and fake accents

I HAVE followed Liverpool since 1967 when I lived in Birkenhead, and for the next decade I was an avid Red, culminating in a rail trip to Rome in 1977. That December I moved to Larne, but have continued my support and still attend as many games as possible, by all means of transport.

Before the arrival of easyJet and Flybe, it was virtually impossible to make a day trip to Liverpool, and because of that, games in London were welcomed. Usually, acquiring tickets for away games meant a casual letter to the home club with a blank cheque, purporting to be a businessman in the city who had an interest in watching the game. The result was nearly always successful, although it still required some more work, including a Manchester accent for the home stand at Old Trafford perfected by watching 'Coronation Street', and doing similar at West Ham where old episodes of 'Till Death Us Do Part' were required.

However, May 1986 was not so successful, so I chose to pay £4 and stand in the old Shed End at Stamford Bridge, stifling my joy when Kenny scored the winner. Disappointment occasionally resulted when I arrived but the game was called off: the infamous cup replay with Luton Town meant arriving at Anfield at 6.30pm to find everywhere deserted and not even a pork pie as consolation, and returning home at 3pm the next afternoon following a night on Crewe station.

My most eventful journey was getting back from Hillsborough in 1988. The return journey (resigned to spending the night at Heathrow) was helped by my seat being adjacent to the aisle, and a mad dash to the queue of buses to take me to the railway station. Owing to the fire at Kings Cross that year, passengers were advised to get off at an unscheduled stop on the outskirts of London. (Nobody mentioned the Underground station was half a mile down the road.) But everything went like clockwork, as I stepped from one line to the other in rapid succession, arriving at Heathrow at 20:40 for a 21:20 flight. Thankfully I was able to transfer my plane ticket, which had been booked for a Sunday morning return. When the security man at the gate said "no need to rush", I had to laugh as I still had to phone home and organise a lift to pick me up from Belfast airport on arrival. Only the production of the match programme in the pub that night convinced people I had actually been at the game.

IAN MCCLENAHAN
Larne, County Antrim, Ireland

'Aldo probably believes I'm stalking him because I've met him so often'

I'VE been supporting the Reds since 1986, although my first journey to Merseyside came five years previously when we were on our way to Coventry to visit my aunt. It was September 1981 and the great Bill Shankly had just passed away. I was only two at the time, but over the years that have followed, Liverpool has become my second home.

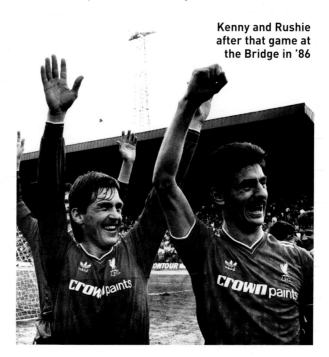

Kenny and Rushie after that game at the Bridge in '86

'The infamous cup replay with Luton Town meant arriving at Anfield at 6.30pm to find everywhere deserted and not even a pork pie as consolation, and returning home at 3pm next afternoon following a night on Crewe station'

I try to get over around 10 or 15 times every season and I've become a member of the Lower Breck Road Supporters' Club. The journeys have included 1,000-mile round trips and sharing pints with Liverpool legends like Aldo – who probably believes I'm stalking him because I've met him so often – Ronnie Whelan, Razor Houghton and Jim Beglin. I've also been lucky enough to meet a lot of the Liverpool managers, from Phil Taylor to Rafa.

Michael Owen's double to win us the 2001 FA Cup in Cardiff was special, but nothing will ever top Istanbul. Like most Reds, I still find it hard to believe. My package for the trip cost £1,453 and some of my mates suggested I was crazy to pay it. But it's the best money I've ever spent. You couldn't put a price on a night like that. It was a dream come true to see Stevie G pick up old big ears and ensure we had possession of our very own European Cup following the fifth win.

Getting to Turkey was a mammoth effort. We started with a bus journey from Bandon to Cork and then got a train to Dublin. After sleeping on the airport floor, we boarded our 7am flight. But a delay meant we had to sit on the plane for three hours. We got to the Ataturk 45 minutes before kick-off and all the programes were sold out. We just got to our seats when Milan went ahead. Thankfully we all know how it turned out.

PATRICK BRICKLEY
Bandon, County Cork, Ireland

Zenden scores his first goal for Liverpool and runs into the Kop, where Jonathan Godfrey was standing

Shaken and stirred

BEING 19 years of age and from Belfast in Northern Ireland, it's not the cheapest thing to regularly watch the world's greatest football team live. But I do, however, make a point of getting to at least one home and one away game a season.

Of those I've attended so far, one match stands out. It was the 2005/06 season and I had tickets for the Liverpool v West Ham United game. We boarded the easyJet flight from Belfast International to Liverpool John Lennon Airport and I couldn't believe who was sat in the seat in front of me...JOHN ALDRIDGE! I had my 'Champions of Europe' flag in my hand luggage, and John was only too happy to sign in for me and pose for a photograph or 10! I then gave him, as a thank you, my Liverpool wristband and to my surprise he was wearing it on Gillette Soccer Saturday. We beat West Ham 2-0 with goals from Alonso and Zenden, who scored his first goal for the club and then ran into the Kop where...he grabbed me and shook me!

JONATHAN GODFREY
Belfast, County Antrim, Northern Ireland

Vive La France!

From left: Chris Dullaghan, Kevin Neely, Clare Neely

THE trip to Marseille started off as a random selection since Ryanair were offering £20 flights to Nice, which was a mere couple of hours drive from the fixture. Being the last game in a group consisting of Besiktas, Porto and Marseille, we never actually considered that this game would be of any significance. But as the date approached and the results transpired, the Olympiakos game was in the forefront of our minds as the pessimists were discussing the possibility of the unthinkable – not qualifying for the knock-out stages.

Kevin and Laurence had decided to share the driving responsibilities once we reached the continent. Kevin, as prepared and organised as ever, reached into his bag to get the sat-nav his brother Gary had lent him, only to discover it had vanished. Finally accepting he had lost it, we set off for Marseille and thankfully the sat-nav in the car, which

Laurence lovingly named 'Mary', outlined the route we needed to take.

The atmosphere in Marseille was quite tense when we reached the ground. In true Scouse fashion, some fans, now accustomed to their French surroundings, started singing "ouvre la porte" in a vain attempt to get into the ground! And once this event DID occur, the singing changed to "fermez la porte" when we realised how cold it was! It was like being in a cattle mart, and that theme continued once we got inside, as we were surrounded by high metal fences.

The Liverpool supporters did their best but were drowned out by the sheer noise emanating from the Marseille section. At one stage, they all turned their backs to the pitch, put their arms around each other, and started jumping up and down, *a la* the Torres bounce. We'd never seen anything like it. It was like a wave of blue and orange (horrible away strip).

Anyway, that was until we won a penalty in the fifth minute or so. The nerves were terrible as the crowd tried their hardest to put Gerrard off, which they did, as he hit his spot-kick straight at the keeper, but fortunately the rebound came back to him and he put it away. That sent the travelling contingent into raptures and seemed to settle the players down. Then came the moment of magic we were all waiting for. Fernando Torres picked the ball up at the corner of the penalty area, gave one of his now-trademark shoulder-drops, and showing great close control, evaded two Marseille defenders before taking another touch to get the ball out of his feet and passing it low beyond the despairing dive of the Marseille keeper. This really got the party started in our end, and seemed to knock the life out of the Marseille support. We scored another two goals after half-time and won 4-0.

CLARE NEELY AND CHRIS DULLAGHAN

Special photo: Sinead with Rushie and Barnesie

'It was almost unheard of in our town for a girl to travel to Liverpool or be a soccer fan'

I AM the only girl in a family of three older brothers, where I follow Liverpool and have done so for as long as I can remember. I now have a son and thankfully he's carrying on the tradition. One of my first trips to Anfield was back in 1992, when it was almost unheard of in our town for a girl to travel to Liverpool or be a soccer fan. It meant I was travelling on my own. The first part of the journey involved getting a coach on a Friday evening. This took me to the Dublin port from where I caught the ferry to Holyhead, a four-hour journey, with the boat usually arriving in Liverpool around 5am on Saturday morning.

I usually went straight to the Adelphi hotel in town, where I was allowed to sit and wait until breakfast, provided I paid for the food. Straight after breakfast I'd jump in a taxi up to Anfield and start queuing for the Kop. And if I was lucky enough, I'd usually get to stand behind the goal, which was a fantastic experience. At midnight on the Saturday I would leave Liverpool a happy person and make my way back to the boat before eventually arriving home on Sunday evening. On numerous occasions the boat would not travel owing to bad weather, and there was one particular occasion where I spent 24 hours on board because of the conditions. But it was worth it. Now I travel by plane, usually getting over twice a year.

SINEAD O'REGAN
Ballinamoe, Shinrone, County Offaly, Ireland

Red stars and Red Rums

LIVERPOOL FC v Ipswich Town, 9 April 1994. That was the game I had earmarked to finally experience the Kop atmosphere for the first time. Although I had been at Anfield before, I had yet to stand on the famed terrace for a game.

Once we arrived in Liverpool we headed to the usual

'In true Scouse fashion, some fans, now accustomed to their French surroundings, started singing "ouvre la porte" in a vain attempt to get into the ground! And once this event DID occur, the singing changed to "fermez la porte" when we realised how cold it was!'

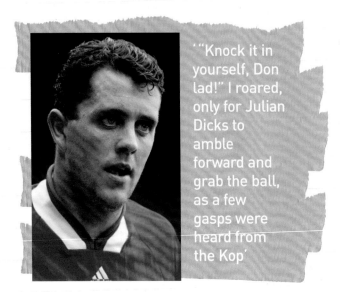

' "Knock it in yourself, Don lad!" I roared, only for Julian Dicks to amble forward and grab the ball, as a few gasps were heard from the Kop'

haunts. The Lord Nelson Hotel, all the hotels on Mount Pleasant Street, even The Moat House was tried, as if I could afford it. Everywhere was full. All I could hear from my mate was something about it being a huge weekend in the city and horseracing. After three Red Rums we headed to Lime Street where there was always an assortment of B&Bs. The fact that many of these establishments were available on this, the Grand National weekend, should have been a clue to our abode, not that I cared too much. We were relieved to get anywhere to put our heads down, and at £12 a night we shouldn't have expected too much, although a light bulb would have made the weekend extra special.

It was a tradition for Liverpool or Everton to play their home game on Grand National Saturday as an 11.30am kick-off so the locals could attend the great racing spectacle later in the afternoon. After waiting until dawn, so we could have some daylight in the room, we got ready for the game. We had to get there early, as the Kop was not all-ticket, and cash was being taken at the turnstiles; even so, a large crowd had gathered to get in early and grab their usual vantage points. Plenty of out-of-towners like us were in the vicinity, but I was in and that's all that mattered. At last I was on the Kop for a game, and there would only be two more games after this for the standing Kop as well. What a close shave.

The banter was as I had expected it to be. We weren't setting the world alight that season, but Ipswich were having an awful time and would finish bottom. 'You'll Never Walk Alone' took on that extra bit of significance for this supporter; I was used to holding my scarf up and singing towards the Kop, but now I was one of them, a Kopite, one small part of the most famous terrace in world football. Nothing can describe that feeling. I can remember it as if it was just last week. Liverpool won the toss, another good omen; we would be attacking the Kop in the second half, yippee! I was sure there would be goals galore in the second half and I would be there to suck the ball in along with the rest of the famous Kopites. Or so I thought at the time.

Well, what a dire affair my game turned out to be. Not only that, but it was a very cold April morning. We had snow, hail and rain, and I was just freezing, despite being surrounded by fellow supporters. I shudder to think what the Paddock and Annie Road end would have been like. After a forgettable first half and equally forgettable second, it was looking bleak until Don Hutchison, who had replaced Robbie Fowler, was bundled over in the box in the 75th minute and the ref pointed to the spot. Happy days. "Knock it in yourself, Don lad!" I roared, only for Julian Dicks to amble forward and grab the ball, as a few gasps were heard from the Kop. "Just drive it down the middle, Dicks" (which incidentally he never managed to do as a golf professional a few years later). Nevertheless, today he delivered, bang, straight down the middle it went. Get in there! It was the last meaningful action in the game to be fair, but I was happy enough. I got my goal at my end, and the three points were in the bag.

Before we knew it we were in a taxi across to Aintree racecourse. Having as much knowledge of horseracing as Everton have of European Cup victories, I was in need of inspiration. Local comic Freddie Starr was on the monitor and I overheard a few punters saying he had a runner in the big one. That'll do for me, so it was Freddie Starr's horse Miinnehoma at £20 on the nose, and back to the ale until the race started. He romped home in style and it was only when I went to collect the winnings that I even bothered to look at the odds: a cool 16/1. This betting lark was a doddle.

What a night in town we had after that. We drank most of it, of course, although I did treat myself to a little something: a spanking new 100-watt light bulb for the hotel room. Well I thought I might as well splash out!

DAVID MOEN

2005 Carling Cup final, Liverpool v Chelsea

From left: Darren Williamson, Grumps (Paul Lynch), Sparky (Adrian Gallagher), Kevin Neely

THREE days before the 2005 Carling Cup final, we discovered that our application for tickets had been successful. This was Rafa's first cup final, and ours.

Flights to Cardiff were expensive, always a problem when booking at late notice. Birmingham and Stansted were the next closest, but the times and costs of trains meant that we'd be better flying to Cardiff. The ferry from Rosslare to Swansea also came into our thoughts, as did Dublin-Holyhead, but the times were such that we'd need to have already left Donegal. In the end, we decided to fly to Liverpool on the Saturday night and hire a car from there to take us to

Cardiff. We got to Liverpool around 11pm and discovered – to our horror – that the Hertz desk had closed! The only desk that was open was Europecar, but they had no cars left.

We had nowhere to stay and getting to Cardiff the next morning would be a big problem as the trains had already been booked up. As we continued to explore what few possibilities we had, the young girl behind the Europecar desk called us over. Someone had cancelled a car and we were in luck! A Ford Fiesta wouldn't have been our first choice but it would do the trick. We flew down the road as quickly as we could. Darren got the shock of his life when he realised how far away Cardiff was – we didn't find our hotel until 4am.

We had only ever seen the Millennium Stadium on TV, and it looked even more spectacular when we were inside. Our view was surreal, high up behind the goal that Liverpool would defend in the first half, and we couldn't have wished for a better start as Morientes crossed for Riise in the first minute to blast home one of his trademark volleys. What a sight it was to see the net bulge. Just 89 minutes to hang on! Chelsea, despite their possession, didn't threaten much, and it was Liverpool that came closest to scoring in the second half when Gerrard just failed to connect with a cross. The skipper, however, would find the target before the game ended, just a pity that it was in the wrong net.

We were gutted. There were only eight minutes to go and we had genuinely believed that the cup was ours. Mourinho was sent off for mocking the Liverpool fans with his shush antics and we could see him exiting down the tunnel on the big screens. The game went into extra-time and we now feared the worse. Chelsea ran out 3-2 winners. So it was commiserating around the bars of Cardiff instead of celebrating.

KEVIN NEELY

Liverpool do a 'Roy of the Rovers'

THE lads I travel with consist of Karl, Thompson, Barry and Kev. There are so many stories we have, but I'll just start off with the 2004/05 Holy Grail season in Europe. I had been to quite a few Premier League games before the Olympiakos tie, but this was our first of the season as a group. We had organised tickets for the match via the ticket hotline, so we all hopped on a 6.30am boat from Dublin to Holyhead before getting two trains to Lime Street.

After collecting our tickets we went straight to our 'local', The Park, which is always the place to get the passion boiling before the game. We were in the Centenary Stand with a

Noely, Thompson and Karl, and the 'Dublin Crew'

'Karl, Thompson and Barry just piled on top of me and I knew the cup was ours for keeps'

touchline view. The atmosphere was absolutely fantastic; I'd never witnessed anything like it. When Gerrard scored that 86th-minute screamer, the whole ground erupted.

When the quarter-finals came around, we travelled over to watch the Reds take on Juventus on the telly. Some people might think we are mad for spending more than six hours travelling just to watch our team on the TV, but Liverpool supporters live for the team.

Our next escapade was the semi-final against Chelsea, when we went via Blackpool and tickets were like gold dust. They couldn't be located for love nor money (well £1,000 probably would have procured one, but I just couldn't afford it), so we watched the game in The Park pub. After the final whistle, the scenes outside the Kop were legendary.

The day after we got back, the first thing on the agenda was to get to Istanbul. We tried every travel agent in Dublin and eventually found something. It would cost us €2,000 each for one night. We left Dublin airport at 5.30am on a direct flight. Unfortunately, our digs were in the Asian part of Istanbul, about two hours away from the ground in a place that had more cats in it than people. We didn't care. We'd made it to Istanbul and were part of Rafa's army.

After a few drinks we were off on a two-hour bus trip to the Ataturk Stadium. It was like we were the Turkish national team returning with the World Cup as we drove along with scarves hanging out the window – we got an unbelievable reception from the locals. Traffic was so bad that we walked the final part of the journey, like pilgrims across the desert to our destiny. We finally got into the ground about 20 minutes before kick-off, only to find we were in amongst the Milan fans. With the way the first half went, it was an absolute nightmare being in that part of the ground. We had to get out of there, and easily made our way to the Liverpool end in time for the 'You'll Never Walk Alone' half-time rallying call.

The second half was like a Roy of the Rovers comic. Every clearance and tackle won by Stevie and the lads was cheered like at no game I have been to before. The penos were just a blur really. I couldn't watch Shevchenko take his, so I turned and faced the other way. Karl, Thompson and Barry piled on top of me and I knew the cup was ours for keeps.

NOEL CARROLL

Our night with legend Carra

IT was the week of the 2006 derby at Anfield. We managed to get word to Jamie Carragher that we were coming across for the weekend and we had a player of the season trophy to present him with. If it had been a Friday morning, we could have dropped in to Melwood and met him after training. Unfortunately, we weren't arriving until later that afternoon. In our minds we thought we might get to meet up with him after the game the next day. On Thursday evening at around half-eight my phone rang and it was the man himself. "I believe you're over for the game," Carra said. "I just wanted to see what your plans are. I'll pass on my number and you can come out to my house."

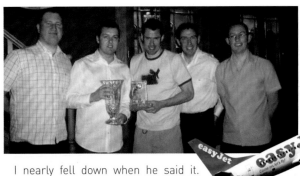

I nearly fell down when he said it. When we got there he showed us his games room where all his medals and shirts were displayed on the wall. He took out his European Cup medal from Istanbul, his UEFA Cup medal from 2001, the FA Cup medals. We were delighted to get our photo taken with all of them. We must have spent half an hour in his house. This was at half six on the Friday evening, and we were due to play Everton at quarter to one the next day. He was so relaxed and telling us about how it was his favourite game of the season.

"Do you think we'll win?" we asked. "Yeah, if we get the first one, they'll have to come forward and we'll pick them off," he replied. It did actually happen that way, with Phil Neville opening the scoring, so Jamie was spot on.

KIERAN POWER
Waterford Supporters' Club

Alan Murphy compares his real Istanbul ticket with a fake one that his mum picked up at a market

Bonding with Bob in the Ataturk Stadium

"WHAT'S bleedin' goin' on?" sobs the loner standing to my left in the Upper East Tribune stand of the Ataturk Olympic Stadium. Crespo has just scored his first of the night, and the Reds are two-nil down. I'm hurting; we're all hurting. But this man – I'll call him Bobby Biscan for want of his real name – is easily the most emotionally distraught man in Turkey, if not the universe. "What's bleedin' goin' on?" he repeats. I pray his question is rhetorical, but his body language suggests otherwise. This unhinged stranger is imploring me for some consolation. What does he want me to say?

Bob arrived at his seat in great spirits, grinning broadly, singing in unison with his LFC brethren. And then 'You'll Never Walk Alone' started. He got only as far as "When you walk..." before slumping onto his seat and suffering an emotional meltdown, the swiftness and severity of which I have never seen the like. I love the Red Army camaraderie as much as the next man, and I patted Bob on the shoulder enthusiastically, telling him not to worry.

This was a fatal error. Bob locked onto my hand with a vice-like grip. It would be 15 minutes before I managed to pry myself loose, but by then it was too late: in Bob's mind we had bonded, and I was now his deflective shield against the onset of a full-blown, football-induced nervous breakdown.

"It's going to be ok Bob. Everything's going to be ok," I chance. "Promise?" he sniffles. I nod diagonally, aiming for as noncommittal a response as possible. Bob takes it as a yes. At that moment, not even Rick Parry has more of a vested interest in AC Milan not scoring a third goal than me. Bob is not the kind of person you want feeling that he's been lied to. The man is enormous. His hulking frame stands only inches shy of seven feet, with the combined girth of Jan Molbian Siamese twins. Appropriately, his decades-old Crown Paints jersey may well not be a jersey at all, but body paint, such is its tightness to his giant exoskeleton.

He's a fellow Dubliner, but he hails from a far tougher realm of the Emerald Isle's fair capital than myself. His beard grows visibly and audibly over the course of the game. This glass-chewing goliath makes Grizzly Adams look like Miss World. Crespo. Three-nil. "You promised," weeps Bob. I'm considering having a crafty cry myself. Half-time arrives, creating a 15-minute void in which shock could easily mutate to depression – not just for Bob, but on a mass scale.

How can Jesus/Allah/Buddha/Vishnu/Tom Cruise allow this to happen? I know they're busy guys, but consider the romance of the occasion: the stadium is awash with Liverpool Red. The Italians? Sure there's only a handful of them: 50 or 60 by my count. My phone vibrates frantically as supporters back home of every non-Liverpudlian hue come out of the woodwork, their gleefully sarcastic text messages laced with the arsenic of gloating and schadenfreude.

We are shell-shocked. It appears that Mr Shankly was right: football really is that important. Never has the beautiful game brought me so terribly low. Strange then, that from the unlikeliest ashes of despair was born my proudest-ever moment as a card-carrying member of the Liverpool faithful. Our club's indomitable, unsinkable fans suppress their personal grief to rally a rendition of 'You'll Never Walk Alone' for which the cliche "spine-tingling" seems scarcely sufficient. The chiselled words echo, crashing against the stadium walls, bewildering the Italians.

It isn't a war cry as such, it's more an act of proud defiance; a salute to our team, who we know are facing (seemingly) insurmountable odds, not through any lack of passion or desire. Moments before the commencement of the six craziest, most euphoric minutes in footballing history, I remember thinking to myself: "Hang on, I've a hunch that Smicer and a couple of his cronies are going to bang in three quick goals here and level the tie." Ok, that is an out-and-out lie. Truth is, try as I might, I can't remember a helluva lot about those six minutes, save the unbridled ecstasy.

It was numbing, and surreal, and I was terrified that any moment it would all be taken away. I remember turning to Bob after the equaliser and saying: "Told you it would be ok", but he was too overcome to register my words. His eyes had

rolled up into the back of his head, and he was rocking back 'n' forth, mumbling a load of gibberish that sounded suspiciously like 'The Anfield Rap', except in Irish.

At 3-3, surely we had exhausted our supply of heroes? Arise Jerzy Dudek. I've never had the pleasure of making the offer personally, but let the record show that Jerzy Dudek is more than welcome to my first-born (apologies, future wife). Or if the Pole needs a kidney? I'm there. In fact, take two! I might even throw in a liver.

With the greatest-ever cup final concluded, and the emotional roller coaster's terminus in sight, I thought I'd throw Bob a congratulatory hug. Welding himself to me, the completely exhausted, borderline catatonic Bob simply would not let go. The minutes rolled by, the stands emptied, the floodlights dimmed, but still Bob held fast, rooted to his spot. I believe we were the last two fans to belatedly leave the stadium.

The man cried from the match's first whistle to its last penalty kick, and it got me thinking: what is it about this great club of ours that can reduce a burly Irishman to a gibbering wreck? What instills in us so much love for a football club whose shores we don't even hail from? We were born on the Liffey, not the Mersey. Why were 10,000 of my fellow countrymen (approximately 20% of the overall travelling contingent) irresistibly drawn to Istanbul, like moths to a flame?

What I would argue is that the attraction transcends football; I don't doubt that the great success of Liverpool in the '70s and '80s was a huge recruitment drive, but to be exalted as the sole reason? Far too lazy, and convenient. I believe there is an intangible, cultural bond between Ireland and Liverpool, and that this bond has always cultivated an affinity between the two peoples. You don't necessarily have to know that in 1850, 25% of Liverpool's population was made up of Irish emigrants.

These cultural memes are not lost, but are passed from generation to generation, not by the memorising of statistics, but through unconscious subtleties: perhaps the warmth and affection with which an Irishman's father speaks of the city of Liverpool, as his father did before him, and his father before him, all the way back to periods such as the 1850s, when the bond was more concrete.

As an Irishman, supporting Liverpool just feels right. I knew it even when I was a nipper.

ALAN MURPHY
Irish Dublin Red

> 'The attraction transcends football; I believe there is an intangible, cultural bond between Ireland and Liverpool, and that this bond has always cultivated an affinity between the two peoples'

'They are due to turn someone over soon'

THE Holiday Inn, October 1979, 15 years old. The day of the Anfield derby. One of the teams was due in the hotel for a pre-match meal and to watch 'Football Focus'. And a team did arrive...Everton. Lyons, Wood, Gidman and King. "Not today, Andy!" (He scored!) "Never mind," said the porter, a friendly staff member nearing retirement. "The Reds will do it today. They are due to turn someone over very soon." This man obviously had the inside track, the local knowledge.

We were barely in our seats when Mike Lyons scored an og. Right about then, from the Kemlyn Road, I caught sight, away to my left, of the Kop. I knew all the legends, but now, there it was – a huge singing, heaving mass of good-humoured devotion. Furthermore, the wall posters, the Shoot Focuses, were all alive and right in front of me. These were not people; these were gods that I only knew from Peter Jones and Alan Parry on BBC Radio 2 at eight o'clock on a midweek night. This was getting better and better, but Everton had not read the script. Kidd and King put them 2-1 up, and we were struggling to get into it.

Suddenly Ray Kennedy scored: 2-2. Now we'd sit back and take the points, but then it all kicked off. Right in front of our eyes a mass brawl and an Everton player sent off. Good riddance, but what's this? That's not Terry McDermott is it? Why is he walking off? Now, Graeme Souness we could believe, but Terry Mac? Fair enough; in hindsight breaking Garry Stanley's tooth with a ring was probably a sending-off offence, but only in hindsight.

Suddenly, a hand across my eyes. What the...!!! "Don't look...don't look!!" Oh my God, what is she doing running across the pitch half naked? Play stopped, Ray Clemence is laughing. The Bizzies arrived and as soon as she was on the pitch, she was gone. Like a Howard Gayle European appearance. And so it finished 2-2 and we were back in the hotel, waiting patiently for the *Pink Echo*.

Here's Alan Kennedy, a gentleman, even with a sponsored Lada outside the door of the hotel. Graeme Souness arrives and meets someone in the bar. Here goes, heart racing!! A long walk. "Mr Souness?" He turns.

"Could you sign this please?" With perfect courtesy, he signs. I thank him and I'm off. Did that really happen? Phil Thompson, back with Mike Lyons, laughing and joking. This was human and real, not staged for TV. And then it's over and before I know it I'm back in Cork. So they didn't turn Everton over, but what a debut game. The following week, away at Man City, a 4-0 win. After all, they were due to turn someone over!

KEVIN J FOLEY

Mr Souness ... could you sign this please?

European glory: it's in the bag

I HAVE been a Liverpool fan for a lifetime. My mother recognised that this Liverpool thing was more than a passing fad. My friends in school began to arrive with kit bags with the names and crests of the teams they supported emblazoned on the side. I begged for a Liverpool bag, and my mother relented after much pressure. She went to the local sports shop and asked the shop assistant if she could see a couple of samples. The guy in the shop duly obliged and my mother spotted the one she was going to buy. "I like this one," she said, pointing to one of the three bags, "but, you wouldn't happen to have one of these in blue by any chance?" Trying to be polite, and I am sure trying to keep a straight face, the assistant replied: "Eh, no madam. You see, Liverpool are the Reds..."

Early memories include watching Liverpool dominate Europe. At the age of eight I watched the Reds play in the 1977 European Cup final against Borussia Monchengladbach (I remember thinking at the time: "How do you sing a song about a football team with a name like that?"). Paisley was at the helm. Keegan wore the number seven. Emlyn held Old Big Ears aloft, and so the love affair with the trophy began. The following year we were at it again. King Kenny weaved in and out of the box in Wembley and scored the only goal of the night. Emlyn once again provided the big toothy grin at the end, and number two was in the bag. Magic. Pure magic.

The original Big Phil ... Thommo lifts Ol' Big Ears

**Walk On ...
the spirit of
Liverpool lives
strong in
Ireland**

A three-year hiatus takes us to 1981. There were some new faces in the team but Paisley was still in command. Loyalties were divided in our house that night. My mother (from the Canary Islands) was rooting for Real Madrid. Of all people, Barney Rubble stepped up to secure number three. This time it was the original Big Phil that raised the trophy. On to 1984. Joe Fagan was the new boss. We played Roma in their backyard. Lawrenson, Whelan and Robinson were all on the pitch at the same time (during extra-time). The hero of the night turned out to be wobbly-legs Grobbelaar. Souey's last act as a Liverpool player was to accept the trophy for the fourth time. This European thing was becoming a bit of a walk in the park.

Heysel. How could this tragedy have happened? It still seems surreal every time you see the video footage of what happened in Brussels. What followed just four years later was the worst day in LFC history. Ninety-six Reds will never be forgotten. You'll Never Walk Alone.

Our first daughter Alicia was born on 25 April 2005. Two weeks after she was born I broke my thumb in the back garden. It needed two rounds of surgery in the space of a week. Having been assured of a ticket for the final by a close friend, my trip to Istanbul was in doubt. I put the case to my wife that it had been 20 years since the last time Liverpool were in the European Cup final and that this might not happen again for another 20 years. (You can imagine the conversation when we got to the final two years later in Athens!) I paid a ridiculous amount of money for a flight that would take me to Istanbul in the morning and depart immediately after the game.

Standing in the queue in Dublin airport on the morning of the 25th of May, I bumped into an old friend of mine, Barry, who grew up around the corner from me in Dublin. Neither of us knew the other was a Red. It was a friendship renewed, as we did the trip to Istanbul together and we now meet up with a gang of fellow Reds for most European nights.

The story of Istanbul is the stuff of legend. We were lucky enough to have been there to see it. The spirit of Liverpool lives strong in Ireland. Hopefully we will be fortunate enough

to see other Irish stars play a role in the search for more European Cups and league titles.

ROBERT MANSON

The birth of a Liverbird called Rhys

ONE match I will always remember took place at Anfield on 9 November 2003: Liverpool v Man Utd. It was the first Liverpool game I took my four-year-old son Rhys to. I normally watched the 'clash of the titans' in the Bot bar in Belfast, usually over some guy's shoulder. I'd dreamt of being at Anfield. Finally, here I was, and the icing on the cake was my wee Rhys being there beside me.

Our seats were in the Main Stand, Kop End. Rhys seemed in awe of his surroundings, especially Peter Sampara, or 'badgeman' as Rhys called him, who would occasionally turn around, face us and burst into song. As the match went on, Rhys got more and more into it, shouting, singing and clapping. In the second half, Man Utd went 1-0 up courtesy of Giggs. Rhys looked disheartened, but I kept whispering with intent: "Never give up, never give up."

Then 10 minutes later Giggs struck again, 2-0, and once more I whispered with an undertone of passion: "Liverpool never give up; you watch." Sure enough, Kewell hit back about five minutes later, and Rhys was up off his seat. He was now a Liverpool supporter. Final whistle: Liverpool 1 Man Utd 2. "Ah well, you can't win them all," I said to Rhys as we walked hand

in hand down the steps. "But daddy you said..." Rhys slipped and missed a couple of steps, giving me a scare, but not as much as it scared him because he started crying and was unable to finish his sentence. None other than 'the badgeman' saw Rhys crying, and thinking he was overwrought with disappointment, he knelt down, looked him in the eye and with a ruffle of his hair said in a strong Scouse accent: "Don't worry kid, we'll get them back at Old Trafford." A Liverbird named Rhys was born.

WEDNESDAY 25 May 2005. Istanbul, AC Milan v Liverpool. Score: 3-0 to AC Milan. It was the start of the second half and I was more than disappointed to say the least; head down, betting slip crumpled. Rhys, who was now six, looked up at me and said: "Remember daddy what you said." I asked him what, to which he replied: "Never give up, never give up."

I smiled that he remembered but also I knew he was right. I suppose in a way that's why Irish people support Liverpool, because of the resilience of the team, the never-say-die attitude that was founded by the Liverpool people more than 100 years ago, and has stayed throughout the team even to this day.

**TONY MCGREGOR
County Down, Northern Ireland**

> 'That's why Irish people support Liverpool, because of the resilience of the team, the never-say-die attitude that was founded by the Liverpool people more than 100 years ago'

'Nothing will hurt more than this'

MAY 20, 1989. We'd just beaten Everton 3-2 in a dramatic and emotional FA Cup final, and we were ecstatic. Amid the euphoria, my dad promised we'd go to see history being made next Friday night against Arsenal: the first-ever double double. I was 11 years old.

We set off on Thursday morning: my dad and sister came along too. It was quite a trek from Northern Ireland to Liverpool as, about a year earlier, the Belfast to Liverpool ferry stopped operating, as did the Dublin to Liverpool ferry. It meant a five-hour bus journey from Derry to Dublin to catch the ferry to Holyhead in North Wales. The ferry docked around 1.30am on Friday morning after a short crossing.

Then we had to wait at the Holyhead train station, which is right on the docks, until 4.30am for the train to depart for Chester. About an hour-and-a-half later we arrived in Chester, and it was already beginning to look like a scorcher of a day. The sun was blasting through the glass roof as we waited for the train to take us to Hooton.

From there we got the underground to Lime Street, arriving at 7.30am, 20 hours after our journey first began. Once there, we had only one thing on our minds: three match tickets. We didn't have any and there were rumours on the boat that there would be a cash turnstile. At 9am we went up to Anfield and checked the Kop. All we could find were 'ticket only' signs. We paid £60 in total, which left us with a fiver for the whole day. It didn't matter; we had tickets to see history being made.

Everyone knows we didn't make

history that night thanks to a certain Michael Thomas. But the two abiding memories that will live with me forever are coming out after the game in floods of tears and my dad saying to me: "Well son, no matter what you see in football during the rest of your life, nothing will hurt more than this."

I looked up at him and thought: "What's he on about?" But over the years, as I understood the game more, those words rang true.

MICHAEL HARKIN
Derry

2001 UEFA Cup semi-final, Liverpool 1 Barcelona 0

MY buddy and me travelled from Limerick to Dublin, got the boat over to Holyhead and then headed up to Anfield. I couldn't wait to get there. After we dropped off our bags at the hotel, we went straight to the ground - the atmosphere was crazy. I cried my eyes out when 'You'll Never Walk Alone' was played. I was in the Kop. My friend was actually a Villa fan and wouldn't sing or cheer for the Pool. Gary McAllister scored a penalty to win the game as we sang all night and partied until 6am.

LIAM MULCAHY
Limerick

A Titanic tale

IN 2005, shortly after Istanbul, I went with my mother over to Cork, to meet up with the Irish side of the family who she hadn't seen in years. While there, we were advised to visit Cobh, which was the last place the Titanic visited before it left on its ill-fated journey across the Atlantic in 1912. Everyone said the town was famous for its Titanic Museum - I commented that the place is more famous because Roy Keane began his career at Cobh Ramblers before being signed by Brian Clough and Nottingham Forest.

After the museum tour we went into the large pub directly across the road. I walked in thinking I might ask the locals a few questions about their 'favourite son', Roy Keane, who would obviously be a legend in these parts. To my surprise, the place was decorated with the red and white of Liverpool FC! There were massive flags, banners, scarves, hats, photos and souvenirs of every sort. There were also lots of framed pictures from the locals' trips over to Anfield. When I asked about Keane, they didn't seem at all interested in him, and just wanted to talk about Liverpool.

I then went on to proudly show the locals my Istanbul ticket stub, which I was carrying around with me in my wallet, and was instantly treated like a celebrity. We had a fantastic next hour or so in the pub exchanging LFC stories, and me exploring all the souvenirs they had pinned up around the pub. It was far more interesting, and enjoyable, than the Titanic Museum.

JOHN JONES
Liverpool

Santa makes appearance in May

A GROUP of us travelled over for the Liverpool v Man City Sunday game at Anfield in May 2008. We'd been promised tickets but they never materialised, so we went out on the Saturday night to get over our disappointment. Next morning, I woke up in some building wearing just my t-shirt and socks. I had no idea what happened, but I had lost my shoes, boxers, shirt, chain, wallet, phone and camera. I was obviously in a bad way as two girls spotted me and took pity on me by taking me into their office and giving me some coffee. They also had a look for some clothes, although all they could find was a Santa suit. Having no alternative, I put it on and went back to the apartment where we were staying. Unfortunately, I was locked out, but the people in the next apartment loaned me some shoes and the cab fare up to Anfield.

I went into The Albert for a pre-match singsong before heading outside and somehow bumping into my mates. We managed to get tickets for the Kop and I went into the ground, still wearing the Santa outfit. Of course we won 1-0 and I even got shown on Setanta. Afterwards, I walked past David Moores who found my appearance highly amusing.

PAUL FAHY

Taken for a ride

AFTER a few hours in work on a Friday morning, I received a call from my friend Adam. He informed me that he was off to Liverpool with Paul, another mate of ours. I went home on my motorbike, got in Adam's van and picked up Paul.

We went straight to the off-licence and then hurried ourselves onto the ferry at North Wall in Dublin port. Quietly enjoying a few beers on board, the first part of our journey was pretty quick. Next was the train to Liverpool, and buses or taxis from there on. However, not all went to plan. Adam, in his merry ways, wandered off while we were waiting for our train.

Paul and I searched Holyhead inside out and, with no credit on our

Many fans from across the Irish Sea have visited The Park pub by Anfield – some travel over to watch the game there

mobiles, he had to be forgotten. Because we were looking for him we missed our train and had to wait for the next one. Holyhead is not the best place to spend eight to 10 hours; it was quite boring! We eventually arrived in Liverpool at 6am on Saturday morning, having left Dublin port at 3.30pm the previous day.

What I didn't mention is that my mate Paul had found out he had a half-sister in Liverpool, and we were to stay with her, so we all had the address if we got lost. Paul and I, still bemused at where Adam had got to, arrived at her house in a taxi at around 6.30am. We knocked at the door and to our disbelief Adam opened it.

Our first thoughts were: "Are you ok?", and then it was: "How the hell did you get here before us?" After a few laughs, he explained he got a taxi from Holyhead to Liverpool, thinking it was not that far. He had wandered off for a bag of chips and didn't know how to get back to the port. So instead of asking someone how to get there, he thought he should get a taxi. £250 it set him back. To make it even worse, or better for us, he's a United fan.

NIALL OWENS
Dublin

Bumping into my Liverpool heroes

I GO over to Anfield a couple of times every year, and in August 2006 I brought my family over: at the time my seven-year-old twin girls and their nine-year-old sister. We had to stay in a hotel outside the city. On the Friday night before our first home league game of the season against West Ham, we were in the bar of the hotel. My girls were dressed from head to toe in their Liverpool gear. I went to the bar for a drink and the girls followed.

There were two men at the bar having a drink and one of them noticed the girls and started to chat to them about their favourite player, etc. He then proceeded to say that his mate beside him played for Liverpool years ago. It was only then that I realised when I looked at his mate that it was David Johnson.

We spoke for a few minutes and I asked my wife to go to the car and get the camera so I could get some photos, which she did reluctantly. We were beside the door of the bar and she took one photo and then proceeded to take another, and who should walk in but Alan Kennedy, who was arranging to meet David Johnson there that night, so we managed to get our photos taken with Alan as well.

The next day after our 2-1 victory over the Hammers we were back in the hotel restaurant having our meal. David Johnson

actually saw us and came into the restaurant and chatted to us about the game, asking the girls if they enjoyed it, etc. He suggested that we go to the bar as he had all his medals there from his playing days, so we could see them. He was an absolute gentleman, who was totally down to earth with no airs and graces about him. The end result was that instead of me bringing my girls to Liverpool to see their heroes that they saw on television every week, I was the one who actually got to see two of my heroes in the flesh. It is something that I will never forget.

PADRAIG MCDERMOTT
Dunboyne, County Meath

Across the Atlantic for a Crouchie hat-trick

I WAS born in Mississauga in Ontario, Canada but my father and all his family hail from Lurgan, Northern Ireland. All of my dad's family still live there. In 2007, a trip was planned to visit them. I had not been to Northern Ireland for a few years, but I was glad to get the chance to do so, as Liverpool were smack bang in the middle of their Champions League and Premier League campaigns. I was excited about Liverpool's first-leg quarter-final against PSV Eindhoven later in my holiday, as it was to be televised. The Arsenal match a few days earlier would be watched in a pub nearby. Little did I know that my dad had pulled some strings to procure tickets for the game against the Gunners.

On the Friday night before the match, my dad handed me two tickets. My hands started to shake and a smile broke out across my face. I could not believe I was going to Anfield for the first time, let alone to see the mighty Reds play against another big-four club. That night I was uncontrollably jubilant and couldn't sleep.

The following morning we rushed to Belfast International Airport. Accents from the north and south of Ireland were heard all through the half-hour flight. Awakening the next morning, I was ready for my first game at Anfield. My grandfather had been here before, as well as my father. I was the third generation of LFC supporters in my family, and I was playing my role in it.

In we went, and I remember being glared at by people in the upper seats as we made our way to the eighth row from the front. I couldn't believe how close we were, and then it hit me. I looked to my left and there it was: within 20 feet of my seat was the Kop. It wasn't quite full at that moment,

but I knew from years of watching matches what it looked like. I could already see it in my head, scarves up in the air, enormous Liverbird flag waving in the centre of the first row behind the net. The Ulster and tricolour flag swaying beside one another in between the red-and-yellow-chequered flag of Liverpool.

Just as Peter Crouch kicked off the game, four Scousers sat in front of us. One heard me talking to my dad and asked where my accent was from. I told him Canada. My dad then informed them that this was my first trip to the ground. All four of them turned around, shook my hand firmly and said: "Welcome to Anfield."

There were a few minutes of knocking the ball about before the giraffe-like Crouch netted our first. We couldn't see it very well, as it was at the Anfield Road End. But we definitely knew a goal had been scored as a terrific sound rose up from the rows of seats. Before the end of the half, Crouchie popped the ball in again to make it 2-0. At half-time my father went out and about the stadium while I sat there marvelling at the sheer magnitude of it all. I still couldn't believe I was actually there.

As the second half kicked off, I was even more excited as Liverpool were kicking towards the Kop. On the hour mark, Daniel Agger headed one in. The first goal I'd witnessed at the Kop End, it was magnificent. The four Scousers in front of us all hugged me and patted me on the back. It was wonderful camaraderie.

Arsenal struck back with one, but it didn't rain on my or Liverpool's parade. Then the tall man did it. He potted his treble with his left foot, a mere 30 feet from where I was sitting. The crowd went ballistic. With three fingers in the air, Crouch ran towards our corner, blowing kisses. It was the closest I'd ever been to a Liverpool player.

The game wound down and we cheered at the top of our lungs, thanking Liverpool for providing us with such great memories.

A man asked my dad to take a photo of him and his girlfriend. They told us they were from South Africa and just came over for the match. It was amazing how the simple sport of football could bring so many people, of so many different walks of life, together.

ROBBIE MCDONALD
Mississauga, Ontario, Canada

Mad rush to the Champions League parade

IT'S 10.30am, 26 May 2005. I wake up with a sore head after the greatest night of my life. I still can't stop smiling about the previous night's madness in the Submarine Bar in Crumlin and the celebrations afterwards throughout

Fans await the Champions League victory parade outside The Albert near Anfield in 2005

Dublin. There isn't a Man Utd fan in sight; they are all in hiding, which makes a change.

I check my phone, only to see I've received more calls and texts in the previous night than I had in my whole life. I have a load of missed calls from my friend John, who's somehow managed to get up for work in the bank. I ring him to see what he wants, and in a panic he tells me he has been trying to make contact all morning. He and two of his work colleagues are standing out in Dublin Port in their suits waiting on the boat to Liverpool, due to depart at 11.00am after pleading for the day off from their boss.

There is no way of getting from my bed in Clondalkin (south Dublin) to the docks (north Dublin) in a half-hour. I hang up gutted at the prospect of missing out on the homecoming of all homecomings. Five minutes later, I get another call from John. He tells me that Stena Line have put on a boat to go to Liverpool at midday for €20 return, and to get out of bed asap and run over to his ma's house to get her to pack a bag for him. I ring Ian and Ronan to tell them to get out of bed too; we're off to Liverpool. Ian's ma kindly agrees to drop us out to the docks. I throw some clothes in the bag and literally run out the door before getting John's bag off his ma, who thinks her son has totally lost the plot.

It's now a race against the clock to get from Clondalkin to the docks. John is waiting with our three tickets. We're all buzzing with excitement. I hand John his bag which his ma has packed when Ian suddenly realises it's his brother's Man Utd training bag. At midday about 300 hardcore fans

from Ireland, half of which are still ill from the night before, are boarding the boat still singing our hearts out.

The trip over is brilliant, with a homeless bloke to our amazement leading the singsongs all the way. We arrive at roughly four o'clock, but are left waiting to dock for about 40 minutes. We finally landed and stopped off at the Ibis Hotel to see if we could get a room for the night, but they were totally booked up and told us that all the other hotels were too. They kindly offered to store our bags for us in the office till after the parade, a big relief for John as he could dump his Man Utd bag at this point. We made our way up towards St John's shopping centre. It was amazing, a sea of Red everywhere and the whole place was buzzing.

There were people hanging out of windows, climbing trees, and on top of buildings. It was just madness. I really believe that we (Liverpool fans) are the most hardcore supporters in England/Ireland, and it was a day like this that really proved it. After about an hour waiting, in the distance we could see blue flashing lights coming towards us and we knew instantly that the team bus was about to finally come our way. As it got closer, we could see Jamie Carragher and Stevie G at the front holding the Champions League trophy with great pride!

Djimi Traore and Djibril Cisse at the back of the bus were dancing like lunatics; Cisse appeared to have no clothes on at all! And as soon as they had arrived, they were gone again. But in that quick passing, we appreciated everything the team had done for us the night before in Istanbul. We were simply there to say: "Thanks, you make us proud to support LFC." The lads had sweated blood to come from the brink of disaster to the heights of heroes. It really was a special moment; one myself, John, Ian and Ronan will cherish for the rest of our lives.

ALAN BOLGER, IAN EARLY, JOHN DUFFY, RONAN CONNOLLY

A family affair

MY family's association with the city of Liverpool goes back about six generations. All of them were coopers, working mainly for Guinness here in Dublin. But they also did quite a bit of travelling as it was a seasonal trade, so every one of them worked in Liverpool at one time or another.

The relationship was cemented further when Ronnie Whelan signed for the Reds in '79. My uncle Matt Butler had been Ronnie's manager at Home Farm Football Club. It was pretty easy to get tickets in those days so I have some great memories of the '80s and early '90s. I still try to go over a couple of times every year but it's a nightmare trying to get tickets, so when I won a trip to the Champions League final

'It was amazing how the simple sport of football could bring so many people, of so many different walks of life, together' in Istanbul, I couldn't believe my luck. It was the most surreal experience of my life. To be honest it took me about nine months to convince myself it wasn't all a dream. But I have plenty of photo evidence to back it up.

SHANE BUTLER
Dublin

€1,200 for three minutes of football

THE story I want to tell is about the game against Barcelona. As usual, tickets were like gold dust, so we had to book through one of the travel companies in Dublin. Excitement in the house was building for weeks. I'd arranged for days off work, and my son was telling all his friends he was going. The day finally arrived and off we went on the plane. We checked into our hotel, dumped the bags and headed for Anfield. I had a knot in my stomach all week, but now we were 'home' it seemed to have gotten bigger. My nerves were frayed.

I had my son on my shoulders so he could see over the crowds. I saw the great Barcelona goalkeeper Andoni Zubizarreta walking along at the back of the Main Stand, and stopped him to say hello and got him to shake hands with my son. We were sitting in the upper deck of the Anfield Road End, in the very last row, my head almost hitting the roof. The teams came out to warm up and we both sat in awe of Ronaldinho with all the tricks he displayed.

The noise coming from the Kop that night was the loudest I had ever heard; the hairs on the back of my neck were standing on end. I shouted 'You'll Never Walk Alone' as loud as I could; the emotions were at bursting point at this stage.

All this time I'd been focused on the pitch and the Kop, and hadn't really noticed my son. When I looked at him he was crying his eyes out. He told me he was scared of the noise. No matter what I tried, I couldn't calm him down. I decided he had to come first so we left the stadium. So after waiting weeks for the game, spending over €1,200 and travelling all that way, we saw approximately three minutes

'The noise coming from the Kop on the night of the Barcelona game in 2007 was the loudest I had ever heard; the hairs on the back of my neck were standing on end'

of the match. We watched the second half in our hotel room. Despite the loss on the night we got through.

I waited almost a full year before risking taking my little lad over again, this time for the semi-final against Chelsea. He seemed to handle the noise much better, even though it was louder than the previous year. However, when the match got started I took a look at him and he was sniggering. I asked what was his sniggering at, and he just said: "Dad, listen." When I heard what the crowd was singing, a little smile crossed my face and I said to him: "Don't you be listening to that." It was of course the reference to Chelsea's lack of history. Not the politest of songs, but it reminded them of just where they were, and who they were playing.

SHAY HURLEY

Brothers in arms

Tom Donohoe (right) with his brother Colin Hamell

I'M an Irish Red. Very briefly, here is my story. I'm adopted, no problem there, but it is relevant. In April '04 I found out at the age of 33 that I have a full-blood brother, only 11 months younger than me, who was also given up for adoption. We met for the first time in May '04 and celebrated a year later by attending our first Liverpool game together; he is also a mad Red! And what a game to pick: Istanbul!

TOM DONOHOE

Risking everything to support Liverpool

I SPENT the first 10 years of my life living on the Wirral and then moved to Northern Ireland. I've supported Liverpool as a child from the early '60s and, as soon as I could afford it, started to travel from Belfast to watch them in the '70s. In 1977, my kidneys failed. I had to go on dialysis two days a week, for eight hours at a time. It meant I was now too weak to travel to any matches, especially the European Cup finals in Rome and Wembley, which I had yearned for.

In 1981, Liverpool reached another European Cup final and after being very ill for a number of years and on a waiting list for a kidney transplant, a couple of my friends, Patrick McGivern and Larry Quinn, arranged a ticket for me to go to Paris. We had to organise the trip between two dialysis sessions. I was given an extra blood transfusion so that I would have enough energy to complete the journey, Belfast to Dublin to Paris and back. My consultant gave me special permission to travel. I was also on a severe fluid restriction and a strict diet, which made life much more difficult. Because of my condition, I couldn't get travel insurance.

Everything went well on the trip and I managed to cope physically, although I was exhausted when we arrived home the next day. Experiencing the Liverpool support was something I will always remember, especially the guys who looked after me on that trip. It must have been fate that brought me to that game, because that was the lowest point in my life and very shortly afterwards I got the 'magic' phone call to say that there was a kidney available for me.

I was transplanted and went on to enjoy 18 fantastic years of 'new life'. During that time I got married, fathered three sons and continued my undying support for Liverpool Football Club, travelling across the Irish Sea as often as I could afford it and using all forms of transport. I also introduced my sons to the delights of Anfield.

Then in 1999, my transplanted kidney failed and I had to return to dialysis. This time it was 'only' for four hours at a time, but every other day. Again it was going to be difficult to get to games. Again I was at a low point in my life. Again Liverpool got to a final, this time in Dortmund. I had to go. A great friend and work colleague of mine, John Moore, organised a ticket for me and I made all the travel arrangements. This time it was Belfast to Brussels to Dusseldorf to Dortmund and back. Everything went according to plan, particularly the result.

Twenty years had passed and I had completed the journey to another final. It was then that I vowed to follow Liverpool to any future finals. So off I went to the daddy of all experiences, Istanbul, still on dialysis, still having to arrange my trips between sessions. John Moore again went on this trip with me, which was a direct flight from Belfast. Athens was next, only this time I took my sons with me. Unfortunately, the result didn't go our way, but the experience was still memorable. God knows when or where our next final will be, but if I'm alive and able, I'll be there.

MICHAEL CONNOLLY
Northern Ireland

Close encounters of the Red kind

"THE tickets are gone. I sold them to someone else." With those words my heart sank. Five minutes earlier, we'd been celebrating the fact that we were off to see the Reds face Manchester United at Anfield the next day.

I've been a Liverpool fan since I was a kid, and this was to be my first live game. Then the phone rang and the bad news arrived. Fortunately, a few hours later another phone call brought us

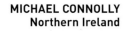

Kuyt scores his second penalty against Everton at Goodison Park in 2007

back up to our previous high. Some replacements had been tracked down and we would be in the Kop for the lunchtime kick-off.

Unfortunately, a late John O'Shea goal spoiled the party after we'd dominated proceedings. Still I'd had a taste of the atmosphere and wanted more. I was due to fly home on the Sunday, but Barcelona were coming to town a few days later for the second leg of our Champions League clash. The decision was made. I'd be staying for the visit of Frank Rijkaard's men. As everyone knows, it was another 1-0 home defeat, but thankfully we progressed on away goals.

That was 2007. Since then I've been back to Merseyside for some other massive occasions. Ten minutes prior to kick-off in our seemingly annual Champions League semi-final with Chelsea, I was again without a ticket. Then a fellow Irish Red miraculously offered my friend and me one each. His pals hadn't turned up. It was in the Annie Road End and proved to be the best seat in the house. Daniel Agger found the net right in front of us to level up the tie, while the glorious penalty shoot-out victory also took place just yards away from us.

The following season I experienced my first away day, even if it was only a short trip across Stanley Park. Again there was penalty drama as Dirk Kuyt converted twice to give us a brilliant win over the blues. It doesn't get any better than that.

JIMMY HYNES
Nenagh, County Tipperary

Continuing the tradition

I'VE been to Anfield twice, with the Reds winning both games. The most recent trip was in April 2008 when Blackburn Rovers were the visitors. On the Saturday we'd flown from Belfast International Airport to John Lennon and then stayed at friends in south Liverpool where I spent most of the evening reading Stevie G's autobiography.

The next morning we had a fry up for breakfast before getting a taxi to the ground, stopping for some wine gums on the way. When the match started Gerrard opened the scoring and we chanted his name. Torres got the second with a header and we sang his name too. Voronin got what we thought would be the last goal, until right at the end Santa Cruz made it 3-1.

JOE HARPER (age 11)
Ballymena, County Antrim

Official LFC supporters' clubs

Ireland

Co Carlow – Rathvilly
Anthony Byrne
5 Woodgrove Ave
Rathvilly
Co Carlow

Co Carlow – Bagnenalstown
Darren Thompson
Carrigbeg
Bagnenalstown
Co Carlow
www.bebo.com/muinebheagkopites

Co Cavan – Kingscourt
Colin Watterson
31 Thorndale Close
Kingscourt
Co Cavan
+353 87 9052991
breandor@hotmail.com

Co Clare
Trina McAuley
5 Lough Gash
Newmarket-on-Fergus
Co Clare
www.clarescousers.org
+353 86 3989780 (Barry O'Keefe)

Co Clare – Killaloe
Denis O'Laughlin
83 Cnoc Ard
Ballina
Co Clare
+353 87 2682414
lockster79@hotmail.com

Co Cork – Buttevant
Pierce Fitzgerald
Ballinguile
Churchtown
Mallow
Co Cork
manton_dave@hotmail.com
+353 87 4164623

Co Cork – Cork City
John O'Sullivan
31 Tiffany Downs
Bishopstown
Co Cork
+353 21 4679159

Co Cork – Duhallow
Charlie Ankettell
Boherbue
Mallow
Co Cork
+353 87 7793205
+353 86 2353811 (Martin Moynihan)
duhallowlfc@yahoogroups.com

Co Cork – Fermoy
Emmett Hull
101 Beechfield Est
Fermoy
Co Cork
+353 87 9321887
+353 25 32536
emmett.hull@sanmina-sci.com

Co Donegal – Castlefin

Wesley Kee
48 Millbrook Gardens
Castlederg
Co Tyrone
07734 237236

Co Donegal – Crozon
Denis Conway
22 Silverhill
Westend
Bundoran
Co Donegal
+353 71 9829369
crozonlsc@hotmail.com

Co Donegal – Inishowen
Joeseph McLaughlin
62 Convent Road
Cardonagh
Co Donegal
+353 74 9374044
joejackie@eircom.net

Co Donegal – Letterkenny
Kevin Neely
142 Meadowhill
Letterkenny
Co Donegal
kneely@eircom.net
www.lfcdonegal.com

Co Dublin – Balbriggan
Mr Tom Devoy
15 Tara Cove
Balbriggan
Co Dublin
tom.devoy@yahoo.ie
+353 1 841 1458
+353 87 2563596

Co Dublin – Tallaght
Mick O'Brien
45 Carrigmore Drive
Aylesbury
Tallaght
Dublin 24
obrienclann@eircom.net
+353 87 7946669 (Sarah O'Connor)

Co Dublin/Dublin
Catherine Brady
15 Huntsdown Road
Mulhuddart
Dublin 15
liverpoolfcdublin@hotmail.com

Co Dublin/Dublin – Mountjoy
John Clarke
C/O Mountjoy Prison
North Circular Road
Dublin 7

Co Dublin/Dublin – Sth Dublin
Declan Greaves
10 The Avenue
Rathdale
Enfield
Co Meath
+353 87 7653212
declan_greaves@lfcsouthdublin
branch.ie

Co Galway
Paul Hehir

Taroman
Clough, Cummer
Tuam
Co Galway
+353 86 8731246

Co Kerry – Listowel
Declan Carty
Coolaclarrig
Listowell
Co Kerry
+353 87 9363817
+353 68 22862 (Sean Brosnan)
cartyelaine@eircom.net

Co Kerry – Tralee
Leo Byrne
17 Westcourt
Caherslee
Tralee
Co Kerry
+353 87 2374993

Co Kildare – Kildangan/Kildare
Town
Warren Delaney
25 The Courtyard
Kildangan
Co Kildare
086 371 3515
info@knlsc.com
www.knlsc.com

Co Kilkenny – Callan
Graham Doheny
Moanamought
Callan
Co Kilkenny
086 870 9668
dohenygraham@eircom.net

Co Laois
Tom Gorry
8 Pattison Estate
Mountmellick
Co Laois
+353 502 44297
+353 86 8882860

Co Limerick – Limerick City
Annette Ingle
53 Clarina Ave
Ballincurra-Weston
Limerick
Co Limerick
+353 87 9062669

Co Limerick – South Limerick
Dermot Horan
'Melwood'
Rockbarton
Bruff
Co Limerick
+353 61 382928
dermothoran@eircom.net
+335 86 8251157 (Hanora Horan)

Co Louth – Dundalk
Richie Watters
Old Road
Bellurgan
Jenkinstown
Dundalk
Co Louth

+353 42 9386948
pcooling@eircom.net

Co Louth – Ardee
Paddy Sharkey
Artnalivery
Ardee
Co Louth
+353 41 6857435

Co Louth – Drogheda
Lorna/Peter McQuillan
128 Pearse Park
Drogheda
Co Louth
+353 41 9832746
lornamcquillan@hotmail.com

Co Mayo – Ballina
Martin Glynn
26 Glenn Ris
Ballina
Co Mayo
Ireland
+353 86 3870842
+353 94 24944 (P Tierney)

Co Mayo – Westport
Peter Flynn
Lios Mor
Kings Hill
Westport
Co Mayo
+353 98 55688

Co Meath – Kells
Barry Smith
36 Maple Drive
Rockfield
Kells
Co Meath
+353 46 9247857
+353 87 2075758 (John Muldoon)
bazsmith@eircom.net

Co Monaghan – Monaghan
Hugh Kierans
Tara
Mullaghadun
Monaghan
Co Monaghan
d26tires@eircom.net
+353 87 9692898

Co Offaly – Ferbane
Liam Coughlan
Athlone Road
Ferbane
Co Offaly
+353 90 6454266
liamoliviacoughlan@eircom.net

Co Sligo
Eamonn Mcmunn
2 Brookfort
Riverstown
Co Sligo
+353 87 8337337
planetautosligo@eircom.net

Co Tipperary – Clonmel
John Fennessy
19 Wheatfields
Clonmel

Co Tipperary
+353 87 9905429
+353 52 28409
+353 87 9272321 (Eamon O'Keefe)

Co Waterford – Waterford
Kieran Power
12 Hazelbourne
Cleaboy Road
Waterford City
Co Waterford
www.waterfordlfc.com
+353 86 3834222 (K Power)

Co Westmeath – Athlone
Sean O'Beirne
Carnagh
Kiltoom
Athlone
Co Roscommon
sonyaobeirne@eircom.net

Co Wexford
Damian Lynch
Faythe House
The Faythe
Wexford
Co Wexford
+353 87 2524120
jg.doyle@eircom.net

Co Wicklow
Terry Leonard
26 Glenaulin Green
Palmerstown
Dublin 20
+353 86 8376993
liverpoollegends@eircom.net

Northern Ireland

Co Antrim – Kilroot
Bob Crawford
23 Queensway
Carrickfergus
Co Antrim
02893 362192
trolsc@hotmail.com
02893 351515

Co Down – 1st Moira
Mark McCormick
3 Castle Avenue
Moira
Co Down
07775575650
paulstirling@vodafone.net

1st Ardoyne
Stephen Thomas
13 Coolmoyne Park
Belfast
02890 74065 (S Gallagher)
02890 770178

Bootle Street
Bill McClure
32 West Circular Cres
Belfast
02890 718820
firemanbill03@hotmail.com

Broadway
Philip Brady
8 Lasalle Mews
Falls Road

Belfast
07903313366
philipbrady63@hotmail.co.uk

Co Antrim – 1st Lisburn
James Ussher
81 Moss Road
Lambeg
Lisburn
Co Antrim
BT27 4NX
02892 667837
07719572252
ashleigh@ussher1992.fsnet.co.uk

Co Antrim – Ballyclare
Alex Agnew
39 Sawmill Rd
Ballyclare
Co Antrim
achi@lineone.net

Co Antrim – Ballymena
James McCloy
64 Gorthahar Road
Rasharkin
Ballymena
Co Antrim
02825 881499
07764533877
jmccloyjoinery@aol.com

Co Antrim – Crumlin
Simon Moore
8 Cairn Walk
Crumlin
Co Antrim
02894 453560 (home)
simon.moore@tesco.net
07971168154

Co Antrim – Larne
Don Dodds
10 Bay Park
Larne
Co Antrim
02828 277685
Fax: 02828 270040

Co Antrim – Rathcoole
Harry Elliott
5 Drumcree Place
Rathcoole
Newtownabbey
Co Antrim

Co Antrim – Seven Towers
Trevor Kyle
19 Farmlodge Ave
Ballymena
Co Antrim
07980485211
02825 648459

Co Antrim – Silverstream
Mr Davy Hill
1 Beverley Avenue
Newtownabbey
County Antrim
02890 221811
07773507606

Co Armagh – Lurgan
Colin Bell
669 Ardowen
Craigavon
Co Armagh
02838 324039
07743191181 (C Bell)

Co Armagh – Richhill
Sonia Kenny
26 Brentwood Park
Richhill
Co Armagh
02838 871863
02838 871429 (J Bunting)
sonia_kenny@yahoo.co.uk
lfc.richhillclub@yahoo.com

Co Derry/Londonderry – 1st Derry
Tony Preston
21 Glencaw Pk
Galliagh
Co Derry
02871 2586271
bigtlfc10@hotmail.com
07979664311

Co Derry/Londonderry – Castlerock
Richard Steen
4 Taylors Row
Coleraine
Co Londonderry
02870 358888

Co Derry/Londonderry – Coleraine
Andy Maguire
18 Loguestown Park
Coleraine
Co Londonderry
02870 354381
andy.m.coleraine@btinternet.com

Co Derry/Londonderry – Limavady
Michael McCloskey
1 Dunlade Mews
Killywill
Greysteel

Co Derry/Londonderry – Waterside
Eamonn McBride
9 Margaret Street
Waterside
Londonderry
lfcwatersidesc@hotmail.co.uk

Co Down – 1st Bangor
Robert Vannucci
25 Bloomfield Walk
Bangor
Co Down
07907520100

Co Down – 1st Dromore
Malcolm Russell
53 Ballynanny Road
Banbridge
Co Down
02840 662453
07929916204
1stdromoreliverpool@jen13.
wanadoo.co.uk

Co Down – Comber
Gary Thompson
75 Crossgar Road
Saintfield
Co Down
dudethompson5@aol.com
Mark Brady
07793367445

Co Down – Newry
Paul Kennedy
Anfield House
23a Derrycraw Road
Newry
Co Down

02830 821369
newrylfc_olsc@yahoo.co.uk

Co Down – Portaferry
Ian Smith
91a High Street
Portaferry
Co Down
02842 728379 / 02842 728696 (Sean Ennis)
07802451892
smith_ian@hotmail.co.uk

Co Down – South Antrim
Joe Lynn
12 Ardfern Park
Downpatrick
Co Down
02890 781000
joelynn62@hotmail.com

Co Down – Warrenpoint
Darren Mullen
25 Temple Hill Road
Newry
Co Down
07881400014 (Jim O'Connor)
07967571386 (Darren Mullen)

Co Fermanagh – Irvinestown
Alan Keys
132a Drumadravey
Lisnarick
Irvinestown
Co Fermanagh
02868 621119
02868 621406 (Trevor Booth)
keysdrumdravey@hotmail.com

Co Tyrone – Dungannon
Ronnie Cowan
17 Killyneill Court
Dungannon
Co Tyrone
ronniecowan@hotmail.com
07737385800

Co Tyrone – Omagh
Andrew Lee
37 Donaghanie Road
Omagh
Co Tyrone
02882 245948
02882 250774 (N Bradley)
andy.j.lee@btinternet.com

Co Tyrone – Sion Mills
Declan Devine
27 Freughlough Road
Castlederg
Co Tyrone
declandevine@btinternet.com

Sliabh Dubh
Hugh Fitzsimmons
26 Colin View Street
Springfield Road
Belfast
07746034161

West Belfast
Pat MacDermott
16 Glenmeen Close
Hannahstown
Belfast
02890 623129
patrick@macdermott.freeserve.co.uk
07985227887 (Larry Claxton)
www.wblsc.co.uk

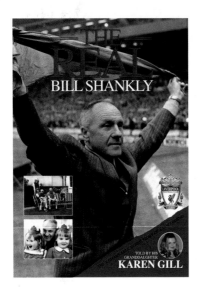

THE REAL BILL SHANKLY (paperback)

SEPTEMBER 29, 2006 marked the 25th anniversary of the death of the man who turned Liverpool Football Club from a struggling Second Division outfit to one of the bastions of world football. Bill Shankly was a remarkable character, but there were many sides to the legendary Scottish manager. Originally released as a bestselling hardback, this publication tells the inside story. THE REAL BILL SHANKLY provides a fascinating insight into the mind of this unique character through recollections from the fans who idolised him, the players who responded to his inspirational team-talks and the family who loved him. The book is compiled by Karen Gill, the great man's granddaughter, who called him 'Grandy' while the fans called him 'The Messiah'.

There have been many Shankly books, but this one, featuring marvellous photography from the unique archive collection of the *Liverpool Daily Post and Echo*, will be the definitive official record of his remarkable life – officially endorsed by Liverpool Football Club. It is a book every football fan will want to read. He was of an age when fans came before commercialism. Every single one of them mattered to Shankly.

Price: £14.99

THE REAL BOB PAISLEY

THE follow-up to the bestselling THE REAL BILL SHANKLY, this long overdue publication celebrates the life and times of arguably the most successful manager in British football history. It seems appropriate that at a time when over 40,000 people recently signed a petition to grant Bob Paisley a posthumous knighthood, his on and off-field life is examined and celebrated. The book offers an inside track, revelling in his life and times 30 years after he guided Liverpool Football Club to their first-ever European Cup triumph.

The complete story paints an accurate profile of a very private man through the eyes of his family, those who knew him the best away from the glare of the public eye. His treasured family album is made public for the very first time, while tributes from some of the game's greatest names only serve to enhance his reputation as one of the finest servants the English game has ever seen.

THE REAL BOB PAISLEY features marvellous photography from the unique archive collection of the *Liverpool Daily Post and Echo*, and will be the definitive official record of his life – officially endorsed by Liverpool FC.

Price: £20.00

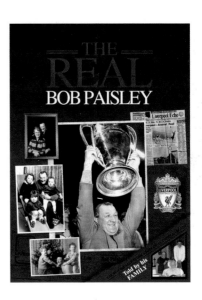

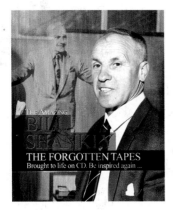

BILL SHANKLY: THE FORGOTTEN TAPES

JOURNALIST John Roberts was the man handed the immense honour of writing Bill Shankly's official autobiography in 1976.

Shanks was less than two years into retirement and still feeling raw as he wrestled with life outside Anfield. Roberts captured the Kop messiah's innermost thoughts on an old-fashioned cassette recorder and these forgotten tapes, featured here, cover all the key aspects of his life.

This is the perfect opportunity to listen to the great man and be inspired again as he talks passionately about his time at Liverpool and discusses the special relationship he enjoyed with the fans as he took a struggling club to the pinnacle of European football.

Price: £9.99

All of these titles can be bought by calling 0845 143 0001

TOPS OF THE KOP: LFC KITS*

A FASCINATING look at the changing face of Liverpool's kit down the years. Every change is noted, taking into account developments in kit design and technology, variations in colour and of course the change in appearance of the famous red shirt, in the form of kit sponsorship.

Now updated to include the 2007/08 strips, the publication is supported by match action and iconic images (which bring the eras to life). It is an ideal companion to be used time and time again.

This beautifully designed publication looks at the kit from 1892 to the present adidas era, through changes which included the change to an all-red strip at the behest of the great Bill Shankly, who believed the players would look more imposing, more intimidating – and so it would prove as Liverpool FC swept all before them.

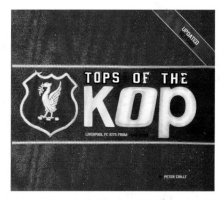

Price: £8.99

* Updated version now on sale

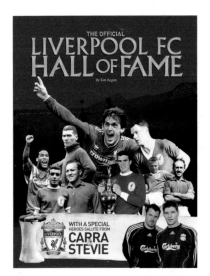

THE OFFICIAL LIVERPOOL FC HALL OF FAME

FIVE TIMES European champions Liverpool Football Club have the richest history in British football. With such a prestigious heritage, the task for a specially selected panel of judges was how to select two iconic players for every decade from the many great players who have represented the club, in order to make up a star-studded official Hall of Fame.

This book provides the panel's answers, with some controversial decisions along the way. This is the definitive guide to the greatest Liverpool players of all time, illustrated with the finest archive photography.

In addition, the publication also reveals the name of every single individual who has played for the Anfield giants, with the 'Hall of Famers' themselves each having a dedicated statistical section.

It is written by Ken Rogers, former sports editor of the *Liverpool Echo*. He has also written the autobiographies of two Liverpool FC icons in Tommy Smith and Phil Thompson, and was co-author of *Liverpool – Club of the Century*.

Price: £20.00

THE OFFICIAL LIVERPOOL FC FAMILY ALBUM

FAMILY photos aren't like they used to be. We take pictures in different ways from the days when we stuffed our holiday snaps in an old book and left them at the back of a drawer. So it is with the other family in your life – Liverpool Football Club.

Thousands of images have been stored digitally over recent years as Liverpool have continued in their old tradition of winning trophies and making special memories for the fans. The *LFC Family Album* is an up-to-date keepsake for all Liverpool supporters who have revelled in the modern-day glory years while still keeping an eye on the past triumphs that continue to inspire future generations.

Anfield heroes like Steven Gerrard, Jamie Carragher, Sami Hyypia and Fernando Torres are among the many who give us their personal take on unique moments captured in time by the camera. Former players and celebrities also contribute, as do the legendary fans that make the club so special.

Just as in our own family albums, there are stories and pictures that will provoke a whole range of emotions and keep you turning the page.

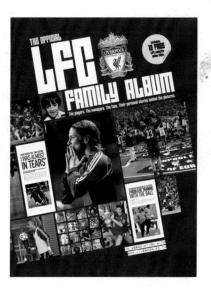

Price: £20.00

Or by logging on to www.merseyshop.com